LIFE STRATEGIES

Doing What Works, Doing What Matters

LIFE STRATEGIES

Doing What Works, Doing What Matters

Phillip C. McGraw, Ph.D.

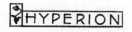

NEW YORK

ISBN: 0-7868-6548-2

Names and identifying characteristics of people in the book have
been changed to protect the privacy of the individuals.

Book design by Holly McNeely

This book is dedicated with love and affection
to my wife,
Robin,
and her gentle and caring spirit,

and to my sons,
Jay and Jordan,
who inspire me
with their vibrancy and energy.

IF EVERYBODY WAS SATISFIED WITH HIMSELF,
THERE WOULD BE NO HEROES.
—*Mark Twain*

CONTENTS

ACKNOWLEDGMENTS

I thank Oprah for awakening in me the desire and inspiring in me the commitment to reach out and share with others that which I believe with such clarity and passion. Without Oprah, there would be no *Life Strategies*, which for me would be a personal tragedy, for I would have missed the enrichment of having completed this task. I thank Oprah for caring, for doing it right, and for sharing her platform with me. She is truly the brightest light and the clearest voice in America today. I thank her for being my true friend.

I thank my wife, Robin, for her undying support throughout our twenty-two years of marriage, and for her love and encouragement during this project in particular. I thank her for the courage to live with three boys, and yet remain a lady. I thank her for being my soft place to fall. She is what succeeding in life is all about.

I thank my sons, Jay and Jordan, for loving and believing in their dad and putting up with the late nights and the long hours of absence and preoccupation required by this project. Their patience and genuine encouragement showed a maturity well beyond their years. I thank them for their warped senses of humor, and for never letting their dad forget how to laugh or what really counts.

I extend my most sincere and heartfelt thanks to my friend and colleague Jonathan Leach, a man of great passion and commitment. He has over the years shown passion for my children and their education, and now for this project. Jonathan poured more work, love, and wisdom into this project than could ever be described. Beyond undangling my participles and organizing my stream of consciousness, Jon cared about and contributed to the content of this book from his heart and mind. I thank him for his sacrifice and late, late-night hours in helping to turn this concept into a book. I could not have done it without him.

I thank Gary Dobbs, my partner, dearest friend in life, and godfather to my children for his never-ending support and encouragement for all that I do. His honesty and candor throughout the last two decades have had tremendous impact on the better parts of who I am. No matter what I do, he is always in my balcony.

I thank my assistant, Tami Galloway, for heading up the logistics of this project and for her tireless commitment to get it right. I thank her for never being too tired and never saying no. Thanks also to Melodi Gregg and Kimberly Rinehart for their assistance in transcribing and arranging the manuscript.

I thank my mother and three sisters for conspiring throughout my life to convince me that besides being the only boy in the family, I truly was something special. I thank my deceased father for being a man of passion and vision, and for teaching me to reach. I thank Scott Madsen for always being there.

Thanks to Bill Dawson, Chip Babcock, Jan and Steve Davidson, and Paul Vishnesky for their friendship, loyalty, and commitment in reading and giving honest feedback on early drafts; and to Hal Zina Bennett, for his editorial input on initial drafts of early chapters.

I thank the thousands and thousands of seminar participants who trusted me enough to allow me to impact their minds, hearts, and lives. I thank them for teaching me about life and about living from the heart.

I thank Jeff Jacobs for his wisdom, experience, and insight in counseling this neophyte author through the maze. I thank him for his interest and caring when it would have been a whole lot easier not to.

I thank Bob Miller at Hyperion for believing in and being

excited about this project. I thank him for his cutting-edge expertise in the world of publishing and his ability to bring it to bear
in unbelievably record time. I also thank Hyperion's Leslie Wells
for her patience and acumen in editing and counseling me on this
project. Leslie's spirit and enthusiasm were uplifting each and
every day. A true breath of fresh air.

LIFE STRATEGIES

*Doing What Works,
Doing What
Matters*

INTRODUCTION

Nine-tenths of wisdom consists in being wise in time.
—Teddy Roosevelt

Target: **America's Sweetheart**
As Oprah moved silently down the long, winding staircase in the pitch black of night, she was totally alone, a rare circumstance given the intense schedule we were following in Amarillo. Since a conventional hotel would have been a security nightmare, we were living in a rambling, three-story house on the outskirts of this West Texas town. The armed guards who kept twenty-four-hour watch around the perimeter of "Camp Oprah" now sat in the dark, huddled against the cold. They had no idea she was on the move; every floor appeared dark and asleep. Except for the familiar low moan and creak of the frigid wind from the north, everything was silent. Descending a second flight of stairs, she tapped lightly on my door with a single fingernail. I knew it was she, and she knew I would know, so she spoke not a word. It was well after midnight. She had gone to bed two hours earlier, but I knew she would sleep fitfully, if at all. It was like that for all of us, but especially for her. Behind enemy lines in cattle country, we all slept light and kept our guard up, alert to the reality of hostile feelings from certain factions in Amarillo.

Over the course of the previous day, I had seen a certain

change occur in her eyes. At the federal courthouse downtown people were not saying nice things; they were attacking her staff in order to get to her. Like a mother lion whose cubs were being threatened, she was up and on the prowl. Could it be the enemy had gone too far?

When I opened the door, she looked forlornly alone, and her face betrayed the painful struggle that was keeping her awake. There were tears in her eyes, but these were not the tears of sympathy and love that millions of viewers had often seen on her television show. In her familiar flannel pajamas and huge fuzzy house shoes, she looked much younger than she was. She needed to talk. It would be a long night.

The private Oprah and the television Oprah are about as close to the same as anyone might imagine. But no one had ever seen her in a situation like this. In some ways, the experience of this trial was foreign to her; in other ways, it was the same old test, different classroom. Oprah's high-spirited, "always on," self-assured persona sometimes caused even me, who had come to know her so well, to forget that she was as vulnerable to hurt as any of us. As I came to learn, the trademark self-assuredness that twenty million Americans see every day springs from her being masterfully in control, even in what may seem like spontaneity and chaos, and from doing what she dearly loves—two conditions obviously not present in her situation in Amarillo. Nevertheless, she remained the trouper, always doing for others, always concerned, even under siege.

But her face at my door reminded me of her humanness, and of how terribly alone one feels when under attack. She wasn't feeling sorry for herself or playing the victim; that's not any part of who she is. But she was hurting, she was frustrated, and she was confused. We were living a strange and high-pressured existence in a surreal world, where it seemed that time had stopped its march long before social progress had been made. The concepts of logic, fairness, and common sense seemed to have been suspended. Members of our group had spotted anti-Oprah buttons with a red diagonal across her face. Hostile bumper stickers were commonplace, even being distributed at the local schools, a stark contrast to the respect and admiration that were the currency of her day-to-day life. Even the president of the city's chamber of commerce had circulated a letter to his staff warning against supporting this "outsider." As a result of these conditions, security was tight, even though tens of thousands of adoring fans were also keeping a constant vigil.

Oprah was facing civil charges of fraud, slander, defamation, and negligence, among other more technical claims. She feared a "kangaroo" court. She was publicly accused of lying and manipulating the truth to sensationalize a story about Mad Cow disease in the beef industry, all allegedly to generate higher ratings. Her integrity and ethics were being trampled, and her accusers were telling America that she was not who she presented herself to be. They had depicted her as a greedy, irresponsible betrayer of the truth. In court, her accusers pounded the table and said that she was not to be trusted—that she should be humiliated and penalized to the tune of over $100 million. The attacks on her professionalism were painful, but it was the attacks on her staff, whom she cared about so much, and also the personal attacks on her that were cutting deep, very deep. Moreover, in contrast to her world, where she could freely answer questions as to the truth, the rules of federal court required her to sit silent, and an ironclad gag order from a no-nonsense federal judge muzzled her in the public domain, at least while the trial continued.

In my opinion, the millionaire power-broker cattlemen who had filed the suit, and dragged her to Texas in the intricate net of a dubious state statute, smelled blood in the water. Through legal maneuvering, they had her on their turf, cornered in their own backyard. Here was an extremely wealthy black female, whom they were portraying as the beef industry's scurrilous enemy, trapped in Amarillo, Texas—the white-male-dominated, undisputed beef capital of the world. All that Oprah could say, all she could feel, was that it was not fair: "I can't believe this is happening. This is so unfair. Surely this isn't happening to me. It can't be real. Why is this happening to *me*? There has to be some reason for all of this."

Hadn't she been the one who refused to sell out to the circus-freak atmosphere that had come to dominate the talk show circuit? Hadn't she been the one to take the high road? Against all the pressure to grab higher ratings through a grotesque parade of misguided humanity, trying to "out-bizarre" one another, hadn't she been deeply committed to staying the course and doing things right?

Was there no justice? Could people not see through the sham of this lawsuit? Oprah just didn't get it. The problem was, I knew that if she didn't get it soon, they were going to get her.

As with any other television or movie star, we are mesmerized by the image of Oprah. We might imagine that in every moment of her life, she's somehow bursting onto a stage, hugely confident and in control, arms outstretched in that familiar wave as music washes over the whole scene. She may seem to be bigger than life. She is not. But even under siege in Amarillo, even in the grip of this inner turmoil, Oprah Winfrey kept up the standard. Millions of viewers had come to rely on her as a daily "rock" in an otherwise crazy world, a breath of rational fresh air. And she, in turn, honored her commitment to those viewers, even while being attacked. She continued to be "Oprah." The show must go on.

January nights in Amarillo are typically freezing, but the quaint Little Theater never lacked for warmth. Every night, as 400 people sat shoulder-to-shoulder inside, it was hard to tell whether their excitement or the brilliant spotlights overhead gave off more energy. "Hollywood" had come to town. The buzzing murmur of anticipation gave way to a hush as a producer in headphones raised a hand, then an explosion of cheers and applause filled the room as the first notes of the "Oprah" theme song suddenly boomed from gigantic speakers.

As Oprah herself strode eagerly out into the lights, there was no doubt that people were in the presence of a star. Everything was perfectly put together, from the set to the music to her personal appearance: all of it sophisticated, colorful, stylish, but at the same time relaxed and unpretentious—something you couldn't help getting caught up in. But everything on the set seemed to be just a backdrop to that smile—a smile that expressed an innocent delight in life, a love of her audience and of what she was doing. And through two consecutive one-and-a-half-hour tapings, the audience returned the love; they cheered and stomped their feet, their applause flowing wave upon wave, in a Texas-style lovefest. It was *her* world again. She was in control; she was doing what she loved; she was Oprah.

For those three hours at the theater, everybody was having fun, and she more than anyone. People wanted to touch her, hug her, as if doing so would win for them some of her warmth and energy. That energy seemed to be bottomless. Long after the theater had emptied, when most of her audience had gone to bed, she would still be there alone with her crew, videotaping promotional spots—still at work, that smile still glowing: America's sweetheart.

But in the quiet house it was after midnight, and I was witnessing the end of the energy. In the near-dark of the basement gameroom, America's sweetheart wasn't smiling. She sat with me on the floor, her hair awry, hugging her knees. Like so many days before, this had been a long day. *Tired* isn't a big enough word when days start at 5:30 A.M. and include being pounded on for nine hours in a courtroom *before* taping two talk shows back to back. Still, sleep would not come. Sitting there with Oprah in the basement, I knew that "they" were getting to her. She was reeling, struggling to find herself.

The broadside attacks were causing unwanted feelings from times long past to float back to the surface. In the face of crisis, Oprah had lost herself. She was responding in a very human way. She was responding with behavior and thoughts that, frankly, are epidemic in American society today. They are behavior and thoughts and patterns that can cripple a life, and cripple a society, for that matter. And whether they are your behavior, Oprah Winfrey's, or those of the society at large, they are the kind of response that promises certain disaster.

As a friend, I wanted to hug her, to tell her that it would be okay and that she shouldn't worry. But I knew better. I knew if she didn't snap out of it and snap out of it soon, she *was* going to lose and she *was* going to be labeled by a verdict, however unfair. What's more, I knew that there were already would-be plaintiffs in a whole slew of other states, waiting to yank her into their own courts if she lost here, all smelling money. But I wasn't there to commiserate with her and be a sympathetic ear. I was there as a strategist to generate a plan for winning this jury's minds and hearts, and winning this trial.

Everyone has something they do. Some people build houses; I build strategies for living. I am a strategist; I study human nature and behavior. Along with Gary Dobbs, my partner, my best friend, and someone I believe to be the best legal analyst in America, I design plans to help get people what they want in life. It's all I do, and if it's your *life* with which I am dealing, the stakes are always high. For Oprah, they were exceedingly high, monetarily and otherwise. Coming in second in a $100 million trial is not an option. I had a plan, a well-thought-out, well-researched strategy, to get the truth out and get it out effectively. This strategic plan had been months in the making. Not surprisingly, Oprah was a huge part of that strategy. Without her, all of her, we could lose this trial in cattle country and lose it big.

We needed her; we needed the totally focused energy that is the essence of who she is—and we needed all of that *now*. Getting Oprah ready was a big part of my job and I intended to do it. The truth was on her side, but make no mistake: the courtroom is no crucible of truth. Just as in life, if you walk into court without a plan, a really good plan, you're kidding yourself. I could wait no longer for her to come around.

This trial was underway and it was building speed every single day. Decisions were being made, plans were being executed, witnesses were coming and going. All of it was building toward Oprah. The press, the plaintiffs, the jury, even all of us—her defense team—were waiting for her to tell her story. But our star witness was struggling with the "insanity" of it all, stuck in denial, and not coming to grips with the fact that this "Twilight Zone" experience was really happening. Not even lead counsel, Charles "Chip" Babcock, Oprah's extraordinarily gifted media trial lawyer, could pull this plan off without her and her complete focus. Every day, Chip asked me, "Is she ready? We must get her ready." Trial lawyers don't come any better than Chip Babcock, but he knew this case was dangerous because Oprah was out of her element. He had successfully defended super-high-profile media people all across America, and although he had a great track record, he knew that nationally, 80 percent of these cases are lost at the trial level. He was good, really good. In this venue, he would need to be.

Sitting on the floor across from this woman I had come to admire so very much, I searched my mind and heart for the right thing to say. We had been talking, analyzing, and working for some time now, but Oprah continued to struggle with the why of it all. What I knew was that, regardless of "why," we were here and she was in the crosshairs. Finally, I just took her hand and said, "Oprah, look at me, right now. You'd better wake up, girl, and wake up *now*. It *is* really happening. You'd better *get over it* and get in the game, or these good ol' boys are going to hand you your ass on a platter."

Now I suppose when you are arguably the most influential woman on the planet, people don't often step up and tell you how the cow ate the cabbage. I saw a flash of anger in her eyes as she instinctively recoiled. But I recognized that her anger had nothing to do with me. To have said any less would have been to cheat Oprah: This was the truth told in a way that she would hear. She deserved no less. As direct as I am, it was hard for me to be so blunt with her, but Oprah knew me, and she knew that my interests were her interests. She looked me in the eye, and with a resolve I had not heard in all of our previous work together, said, *"No they will not."*

I truly believe that at that precise moment, the cattlemen lost their case. Until that instant, Oprah had been fretting over whether this deal was fair or unfair, rather than accepting that, either way, it simply *was*. She had been philosophically distracted instead of focusing on what she must to do in order to win. From the very beginning, she believed deeply in the rightness of her actions; she believed passionately in her First Amendment freedom to hold an open debate on public health and safety, including our food supply, whether the mega-millionaire beef factories liked it or not. But the viciousness of the attack on her person and profession had so unsettled her that she had stopped being Oprah Winfrey. She fought back from her head, but not from her heart. She had done a lot of right things to help in her defense: moving her show to Amarillo, agreeing to be in trial every day, working and studying the facts every night. But she had been hung up on the belief that because it was unfair, something would derail the problem and it would go away.

The nonstop attacks on her production staff had also seriously distracted her, because she viewed Harpo Productions and all of its people almost as family. Preoccupied by what she believed to be the totally disingenuous nature of the complaints, she had given her power away. I saw that she was letting these men, the judicial system, and the whole circumstance of being under such vicious attack deprive her of her identity. Had she taken the stand in that state of mind, full of self-doubt and distracted by that inner turmoil, to face the three days of relentless, tedious, manipulative, and grinding cross-examination, it would not have been good. Without a strategic plan that included clearly defined objectives, she probably would have sent a very bad message to the jury. They would have wondered, "If Oprah is not sure, how can we be?"

That night, Oprah faced her demons, some of them spawned by the trial itself—a struggle that she later came to see as a microcosm of her whole life—some resurrected from years gone by. She had a choice: She could continue to resist accepting the situation because she didn't like it, or she could grab onto it and stand up for herself and those being attacked with her. Once she took off the blinders and *dealt* with the real deal, rather than *debating* it, she was "back." She did take the stand, and she looked the jury squarely in the eye, told the truth, and told it effectively. Likewise, she looked her accusers in the eye, and her message to them was clear: "Gentlemen, if you have a problem with that show, I'm your girl. The buck stops *here*. If you have a problem, see me, and *leave my people alone*. You wanted me here; well, you got me. Take your best shot. I am *not* running, I am *not* settling, and I will *not* be intimidated." Oprah Winfrey is a formidable woman. Oprah Winfrey is a winner. And once she committed herself to working the problem and defending herself and what she believed in, her accusers were toast: signed, sealed, and delivered.

CHAPTER ONE

GET REAL

We do not deal much in facts
when we are contemplating ourselves.
—Mark Twain

Now I know we're unlikely to read about your problems and challenges in the *New York Times,* or see you tonight on CNN—at least I hope that's true. I know that you're probably not an international star of television and movies, whose battles, trials, and tribulations are scrutinized minute by minute in the worldwide media. But just like Oprah, you face problems and challenges each and every day. You, too, may feel that what is happening to you simply is not fair, and you may be right. Just like Oprah, you may feel that at times the world spins out of control, forgetting who the good guys are and letting the bad guys go too far, sometimes way too far.

At times, people aren't fair or sensitive, but that's just part of life. Sadly, it seems that the more successful you are, the more potshots people take at you. Either way, fair or unfair, just like Oprah, you have to help *you.*

The fact that your problems aren't headlining the six o'clock news does not mean that your problems are unimportant, at least not to you. Believe me when I tell you that if you don't step up and fight for you, no one else will. At the same time, I think you may find that the person you most need to stand up to in this world is *you*. We'll talk more about this later, but you can probably guess that in this war we call life, most of the decisive battles are fought within *you*.

In the meantime, let's agree that what makes a problem big is simply that it's yours. To the clerk in the store down the street from Oprah's studio, it might not matter a great deal that Oprah Winfrey was under siege in Amarillo with her very character being impugned, but it mattered a whole lot to Oprah Winfrey. Your problems, in turn, may not matter much to your next-door neighbors. It doesn't mean that they don't like you or have good hearts; it's just human nature that they would put their own concerns first. But it does mean your problems need to matter to *you*. If they don't matter to you, they won't matter to anybody who can really change them.

Don't feel as if you should minimize your problems, or apologize for them. Our world has for too long conditioned us not to make waves. We don't want to make a scene or disrupt the flow of things. As a result, we settle, quietly, much too often. If a problem is important to you, then that's enough; that qualifies it as worthy. It's important, because *you* are important.

Nor should you concern yourself with whether your problems seem trivial in the grand scheme of things or not. If I've broken my ankle, and the guy in the next hospital bed has just had his leg amputated, that's terrible, but it doesn't make my ankle hurt any less. If it's your problem, then of course you should care about it. Also beware of getting bogged down in a debate about the fairness or unfairness of what has befallen you. If it is unfair, then it's unfair, but you still have to deal with it.

Your life really can be different—you just haven't had the tools, the focus, and the "inside scoop." Keep moving along with me, assuming that your problems do count and that maybe, just maybe, there is something here for you, something you deserve. I realize that at this point, you don't know where all of this thinking is headed. But *what if* this book is exactly what you need to have what you've been wanting in your life? A closed mind or attitude of resistance could cause you to cheat yourself out of an important chance for a better "ride." If what you're doing isn't working, you might as well at least consider an alternative approach. You can start by admitting you may not know everything you need to in order to get what you want.

Oprah didn't have any experience in the courtroom. She had plenty in life, but not in the courtroom. She was willing to admit what she did not know, and hook up and learn it. She was not resistant to learning, and when she did learn the rules of the game, she created victory. So can you. Learn how to play this game and you might be surprised at the result. The courtroom is relevant here, because it is indeed a microcosm of life. In any trial, somebody is trying to take something away from somebody else. So it is in life. That is why I shared with you Oprah's experience in Amarillo. In that compressed life drama are a series of valuable lessons.

Trials reflect the competition that characterizes so much of our lives, although trial results are often more sharply focused: at the end of the day, there's a clear winner; there's a clear loser; freedom may be lost; money may be taken away. But by far the most compelling parallel is this: In life, as in the courthouse, when the competition starts, or when the world starts coming after you, you'd better have yourself a really good strategy *and* know the rules of the game, or the bad guys will be dividing up what *used to be* yours. They'll be getting your paycheck, or dating your sweetheart, or in some way cutting you out and taking your turn.

Ask yourself right now: Do you really have a strategy in your life, or are you just reactively going from day to day, taking what comes? If you are, you simply aren't competitive. There are "a lot of dogs after the bones" out there, and just stumbling along is no way to succeed. The winners in this life know the rules of the game and have a plan, so that their efficiency is comparatively exponential to that of people who don't. No big mystery, just fact.

You, too, need to know the rules of the game and have a plan and a map. You need to ask yourself: "Am I really headed where I want to go, or am I just out there wandering around?" "Is what I'm doing today really what I *want* to do, or am I doing it, not because I want to, but because it is what I was doing yesterday?" "Is what I have what I really want, or is it what I've settled for because it was easy, safe, or not as scary as what I *really* wanted?" Hard questions, I know, but don't you really already know the answers?

The Epidemic

Oprah's situation in Amarillo highlights lessons of widespread application that can show you where the rubber meets the road in your own life. What makes Oprah so appealing is the fact that she is so real, so human, and has the same frailties that we all do. Her initial reactions to the Amarillo attack, the tendencies that she at times demonstrated during that experience, are identical to those I see being applied by people from every walk of life in the face of day-to-day challenges. In fact, those very behaviors are present in epidemic proportions in America today, infecting the lives and goals and dreams of millions of people, young and old, sophisticated or not.

The difference may be that Oprah has developed her life-management skills to the point that it takes a huge crisis to throw her off track. For you, the breakdown may occur way short of a $100 million lawsuit, where the entire world watches as you are personally attacked. That's okay; I will meet you wherever you are. It doesn't matter whether you have a good life that you wish could be better, or a horrible life that you know you must change. This book is designed to give you the tools you need for purposeful, strategic living. Taking a long, hard look at the negative behaviors in your life, and at your current life strategy—if you've even got one—can be more than enlightening; it can be the beginning of a Life Strategy. This self-check of how you are living day to day is of tremendous importance, since you will be, and are, *accountable for your own life*.

Most people, and I'll bet you are no exception, cheat themselves by not asking themselves the hard questions, not facing their true personality and behavior, and therefore not addressing the nitty-gritty issues undermining their efforts to succeed. My position is this: Let the rest of the people live in a fog of self-deception. You take off the blinders and deal with the truth, and you'll leave them in the dust.

So what are the patterns that threatened Oprah in her challenge in Amarillo, and which are also so commonplace in America? What are the patterns that may be destroying your chance to change your life and have what you want?

The first common tendency is denial. Oprah resisted accepting that something so unjust could happen to her and her staff. And all the while it was, in fact, very much happening. Failing to acknowledge that actuality, one that would only grow more complicated with neglect, she fixated on why it shouldn't be happening, rather than dealing with the fact that it was. Her reaction was totally logical, because she knew the truth about what she had done, and she understood the *real* motives of her accusers. But the world is not always logical. Often you are forced to deal with what is, not just what should be. Oprah, for example, felt bad about even being involved in the matter in any form or fashion. She felt the process was nonproductive and a waste of everyone's time. She would never have chosen to be there. That was part of the "denial dialogue."

But you don't always have a choice. For example, having arrived at a nice restaurant, you most likely would not start a fistfight in the lobby. But suppose you just happen to be standing in that lobby when some jerk goes nuts and starts swinging at you—guess what? You're in a fistfight. What's more, you'd better deal with it or make plans to get your dentist out of bed, because it *is* happening. Denial can take the form of totally failing to see what *is*, or seeing it, but resisting it, because you don't like it. Either way, denial is dangerous. This common mistake can have uncommonly bad results.

The second pattern involves making initial assumptions, then failing to test them for truth or accuracy. If you adopt some position, opinion, or belief, and fail to test or verify it, subsequent thinking that is otherwise totally sound and logical can lead you to conclusions that are way wrong. Oprah *assumed* that, because the lawsuit against her was so obviously insincere and "unfair," it would ultimately be revealed as such, and then vanish in a puff of smoke. She *assumed* our justice system would ferret out and eliminate the frivolous. She *assumed* that someone in authority would intervene and tell these cattlemen they could not abuse the court system to try to get richer. She clung to these assumptions because *she wanted them to be true*. Had she tested those assumptions unemotionally, she might have awakened sooner to the fallacies of our justice system and her assumptions. But if you trust yourself and therefore have confidence in the rightness of what you believe to be true, it can be very easy to close your mind to additional possibilities.

The third problem is inertia: paralysis caused by fear and denial. Picture an airline pilot sitting motionless in the cockpit of his fully occupied but disabled jet as it rapidly loses altitude; imagine him saying, "Golly, I can't believe this is happening. There's bound to be some divine intervention in a minute"; or "It can't be all that bad—I've never crashed before. Something will happen to save us." If you deny things that seem too painful to accept, then let their impact, once realized, rob you of efficient, energetic acts of self-preservation, you will fail. Oprah Winfrey rose to a challenge, but she had to grasp it and its gravity first. So, too, must you grasp your true challenges before you can efficiently mobilize. Inertia takes your greatest resource out of the game.

Another pattern involves deceptive masking. Oprah, like so many of us, can wear a mask. Her persona can be so mesmerizing that people forget that she has needs, too. Sometimes we adopt a "stiff upper lip" because being in need, and admitting it, can seem to us to be a show of weakness. But by insisting on "toughing it out," you may close yourself off from forthcoming help, since others are taken in by your show of strength and fail to recognize your needs.

Many people also fail to grasp that, when you choose the behavior, you choose the consequences. By choosing to keep her focus on the "unfairness," Oprah could have continued to let precious time and energy slip away, time and energy that could have been focused on working the problem rather than resisting it. This behavior was a choice on her part. No matter what her rationale, she was *choosing* the behavior of denial, and in so doing, *choosing* the consequences of falling behind the power curve of defending herself. Fortunately, in a dramatic turnaround, she chose not to keep resisting, and to start coping. She made a choice to take action, and thereby chose the consequence of her eventual victory.

These are all interrelated and common mistakes that when mixed with a dangerous set of circumstances can spell disaster. Obviously, the bigger the problem, the bigger the downside if it is mismanaged. As you think back through your life—and surely there are key events that stand out in your memory—what results were created when you were living in denial, or basing your decisions on what turned out to be faulty initial assumptions? What was the effect when you were stuck in inertia and, by hiding behind your mask, you blocked others from helping? Perhaps most importantly: What choices have you made that set you up for an outcome you did not want or need? Have your problems been mundane, or have they been monumental?

You may have known people who seemed to have stepped blindly into a disaster, and your first thought was, "What in the world could they have been thinking?" I predict that before you are through with this book, you will very probably step back from your own life and wonder how in the world you could have been thinking what you were thinking, not seeing what you were not seeing, and choosing the behaviors you chose. Your challenge, at least in part, is to determine what these patterns have done to your life, your dreams, your needs. Are they alive and going strong, or are the epidemic behavioral patterns silently raging in your life, allowing your problems to fester, poisoning your dreams?

Even in everyday life, we see dramatic examples of dreams that die from that which we choose not to see. Perhaps it is parents deluding themselves that their son is not on drugs until his body is found after an overdose; a woman denying that there is a lump in her breast until it progresses beyond treatment; or the spouse who foolishly believes his or her mate is really an agent for the FBI, with only weekend-night assignments. In each of these cases, the result is the same. Problems and challenges almost never resolve themselves; they don't get better with inattention. The only thing worse than having a child on drugs, a serious disease, or a philandering spouse is having the problem but not recognizing it, or, worse yet, knowing it but pretending it isn't true.

Reading this book is not intended to be a passive experience. As you progress through it, you'll see that it is interactive: the key principles in later chapters rely on themes developed in the earlier ones, and all of it calls on you to play an active role.

Assignment #1: Your first assignment is to challenge your beliefs right now, by listing in order of significance the top five things in your life that you have simply failed to fully and completely admit or acknowledge to yourself. This requires some new thinking. You may think, "If I know it, I'm not denying it," or "If I'm denying it, how can I know it to write it down?" I said new thinking. Ask yourself some of those hard questions about what you would rather not think about. Write them down, because you'll be referring to them later. What is it that you know in your heart is a problem not acknowledged or at least so painful that you avoid it?

Be advised that you are going to be writing down a lot of things as we progress through the rest of the book. I recommend that you get some type of journal where you can do all of the "homework" that arises as we move forward. I recommend a spiral notebook, where the pages are attached and can therefore be kept together. This journal is highly confidential and should be for your eyes only. Treating it as such will allow you the freedom to be totally honest.

I would wager that whatever made your list is at least in part a product of your own behavior. I also suspect that the main difference between your problems and the more terribly tragic situations we hear or read about is the result, not the behaviors that led up to it. For aren't the patterns in your life, and those present in the more tragic stories, very likely the same? You've driven a little too fast down a neighborhood street; you've left the kids unattended while you ran next door "for a minute"; you've driven yourself home from happy hour, when discretion should have told you to hand over the keys; you've engaged in unprotected sex; you've fudged on your income tax. The "shocking stories" are often about people who have done the very same things. But only because of a tragically different outcome, they wound up in jail, or burying a child, or dealing with HIV.

Maybe your driving drunk or speeding through a neighborhood didn't leave anyone dead, unlike the person you see on television who did the same thing but ran over a child. You're not audited, whereas the next person is. Your kids are still safe when you get home. It's not that you behaved or chose any better; you just got by with it. But if you are habitually practicing poor life-management skills, you are playing with fire. You may not be getting away with as much as you think you are.

You don't live, choose, or manage your life in a vacuum. It happens in a context called the world. Given the current state of the world, naïveté or a rose garden perception will likely land you in trouble you don't want. You don't live in Mayberry, because it doesn't exist. These days, when you hear people use the word *coke* in a conversation, the odds are that they are not talking about the soft drink. If you decide to take your honey for a midnight swim, you're likely to end up in jail for trespassing, or worse, glowing in the dark because you were bobbing around in a toxic dump or Superfund site you only thought was pristine. Take a twilight stroll down the lane or through the park, and you might not be sleeping at home tonight (don't you hate those hospital gowns?). Oh, and before you leave the house, you might also want to write your name on your arm—better yet, write it on your leg, since that's less likely to get smudged if you decide to fight back.

The world has changed; it is tough out there, of that there can be no doubt. I am sorry to sound like a cynic, but you know I'm right. This world we have conspired to create is drastically different from the one our parents and grandparents knew. If there ever was a Mayberry, there certainly is none now. As we hurtle headlong at breakneck speed toward the millennium, we are caught up in the fastest-paced, most rapidly changing society in the history of humankind. Our world is like an unguided missile, with more speed than control.

You've got a mess on your hands, for sure. You don't

need a Ph.D. in behavioral sciences to know that in virtually every dimension of human functioning, America is, in varying degrees, failing. The divorce rate in the United States is estimated by some authorities to be as high as 57.7 percent, and the average length of new marriages is twenty-six months. Sixty-two percent of our society is obese. Reported emotional neglect of children has increased 330 percent in the last ten years. One in four women has been sexually molested. Suicide is increasing at an exponential rate. At least one out of every six of us will experience a serious, function-impairing depressive episode at some point in our lives; thus, antidepressants and anxiety-reducing agents are now a multibillion-dollar industry.

Violence is rampant, not just in the streets, but at home. Each year, our society witnesses nearly forty million crimes: 74 percent of us are victims of property crimes, while 25 percent of us fall prey to violent crimes. Our teenagers are headed in the wrong direction, as well. Teens between the ages of fourteen and seventeen commit approximately 4,000 murders a year. Each year, over 57 percent of public elementary and secondary school principals report at least one incident of crime to law enforcement authorities. Perhaps the saddest statistic of all: by the time they reach the eighth grade, 45 percent of American children have experimented with alcohol, and 25 percent with drugs.

As a society, we are losing it. When it comes to managing our own emotional lives, and training our children how to manage theirs, we're out of control but desperately pretending otherwise. We project an outward image of "I'm all right. I can take it. I'll be okay," because we fear judgment. Well, it's not okay, and we'd better start changing this world one life at a time, or God only knows what the millennium will hold. The life for you to start with is your own. If you want to be a winner instead of a statistic, you can do it, but lean forward, because it is not easy.

In every church I have ever attended, the people with real problems hid them rather than seeking support, and those who didn't hide them wished that they had, after the doses of guilt, judgment, or alienation they received. We hide our problems, and judge those who don't or can't hide theirs. It's not working, people—not even close. We have forgotten the basic laws of living in general, and living together in particular, and therefore violate them constantly.

I am convinced that the fundamental Life Laws that govern our world and dictate the results of our conduct have not changed. Certain characteristics of the game are different, sure, but it's the basic Life Laws that still dictate our results. Understandably, living in ignorance of or consciously ignoring these Life Laws has created huge problems and a society desperate for answers, one desperate for guidance and knowledge about human experience. Count on us, as a society, to try to quench that thirst with answers that are often harmful, silly, or both.

If you want to know why we as a society are spinning out of control, consider what sorts of "solutions" we're currently being offered. As for psychology as it is practiced today, I am not too much of a fan. In my view, it's too fuzzy, it's too intangible, it exists in a world of opinion and subjectivity. Maybe that's okay if you live in some ivory tower and can afford to pontificate about ambiguous and abstract elements of life. But I don't think that's what you want and I don't think that's what you need. You're living in the real world and dealing with real problems that need real change. You don't just need insight and understanding into your problems; you need them to change, right now.

Consider, too, the "self-empowerment" industry that dominates our culture. It really has very little to do with empowerment, and lots to do with somebody else's bottom line. It is largely unfocused, lazy, gimmicky, politically correct, and above all, marketable, often at the expense of truth. The gurus seem to have everything but verbs in their sentences. You're trying to pay the rent and get your kids to go to college instead of jail, and they want you to play with your inner this or your inner that, or yourself; perhaps a poor choice of words, but appropriate.

You are sold "self-improvement" the same way you're sold everything else: it's easy; five simple steps; you can't help succeeding, because you're so wonderful; your results will be fast, fast, fast. But we are paying dearly—in more ways than one—for this polluting flood of psychobabble. I say polluting, because, instead of stripping away our excuses and jacking us up to deal with our true lives, the psychobabble provides us with a whole new set of excuses. The result is more distraction and more problems.

To the extent that our current pop psych does identify legitimate disorders, those terms are now so overused as to obscure those cases that are genuine. A mom who despairs over the behavior of her spoiled-rotten brat is told that her child is "hyperactive" and is "engaging in negative attention-getting." Outrageous behavior in the classroom is routinely ascribed to "attention-deficit disorder." If you're shooting it up, snorting it, or drinking yourself to sleep with it, you're suffering from a "substance abuse problem." When a middle-aged woman, longing for something more in her life, certain that there's something missing, picks up a book that at last promises answers, it tells her that the answer to her yearnings lies somewhere in her exotic ancestry, several incarnations back. Tell them what they want to hear: it's not their fault; they are victims. What's astonishing is that *we are actively participating in the game, gobbling up these illusions.* You would think that if a ship just kept on sinking faster and faster or was getting farther and farther off course, somebody would finally stand up and say, "Hey, anybody notice this ain't working?"

Well, I'm saying it. I'm shouting it. You need a new strategy, badly. It may not be "nineties en vogue" or politically correct to say so, but I just don't too much care about providing you with vague philosophical pronouncements, rah-rah rhetoric, clever buzz words, or quick-fix solutions as to how life should be or why it should change. What I *am* interested in is your having a clear knowledge-based strategy for winning by overcoming your problems, patterns, and obstacles, and getting what you want in this life, for you and those you care about.

Whether "winning" for you means healing a relationship or a broken heart, having a new job, a better family life, a skinny butt, some inner peace and tranquillity, or some other meaningful goal, you need a strategy to get there, and some guidance on how to create one. Why should you listen to me? For one thing, I am not suggesting that you substitute my judgment for your own, not at all. Challenge every word I say, but first hear it. I've studied the Life Laws, gathered them into one place, and am going to explain them, I hope, clearly.

I have had the privilege, over the years, of designing winning strategies with and for thousands of clients, people from all walks of life, and in every imaginable predicament. I have addressed their problems the same way I want you to address yours: with a real-world focus on *results,* not intentions. There is a science to strategic living. Not to know it in this complex era is tantamount to being illiterate. I did not do it for them, I did it *with* them, and that is my plan with you.

So who am I? I'll bet with the exception of having chosen a different career and course of life study, my background may be a lot like yours. My parents grew up poor. Both my mother and father chopped cotton in the middle of Texas when they were growing up. They were raised by good-hearted but uneducated parents. When, after returning from World War II, my father announced he would go to college on the GI Bill, his family openly ridiculed him for wanting to "play student," wasting his life in a book instead of getting a real job. Nonetheless, ultimately and with great sacrifice to us all, he earned a Ph.D. in psychology, which he practiced for twenty-five years. In 1995, he collapsed and died one Sunday morning while teaching at his church. My mother, to whom he was married for fifty-three years, has a high school education and has worked on and off throughout my life. She raised me and my three sisters with love, affection, and sacrifice: a truly noble woman.

During my high school years, my father and I, separated from the rest of the family while he pursued his internship, lived in apartments that often had no utilities, because we couldn't afford them. Being pretty shallow and status conscious, I was embarrassed to be poor and didn't know enough yet to understand that it did not matter. Among my teenage friends, I was the one with no nice clothes, no car, no money, and no prospects. I had little or no supervision, and if it had not been for athletics, I would probably have never finished high school. Like many families, we lived paycheck to paycheck, got around in old rattletraps, and spent a lot of time doing without. But we loved one another, stuck together, and kept ourselves involved in life.

Had I not won a football scholarship, I probably would never have gone to college, and probably wouldn't be writing this now. I became a psychologist, but found I liked building strategies better than doing therapy, so I began creating and finding forums to instruct people on how to change their lives and attain their goals using the ten Life Laws. I didn't spend much time focusing on why people, businesses, or clients were doing what they were doing unless it directly affected how to change. I instead focused on helping them design a plan to move forward from where they were.

Quite predictably, that approach got us to dealing with solutions much more quickly. It placed the true problems at center stage. Too often, problems get pushed aside because it is painful to deal with them and it seems easier not to. I say "seems" because, while the pain of dealing with problems is an acute, easy-to-identify pain, the pain of avoiding them is also profound, even if more subtle. If you are part of the epidemic of lives not managed, you may find yourself in one of these categories of existence:

—Frustrated that you are not making more money in your job or career

—Capable of more than you are accomplishing

—Stuck in a rut and not getting what you want

—Bored with yourself

—Silently enduring an emotionally barren life or marriage

—Trudging zombielike through a dead and unchallenging career

—Consistently failing in the pursuit of your goals

—Just "going through the motions" of your life with no passion, no plan, and no goal

—Living in a fantasy world in which you think you are bullet-proof, when in fact your actions entail incredible risks

—Living in a comfort zone that yields too little challenge and too little of what you do want, and too much of what you don't want

—Living a lonely existence with little hope for change

—Suffering financial burdens you can't handle, or

—Living with lingering guilt, frustration, or depression

It is not okay to simply accept burdens like these. This book is about how to reach, in a *strategic* way, for something better. You have both the capacity and the right to do so. But first, you have to stop being part of the epidemic. You have to eliminate the behavior that has become so much a part of our country's obsession with the theory of relativity. Einstein probably had no inkling of how a society might apply his scientific thinking to social mores. Americans act as though everything is relative; there are no absolutes anymore. There's no good or bad, no right or wrong, there is no standard to achieve. Everything is a compromise. Think about how often you have said or heard comments like:

"Well, we're doing *relatively* well."

"It's not what I really want, but what are you going to do?"

"I'm trying, but you know, it's hard."

"Well, compared to what we could have had to endure, we're not doing so badly."

Such ideology is seductive, because if there is no clear
standard, no clear finish line, then you can pretend you aren't a
loser, even if you are not getting what you want. It's fuzzy; it's
easier to hide. Seductive as it may be, that thinking is a myth. You
are either winning or losing in your life, plain and simple. You
live in a competitive world, where outcomes are determined by
the distinct Life Laws that I want to reveal to you.

Here's the deal. The next several weeks, months and years
are going to go by, whether you are doing something about your
life circumstances or not. The weeks and months and years will
go by, whether you learn and embrace the Life Laws or not.

Resolve now that you will no longer live by the old adage
that "ignorance is bliss," *un*blissfully allowing your choices and
behaviors to cause you pain and fear rather than peace and joy.
Life Laws, accountability, and hard questions and decisions may
not be what you want to hear about, but good deal or bad, they're
the only deal you've got.

Reality Check

*Assignment #2: It's time for you to do a little homework,
in part to see if you're willing to recognize your self-defeating
excuses and rationales. I want you to sit down and write a story.
The story is entitled: "The Story I'll Tell Myself if I Don't Create
Meaningful and Lasting Change After Reading and Studying This
Book."*

*I want you to be honest. You know your patterns. You
know your typical excuses, rationalizations, and justifications for
failure. Just look ahead, see which excuses you are most likely
going to rely on, and write them down in a story. I suggest that
you begin it by writing: "After reading and studying this book, I
did not create meaningful and lasting change because . . ."*

*As you go through this exercise, I want you to be creative,
thorough, and brutally honest about the things you will say to
justify your failure. You know you con yourself and let yourself off
the hook when the going gets tough. This is a test to see how
willing you are to recognize that con job that sabotages yourself.
It is a test to see if you can tell it like it is, or if you want to just
live with the same old, tired excuses and be right instead of happy.*

Now that you have finished writing, let's reflect on what you've done. You have just argued your limitations. You have just created a record of the thoughts and beliefs that you use to sabotage yourself in every endeavor you undertake. There, on paper, are the same thoughts and beliefs you will use to prevent this book from changing your life for the better. The more candid it is, the more self-critical it is, the more valuable it is. Are any of the following excuses familiar; did some of them get on your list?

—It was just too hard.
—He doesn't really understand me.
—That's all for other people.
—I couldn't focus because of the kids and my job.
—He's just too harsh; I need a more gentle approach.
—My problems are different.
—I need to read it again.
—Until my spouse reads it, I'm just spinning my wheels.
—I'm right and he's wrong.

Try something new with me for a while. At least during the period of time that you are reading this book, you can help yourself immensely if you evaluate your life, behavior, and thinking very differently. Instead of asking whether the way you are living, behaving, and thinking is "right," I want you to ask whether the way you are living, behaving, and thinking *is working or not working*.

I suggest that if what you are choosing is not working, that by itself tells you that those things are worthy of change. This ought to make perfect sense—unless, of course, you're more concerned about being right than you are concerned with being successful. If, on the other hand, your priority is winning and getting what you want, then at least for the time that you are reading this book, be willing to "move your position" on anything and everything that we deal with.

You can always go back to your old way of doing things; resolve that if what you are doing is not working, you will be willing to change it. I don't mean that figuratively, I mean it literally. If your marriage isn't working, change what you're doing. If your self-management is not working, change what you're doing. If your "child management" is not working, even though you're dead sure you're right, change it. What have you got to lose? Forget about being right or winning the argument about who is right. If what you're doing is not working, change it. Measure your thinking and behavior by that simple yardstick: Is it working or not working? You've been right long enough; try being a winner instead.

Having read only what you've read so far, you've arrived at a crossroads. In the next few moments, you'll be making one of the most important decisions in your life. Will you choose to learn the Life Laws, fold them into a life strategy and begin to live purposefully, or will you just continue to bob along with your hands in your pockets, taking what comes your way and complaining about what you don't have?

There never is a "good time," so there's no better time than right now. There's no better place than right here. This book is for people who are saying, "I have had it. I am sick of this. Show me the Life Laws, show me how to live strategically and show me how to create what I want in my life. I am ready."

The game has just begun. It's not too late. Whatever your situation—whether it's just that you suspect there's something missing from an otherwise quality life, or your life is a shambles—there is a strategy that will make you a winner. Together we're about to make you bottom-line streetwise and real-world savvy. Enough whining about "bad genes" or "bad luck" or "bad timing." It is *your time* and *your turn*. But you have to have the guts to face the truth about yourself. Get your feelings hurt, decide it's all too harsh—and your life is back where it started. But consider these two truths: First, you've got what it takes, and you're worth the effort it will take to find that truth and build that strategy. Second: nobody is going to do it for you. But that's okay, because you don't need a brain transplant; you don't need a spine transplant; you don't need anything that you don't have within you.

When I confronted Oprah that night with the accountabilities and results swirling around her, she came quickly to attention. No longer willing to be a spectator at her own dismemberment, she became committed and focused. She immediately stopped living with the epidemic behavior. She stopped doing the things that were going to prevent her from overcoming her obstacles. Just as importantly, she actively adopted and began living consistently with the Life Laws that govern our world. As we work together to provide you with strategic control of your own destiny, you will get the chance to learn those same laws, and, I hope, incorporate them into your life.

Life Laws are the rules of the game. No one is going to ask you if you think these laws are fair, or if you think they should exist. Like the law of gravity, they simply are. You don't get a vote. You can ignore them and stumble along, wondering why you never seem to succeed; or you can learn them, adapt to them, mold your choices and behavior to them, and live effectively. Learning these Life Laws is at the absolute core of what you must master in this book to have the essential knowledge for a personal life strategy.

CHAPTER TWO

YOU EITHER GET IT, OR YOU DON'T

We don't like their sound,
and guitar music is on the way out.
—Decca Records executive, rejecting the Beatles in 1962

Life Law #1: You Either Get It, or You Don't
Your Strategy: Become one of those who get it. Break the code of human nature, and find out what makes people tick. Learn why you and other people do what they do, and don't do what they don't.

This is a law so fundamental in its truth that you should treat it as a personal challenge in developing your life strategy. Obviously, if you are not already, you want to start being one of the people who get it, one of the few people who has figured it out. In almost every situation, there are people who get it and there are people who don't—and it's really easy to tell them apart. Those who get it are enjoying the fruits of their knowledge. Those who don't spend a lot of time looking puzzled, frustrated, and doing without. Those who don't get it can often be found beating their heads against the wall and complaining that they never seem to get a break. Those who get it seem to be tuned in and not just playing, but actually controlling. They don't make foolish mistakes, because they have figured out that there is a definite formula for success, and they have broken the code. They have the formula. These people are invariably successful because they have acquired the knowledge they need to create the results they want. In short, they get it.

The "it" that you need to get may change from time to time and from one situation to another, but there will be some important common elements. The "it" whose code you need to break may be in relationships, self-management, or career competition. You may need to come to grips with your emotional life. Whatever "it" is, once you truly understand how things really work, you are functioning from a position of knowledge and strength. This is obviously a good thing, particularly if you now belong to an "informed minority," while the rest of the herd continues to plod along in a blind trial-and-error fashion.

If you break a criminal law, such as those prohibiting theft or assault, you will pay a fine or go to jail. If you violate a physical law, such as gravity, you can experience pain or—depending on your elevation when you commit the violation—even death. Just as with these types of laws, if you break a Life Law, there are penalties, some quite severe. I will bet that you have been paying dearly for those violations throughout your life.

You break the current Life Law whenever you operate without the necessary information and skills to create the results you want. When you don't understand the rules of the game, such as which behaviors will get which results, or when you lack a strategy, you are likely to run afoul of conditions and requirements that would guarantee your success. In competition with those who do get it—that is, they do have the skills, know the rules, and have a plan—you are not even a threat; you are just a patsy. In addition to making you noncompetitive, not understanding how life works can also definitely put you in conflict with authority figures. If you aren't playing by the rules, bosses and others with leverage and control can write you off in a hurry, or penalize you for being unprepared.

When I see people who just don't get it, stumbling along in life, I wonder how they ever survive. It's painful to watch people do things when you know, before they ever do it, that their fate is sealed. They are trying, they have hopes and dreams, but you know their outcomes are doomed because they just don't get it. If you are one of those people, isn't it time to tune in and quit losing before you ever start because you just don't get it? Violators, invariably, continue to miss clues to their ineffectiveness and continue down the path of destruction. Those who do get it pay attention and make adjustments. As I was growing up, I had a number of "educational opportunities" regarding this law long before I had any fancy schooling. Time and again, the world would just hammer me when I didn't get it. I learned the hard way that the more tuned in I was, the less often I got burned, and vice versa. And above all, I learned I had to pay attention.

During my high school years in Kansas City, I worked the night shift at the Hallmark card plant downtown. When you get off work at two or three o'clock in the morning, it's a different world than what people see during the day. We were night owls looking for trouble, and we usually found some. A buddy of mine, who also worked at the plant, owned a Chevy Chevelle muscle car with over four hundred horsepower. After work, we liked to race around the deserted streets at ridiculous speeds, looking for a drag race with some other late-night moron with a hundred dollars to bet.

One night, during the Christmas holidays, we had two passengers on our late-night prowls: a long-time friend visiting me from a small town, and a friend of the driver's whom I had not met before. Under my then-theory that stupidity was a virtue, we were doing well over a hundred miles an hour on Main Street, right on the fringe of downtown Kansas City, when an unmarked patrol car appeared out of nowhere, clinging to our bumper. His car was apparently pretty fast, too. He didn't seem to want to race, I was pretty sure he didn't have any beer to share, and boy, did he look mad.

Skipping the usual practice of flooding us with spotlights and calling for backup, the patrolman pulled us over and leaped out of his car, slamming his door so hard we could feel it. I don't know if this cop was truly a giant, or just looked that way that night, but he looked big enough to have his own weather systems, and it definitely looked like a storm was brewing.

As the officer stomped up to the car, my buddy's friend panicked. Wriggling and sliding out the rear window, he dropped head first to the sidewalk and took off running. If that cop wasn't mad enough before, he was now. It was bad enough that we had violated his turf; now, because one of us had run away, we had further insulted him and defied his authority.

The policeman yanked the driver's door open, grabbed my buddy by the collar, dragged him out, and ordered us to follow suit. Holding my friend by the collar, he said, "I'm going to ask you one @!&Z$ time: Who is that boy that ran off?"

In his most surly and sarcastic tone, my buddy snarled, "Well, his name is . . . Sam Sausage! What of it?"

In retrospect, it was at that moment that I recognized this first Law of Life, and perhaps even formulated how to express it, because I remember thinking, "Buddy, *you just don't get it*." That cop hit him so hard it almost broke *my* nose.

Up to that point, I had been worried about getting a ticket or an impounded car. Given the turn of events, that would have been a godsend. Apparently, this particular officer was not real big on paperwork. My small-town friend was, unfortunately for him, next in line. His problem was, he really didn't know the runner's name, and neither did I, so my prospects were not looking too good, either. Now the cop ran the same drill. Grabbing the collar of my friend (who was now wishing he could "beam" back to "Nowhere, USA"), he looked him in the eye and said, "I'm gonna ask you one @!&Z$ time: Who is that boy that ran off?"

Well, as I said, my friend may not have known his name, but he did know what probably wasn't going to be the best answer. With absolutely no surliness and no attitude, and with all the sincerity that a petrified, cotton-mouthed kid could muster, he said, "Sir, I swear to you on my mother's grave (she was of course alive and well back in "Nowhere"), I don't know his name, but, sir, I can promise you this: I am absolutely certain it is not Sam Sausage."

As scared as I was, I instantly thought, "Now, he gets it. We may live through this yet." I said not a word, figuring this cop needed a really good leaving alone. My dad had taught me there are times in life when you just don't want to miss a good chance to *shut up*. This was clearly one of those times.

One guy did not get it, and he was kissing the pavement and would sport two black eyes for the next several weeks. One guy did get it, and he was still vertical and could see out of both of his eyes. A stark contrast. I can assure you that we never traveled at over twenty-five miles an hour on that cop's beat again, ever. Life just goes better when you are one of those who get it.

At this point, your question should be, "I don't want to kiss the pavement in life, so what am I not getting in the important areas of my life, and furthermore, where and how do I get it?" Clearly, you have to be willing to learn some things you don't know so you can begin to make better choices and decisions. To avoid "kissing the pavement," you have to be willing to learn the

Life Laws and how things work so that you can fold all of that into your life.

These undeniable Life Laws that are our current focus can take all the guesswork out of your decision making. This current law, and the nine others that go with it, will explain a lot of events and outcomes in your past life that may have seemed, at the time, like randomness or dumb luck.

Know this: If you learn the ten Laws of Life presented here, you will definitely be one of the people who get it. You will never again have to fail because you just didn't know how you or the world worked. These Life Laws will tell you how, and they will tell you why.

The Edge

The kind of knowledge I want you to have is that which defines and makes the difference between really living and just existing. Existing is instinctual; it is involuntary, reactive self-preservation, with the primary goal of just getting from one day to the next, without regard to quality. Living, on the other hand, is the exercise of certain learned skills, attitudes, and abilities that you have acquired and honed to a sharp and focused edge. The primary goal is to have a quality of experience that is unique and rewarding. The skills you need to create that quality of life are the skills of understanding and controlling the cause-and-effect relationships of life: in other words, using your knowledge to make things happen the way you want them to. That means learning how and why you do what you do, and don't do what you don't do; and how and why other people do what *they* do, and don't do. That knowledge can give you an incredible edge in the competition of life.

If you'll reflect on it, I'll bet there's not a single situation you can think of where superior knowledge, that would allow you to predict and control the actions of yourself and others, would not have been a good thing. We live in a social world. Virtually everything you do requires interactions with others. Whether you are buying a loaf of bread, working with others at your job, living within a family unit, dealing with your roommate, or you're just out there navigating the terrain of life, you have to deal with other people.

Examples are so plentiful as to seem simplistic. If you've applied for a job running a computer and you know how to run it, obviously that knowledge gives you the power to get the work done, and is an essential condition to your getting the job—but it gives you the advantage only if you can convince the interviewer. If you find yourself deep in a forest, but know how to get out—bingo, good thing. If you and several other people are deep in that forest, and you're the only one who knows how to get out—double bingo, that's really a good thing. Now your knowledge makes you the one in control. You are the one everyone else will follow, the one who enjoys the special peace of mind and confidence that comes with self-reliance. It won't be because you're attractive or rich or have a great personality, but because you get it. Knowledge is power.

Think about the people who are running your world: people who are successful in business, politics, athletics, love, or just life in general. I'd be willing to bet that almost all of them know how to get others to do things they want or need them to do. They know what buttons to push to get people to move in their direction and adopt their ideas, values, and beliefs. They can also predict what other people are likely to do or not do, because they have a masterful understanding of the factors that determine human behavior. Being able to predict the behavior of others can be almost as powerful as being able to control it. This is particularly true of your quest to motivate and control yourself.

For example, if you suddenly understand why you always seem to quit before you achieve what you want, and you understand how to change that pattern, then your life is different and it's different right away. The applications are endless. If you suddenly know why your spouse does what he or she does, and you know how to get him or her to change, you've just made a major step toward improving your marriage. Consider the advantages this information affords you in raising your children, competing in the workplace, selling yourself or your products, or winning the confidence, trust, and affection of those you respect and value. That is an incredible edge.

Because you know how the game is played and you know the pressure points that drive the results, you create a level of mastery necessary to win. If you know which behavior gets which result, you eliminate the errors. And who wins? You do.

I want to stress that these are *learned* skills, and this is acquired knowledge. No matter how smart you are, no one expects you to start speaking Russian until somebody has taught you how to do it. No matter how smart you are, if you haven't got the training, we cannot strap you into the cockpit of a 747, launch you off the end of the runway, and expect you to know how to fly that airplane. The problem is that when it comes to succeeding at the game of life, nobody ever really taught you the rules, let alone how to play the game.

When I look at the behavior patterns in American life today, I don't ask myself why our society is in decline. I ask myself, "Why not?" Given our lack of preparation, I would expect no other outcome.

We're hardly literate enough in human functioning to recognize what the problems are. Think about it. Why do so many marriages fail? Because *nobody gets taught how to be married.* We're not taught how to pick a mate, or why to pick a mate; we don't know how to manage our emotions once we're in a marriage; we don't know how to resolve marital conflict. Married people have never been taught why they or their spouses feel the way they do and act the way they do. Nobody has ever taught us the fundamentals. Why, if you're an American, are you more likely than not to be obese? Because no one has ever taught you how to manage your impulses. Nobody ever taught you how to program yourself for health and well-being. Why are our kids turning to drugs, at younger and younger ages? Because nobody has ever taught people how to parent their children in a way that keeps them from needing to turn to drugs to feel the way they want to feel.

Since we do not get formal training from society, we've been relying on the role models in our lives. But isn't it true that most of us were raised by parents from an era that put little or no emphasis on human functioning? Where life management was concerned, people of earlier generations did get strapped into the cockpit and launched off the runway, ready or not. If our parents were never *trained* to be effective mothers, fathers, spouses, then what kind of role models could they be? In fact, I submit to you that if you have been fortunate enough to have positive role models in your life, you—and they—can thank Providence or blind luck or even trial and error that they got it right, but it's a safe bet that training and preparation had nothing to do with it. Simply put, this means not only that you may lack certain crucial information, but that the information you do have may be wrong. Sometimes, the hardest part in learning something new is unlearning the old way of doing it.

Assignment #3: Adopt the attitude of questioning and challenging everything in your life that you can identify as having been accepted on blind faith or as having been adopted out of tradition or history. Using your journal, make a list of all of those things you can think of that fit that definition. Consider patterns in your personal, professional, family, and social areas. I think you will be surprised at how much of your life involves patterns where you do things in a certain way simply because someone else who didn't know any more about it than you did them that way. You will, of course, find certain things that withstand the challenge and therefore should be embraced and continued. You will also identify things that do not withstand the challenge and therefore should be modified or abandoned.

Clearly, all you can do is what you know how to do. It is my intention to put you on alert that there is a lot more to know, and that what you do know may be wrong. The next nine Life Laws are organized to provide you with reliable knowledge that you may not find in a textbook, but that truthfully and accurately reflects how the world works. Maya Angelou has eloquently said, "You did what you knew how to do, and *when you knew better, you did better.*" It's time you knew better.

Obviously, not everybody in this world is lost, but you must be careful and discriminating about where and from whom you accept input. There are idiots with fancy degrees who don't have enough sense to come in out of the rain. And there are wise and insightful people without any highbrow education. You can also find a few who have both education and wisdom. It is up to you to choose solid, reliable teachers. Not so that you can substitute their thinking for your own, but so you can add to your personal knowledge.

If you have ever been involved in any sort of organization, you know what I am saying. Some authority comes from the shiny nameplate on the door—and then there are those whose influence, simply but powerfully, comes from the fact that they just know "the ropes."

Your job, of course, is to find sources of information and influence whose credibility is not a function of a nameplate on a door, but instead is proof of the fact that, however they gained the knowledge, they do "know the ropes." Fortunately, there are those kinds of people around. I am sure you have encountered them in your life and maybe have been that person who "knew the ropes" in different situations and circumstances along the way.

Think back. Early into a new job, when you were still the "new kid," someone may have said to you, "Stick close to that old gray dog over there—he knows the ropes around here.'' What people respected about Gray Dog (G.D.) was that he (or she) understood that particular *system* and how to make it work for, rather than against, the people in it: Better than anyone else, this person knew the rules, the beliefs, the biases, and the guidelines that drove that particular system. Now, your office wall may have been cluttered with diplomas; your first week's workclothes may have cost more than G.D. made in a month; but no matter how sophisticated your background, no matter how much expertise you thought you were bringing to your new position, you learned pretty quickly that G.D. had wisdom.

When the power goes off, or the computer network crashes, don't bother telling the specialists; just call G.D. He'll know whom to contact and what to say. When the copier people say that they can't possibly service the machine until next week at the earliest, have G.D. call them; she gets results (or she may know just where to kick it herself). And when layoffs are imminent, somehow G.D. is going to be the first to know the details.

While other people at the job know ''things,'' G.D.'s particular expertise lies in the human behaviors that govern that workplace. Early into that new job, you learned that if you could just know what he knew, you'd avoid breaking a rule (written or otherwise), embarrassing yourself, and alienating the boss. He could tell you what the higher-ups were looking for in an employee. He could tell you what they needed to see and hear from you in order to decide that you were okay. He could tell you the ''rules of the game,'' some written, some—usually, the important ones—not. He might even share with you the secret formula to get ahead.

G.D.'s *experience* had given him knowledge, and that *knowledge* made him powerful. He had learned how to work the system—that's how he got to be so gray. He knew what you could get away with and what you couldn't. He had studied the policy manual. More importantly, he had observed how the real world worked. G.D. had broken the code.

Now you may be that person at your job, or you may know someone who is. There's an old G.D. just about everywhere. You see him in prison movies—he's the older guy with the watchful eyes, slouching by the wall, saying little. He's in movies about the police force, or the Mafia, or the battlefield. He knows the politics, and he knows when to push and when to give. He knows how to stay alive. You can find him in the corporate cafeteria, and you can find him living under the bridge, among the homeless. There's always that person who can reliably tell you, "I don't care what they say, or what you believe, or what you learned in school, or what you thought it ought to be; I'm telling you how it is."

When I imagine Gray Dog, I picture him telling me how it is—sharing with me the kind of commonsense wisdom that you don't get out of a book. Nothing fancy, just the nitty-gritty that you only know from experience and paying attention. He may not be eloquent, but you can tell he gets it. You might expect to hear:

Gray Dog Wisdom

Fact: "There ain't no Santa Claus, there ain't no pony, and Elvis is *way* dead. If your life is going to get better around here, it will be because *you make it better*. Pray to God, but row for the shore."

Fact: "Before your life can go in the right direction, you have to pull your head out and *stop* going in the wrong direction."

Fact: "You don't have to stick *your* hand in *your* blender to know that it is not the best idea to put hands in blenders."

Fact: "Make a plan and work the plan. Life is not a dress rehearsal."

Fact: "They will use you if you let them. When they come around thinning the herd, or taking away people's lunch money, get a really serious look on your face, and dig in."

Fact: "Life *is* a competition. They *are* keeping score, and there *is* a time clock."

You and I

In this book, the "system" we address is your *life,* your relationships, your career, your family life, your spiritual life, your participation in society, and most importantly, your relationship with yourself. So unless you won the lucky sperm contest and came into this world as a ridiculously endowed trust-fund baby, you need to learn the system, or get used to being a have-not. As clichéd as it may sound, life is a journey; as with any other trip, if you don't have a map and a plan and a timetable, you will get lost. On the other hand, with a well-thought-out, realistic, serious plan, you will be amazed at what can happen. If you don't have a clue about making a life strategy, you're not stupid; there is a science to these matters, and you can learn that technology. You need a guide who knows the system of life and the science, and you need a guide who will tell it like it is, even though how it is may be difficult to hear.

I'm more of a bald dog than a Gray Dog, but if you're willing to learn, I'm ready to tell you how it is. I do know the bottom line, and I've worked long and hard for that knowledge. I want to save you the trial and error I had to go through to get it. To the extent that life has a "policy manual," I've read it backward and forward; just as importantly, however, I've made it my business to understand the push and pull of human behavior. I have paid careful attention to the social hydraulics that are affecting your life right now.

For example, having helped to build strategy in Oprah's and hundreds of other lawsuits, and thousands of lives, I have learned that it is possible to turn situations around. Victory *can* be snatched from disaster. I have learned that anybody can handle smooth water, but that the people who succeed do so consistently and know how to stay afloat when storms are raging. I want to tell you what they know. I want *you* to be among those few in the crowd who get it. As when the magician spreads the cards out face up, and shows you how the trick is done, you may be surprised at how dramatically your results can change when you learn and follow the ten Life Laws.

The challenge of creating a strategy for Oprah's trial was a recent example of how that edge of knowledge was used to create a desired result. I had to develop a strategy that would get people to embrace her view of the events in question. To do that, I had to know what was important to those jurors and what to emphasize to get them to conclude rightly. As you've already seen, the hill we had to climb was incredibly steep, in that we were trapped in cattle country (several jurors even raised cattle themselves!). It was nonetheless a challenge I approached with passion and resolve. The strategy had nothing to do with duping a jury, or creating some "smoke and mirrors" defense. The strategy was to get twelve intelligent, moral people to overcome any misguided loyalty they may have felt toward these millionaire "factory" cattlemen, and to deal with the truth as it really was.

Planning that strategy involved the same kinds of things you need to know in order to plan your strategies to persuade the people in your world to support *your* goals. In every strategy involving people, there are always at least two things you must do:

You must overcome their resistances and excuses, and then get them to accept your view of the world. In Amarillo, I had to figure out how to overcome the powerful human tendency to "take care of your own." Oprah was the outsider, up against the local boys. I was convinced the jurors would not be consciously biased, but a bias about which someone is unaware can be potentially even more dangerous than if they were partial and knew it.

I know Texas, and I know people in general are suspicious of those they don't live with, work with, worship with, and grow up with. We had to meet that jury where they were in terms of what they believed, and yet persuade them to move their position to our way of thinking. You must understand someone and know what makes them tick before you can connect with them. They need to see similarities between you and your values and their own. That is the basis of bonding. As a result, we had to figure out the same kinds of things you will have to know to deal effectively with the people you hope to influence in your life: Whether it's your children, your spouse, your boss, or others, you have to know them to move them. You have to sell them on the fact that you aren't some off-the-wall "wacko" with strange ideas.

To really understand someone, what is it you need to know? What information will truly tell you who they are? If I want to genuinely know what someone or some group is really all about, so I can know what I have to offer that will be of interest, I, at a minimum, want to know:

1—What do they value the most in their lives: Are ethics a big deal? Do money and success define them? Do they value strength, or compassion? What really matters in their outlook on life?

2—What are their expectancies and beliefs about how life does and should work?

3—What resistances or predispositions—fears, biases, prejudices—do they have?

4—What positions or approaches or philosophies are they most likely to reject or accept?

5—What do they need to hear from a person in order to conclude that that person is fundamentally "okay" and to be trusted?

6—What sorts of things do they consider relevant?

7—How do they feel about themselves?

8—What do they want most in their lives?

As you make a conscious commitment to learning about how and why you and others do what you do, you will find that different things drive the behavior of different people. Life Law #3, *People Do What Works*, describes the different categories of payoffs that control behavior, so I will defer a detailed discussion of that law until later. However, there are some important common truths that are fundamental to human functioning.

These commonalities apply in a vast majority of the cases and therefore should become the ABC's of your knowledge base about people. Obviously, if you know these common characteristics of human functioning, you can use them in your strategic planning for yourself and others. I constantly use these common characteristics in formulating strategies that involve not just jurors, but people in all walks of life. Write these things on the back of your hand if you have to, because incorporating them into your social interactions will change the course of your life, starting right now. The ten most significant common characteristics I have identified are:

1—The number-one fear among all people is rejection.

2—The number-one need among all people is acceptance.

3—To manage people effectively, you must do it in a way that protects or enhances their self-esteem.

4—Everybody—and I mean everybody—approaches every situation with at least some concern about "what's in it for me?"

5—Everybody—and I mean everybody—prefers to talk about things that are important to them personally.

6—People hear and incorporate only what they understand.

7—People like, trust, and believe those who like them.

8—People often do things for other than the apparent reasons.

9—Even people of quality can be, and often are, petty and small.

10—Everybody—and I mean everybody—wears a

social mask. You must look beyond the mask
to see the person.

Having read this list, you may be thinking, "Boy, this guy
is a pessimist about people." Not true. I'm not a pessimist; I'm a
realist. I'm just telling you how it is, and if you will honestly
assess your experience, you will find that you, just like me, are
living proof that those ten observations are accurate.

These two lists—the personal information you need to
know to really understand someone, and the ten most common
traits among people—are exactly the kinds of things that you need
to know if you are designing a life strategy that requires you to
persuade someone to see things your way, in order for you to
succeed. Whether it involves your spouse, your child, a customer,
some authority figure, an employer, a coworker, or yourself, if you
use these lists as guides to your thinking and behavior, you are
operating with a plan of approach that gives you the edge.

In fact, to ignore these "givens" about human behavior
would be wrong thinking. Wrong thinking can seal your fate before you even begin. Failure is no accident. You set yourself up
for it or you don't. You can and will avoid failure if you use this
information in your attempts to manage yourself and others. Even
using just these two lists means you have a strategy, instead of
just reactively plunging into intersections. But the points of focus
on these lists are just the beginning of understanding how people
and therefore the world works.

That means that you've got to commit to becoming a student of human nature. This is a social world and you are a social
animal. Now, I recognize that this is probably the third time I've
told you this since you started reading this book, but I intend to
pound it into your head: If you understand why the rest of the
herd does or doesn't do what it does or doesn't do, you will not
be caught unaware by yourself or anyone else.

I've told you that the next nine laws will address, in great detail,
how our world works. You need to be willing to learn these laws
and to go beyond what you learn in this book by becoming an
attentive student, gathering data every single day as you're moving
about the world. It's all about attitude. Open your door tomorrow
with a commitment to pay attention to how people are behaving
and why. Use your two lists as a place to start figuring out yourself
and those you deal with.

Try a simple experiment tomorrow by testing a few of the common characteristics on the above list. Characteristic number two, "The number-one need among all people is acceptance," can be tested quite easily. If you go to a restaurant, a store, or have some interaction at work, take time before you conduct your business with the person to acknowledge him or her directly. You might try commenting on how hard they are working or how difficult their job might be. This will convey a message of acceptance to the person, and you will immediately see an upturn in their attitude and service toward you.

If, for example, you are in a restaurant and service is slow, when the waiter finally gets to you, try saying something like: "Boy, I can't believe they have you running so hard and fast today. As fast as you are going, you need roller skates. We appreciate you getting to us." As superficial as that may sound, give it a try. I think you will come away concluding that the ten things on the common characteristics list were not put there indiscriminately.

You know that certain people are successful and other people are not. Make a study of how they differ. Search for explanations of why they differ.

As a kid, I always fantasized about being Superman, particularly having his X-ray vision. As a healthy, growing boy, you can probably guess how I would have used that particular gift. (*Hint:* It wouldn't have been to see who was locked in the basement.) In any event, isn't that what we're talking about here: being able to see what others cannot? Probably not as fun as X-ray vision, but a whole lot more useful. There is a whole other level of functioning going on out there; pay attention to it and it will yield big dividends.

You probably think that I'm teaching you how to be manipulative. You're right. Manipulation is not, in and of itself, a bad thing. The fact is, I am attempting to manipulate you right now. I say that openly and freely, and I make no apology for it. Manipulation is only a bad thing if it is insidious, selfish, and works to the detriment of your target. But if I can manipulate you into learning about becoming and then actually being a more effective individual, mother, father, husband, or wife, what is there to complain about? That kind of manipulation is a good thing, particularly since I'm telling you up front that I'm engaging in it.

And let's not forget that one kind of manipulation reigns supreme. Even more important than having the knowledge to pre-

dict human behavior or control other people is having the knowledge to predict and control yourself. Knowing how to be an
effective manager of others can be helpful; it is exponentially more
important to be an effective manager of yourself. No matter where
or in what circumstances you encounter people—whether in your
home, at work, or at play—the one common denominator in all
of those situations is you.

The person you spend the most time with is you. The
person you most need the power to influence and control is you.
The person whose negative characteristics and behavior patterns
you most need the power to minimize or eliminate, and whose
positive characteristics and behavior patterns you most need to
maximize, is you. Whether the characteristic is depression, insecurity, anger, apathy, loneliness, or any of a number of other possible characteristics, you are the one who will have to minimize
or eliminate it. Doing so will require knowledge. It takes knowledge about how you developed that negative characteristic, why
you persist with it, and, more importantly, how to replace it with
more positive, constructive characteristics.

How many times in your life have you looked at others
and thought, "I wish I could be that happy," "I wish I could have
that self-confidence," "I wish I could be as together as they seem
to be"? If you're honest, I'm sure you've said that to yourself at
least occasionally. That's okay: Not every day is a great day. Nor
is it at all unhealthy to see, in other people, qualities and characteristics that you'd like to emulate. But the paramount issue is that
you have to understand how you work, from the inside out; what
makes you feel the way you feel.

To appreciate the importance of being among those who
get it, you have only to consider the alternative state in which you
may now be living. Although the opposite of knowledge is un-
doubtedly ignorance or the lack of knowledge, the more dangerous
alternative is the presence of wrong thinking or misinformation.

We usually find this a lot easier to recognize in other
people than in ourselves. How many times have you encountered
some guy who has not one clue about what people value, and not
one shred of sensitivity to his impact on other people? This clod
will embarrass himself with offensive behavior and statements,
painfully unaware of the rolled eyes and jokes behind his back.
People get the same strained smile or grimace on their faces as
they do around a really bad odor, yet he wrongly thinks he has

impressed everyone. (You may recall Cousin Eddie from the *Vacation* movie series.) He just doesn't get it.

Now contrast this clod to the person who clearly has made a study of human nature. He or she skillfully and effectively inspires in others the kinds of responses that pave the way to personal success. People seek out this person because they know they'll be treated well; the encounter leaves them feeling better about themselves for having had the interaction. The moral of that story is that while you are paying attention to how the world works, pay special attention to how it is reacting to you.

We cannot leave a discussion about the power of knowledge without mentioning the clod's first cousin, the "know-it-all." Know-it-alls are a useful illustration of what it means to lack a willing spirit. Not only are these insufferable bores tedious and harmful to others, they suffer their own form of self-paralysis: If they already know it all, why would they be the slightest bit open or sensitive to opportunities to gain new information? They already have all the information, so there's no reason to look for more. Any effort to get them to consider something new is "irrelevant" and causes them to shut down, like a turtle pulling back into its shell. They are totally closed to any opportunity for learning information that may contradict their strongly held and poorly founded beliefs. They fossilize into this state, stuck in wrong thinking, and are proud of it. This paralysis, in turn, paves the way for prejudice, bigotry, and all manner of closed-minded, judgmental behavior. Having picked up misinformation about an entire group or race of people, they treasure that false knowledge; they treat it as the gospel. Their motto is "Not always right, but never in doubt." It's a very common human trait, and it has spawned wars, and all kinds of human suffering, for centuries.

In other words, don't assume that the current discussion and law applies to everyone but you.

You either get it or you don't. One of the worst ways to not get it is to think you do when you don't. Adopt the attitudes set forth in this section, and immerse yourself into the process of learning the next nine laws, and you will become a member of the "gets it" club. Let's hope you have given your last "Sam Sausage" answer to the questions of life.

So just as knowledge is power, the lack of knowledge, or a reliance upon misinformation, is crippling, misleading, and harmful. Resolve now that you will gather knowledge about how and why you and those you encounter in life do what you, and they, do. I can imagine no better starting point for putting this plan into action than learning the next nine laws. Let them become the bedrock of your knowledge.

CHAPTER THREE

You Create Your Own Experience

The sower may mistake and sow his peas crookedly; the peas make no mistake, but come up and show his line.
—Ralph Waldo Emerson

Life Law #2: You Create Your Own Experience
Your Strategy: Acknowledge and accept accountability for your life. Understand your role in creating the results that are your life. Learn how to choose better so you have better.

The law is simple: you are accountable for your life. Good or bad, successful or unsuccessful, happy or sad, fair or unfair, you own your life.

You are now accountable; you have always been accountable; you will always be accountable. That is how it is. That may not be how you want it to be, but that is how it is.

Please understand: I am not talking about this as a ''general proposition.'' I am not presenting this as a theory. I'm telling you that you create the results in your life, not some of the time, but all of the time. If you don't like your job, you are accountable. If your relationships are on the rocks, you are accountable. If you are overweight, you are accountable. If you don't trust members of the opposite sex, you are accountable. If you are not happy, you are accountable. Whatever your life circumstance is, accepting this law means that you can no longer dodge responsibility for how and why your life is the way it is. And taking responsibility doesn't just mean giving "lip service" to being accountable by saying, "Okay, I'm accountable."

Let me tell you *why* this is so important. If you don't accept accountability, you will misdiagnose *every* problem you have. If you misdiagnose, you will mistreat. If you mistreat, things won't get better, plain and simple. Even if you think there can't possibly be a link between your problems and yourself, assume I'm right and keep digging for your role in the problems. It is there, I promise you. Trust me.

Since this law is absolute truth—since it is how the world works, like it or not—then your resisting or denying this law keeps you stuck in the realm of fantasy. By convincing yourself that you are a victim, you are guaranteed to have no progress, no healing, and no victory. Your flight from responsibility will prevent you from taking the bit in your teeth and going to work on controlling your life. If you truly want change, and you truly acknowledge that you create your own experience, then you must analyze what you've done or haven't done to create the undesirable results. Genuinely acknowledging your accountability means that you should be willing to ask yourself questions like the following:

What is the life circumstance that I do not like?
What did I do to arrange the situation so that it happened in the way that it happened?
What did I do to make the result possible? I accept that I'm the one who did it, so what was it?
Did I trust foolishly?
Did I miss important warning signs?
Did I fail to be clear about what I wanted?
Did I con myself because I wanted it to be true?
What choices did I make that directly led to the result I did not want?
Did I choose the wrong person or the wrong place?
Did I choose what I chose for the wrong reasons?
Did I choose the wrong time?
What did I *fail* to do that directly created the result I did not want?
Did I fail to take needed action? If so, what was it?
Did I fail to stand up for myself and claim my rights?
Did I fail to ask for what I wanted?
Did I fail to require enough of myself?
Did I fail to tell somebody to go jump in the lake?

Did I fail to treat myself with dignity and respect?
What actions do I now need to take in order to change?
Do I need to start certain new behaviors?
Do I need to stop certain old behaviors?

We need to call time out at this point, because I want you to understand what's at stake. If you fail to accept this law and continue to perceive the world and react to it as a victim, clinging to the belief that you are "right" so the problem can't be your fault, you will not successfully create meaningful and lasting change in your life.

Don't let this be some dry rhetoric in a book. Read this as though I am speaking directly to you: If in any part of your life, you are angry, hurt, or upset in any other way, then you own those feelings and are accountable for their presence in your life.

There is more than one way to play the victim. You can insist that someone is being mean or unfair or ugly to you. Another way—in fact, the most common way—is to believe that you are right in your position, those who disagree with you are wrong, and therefore it is not your fault that things are at an impasse. But even if you are right and they are wrong, you still have ownership of the problem. My question to you would be, "If you're so right, if you're so smart, then why can't you create the results that you want?"

You can answer, "They just won't listen," and again I would say, you own the fact that they won't listen. The fact that they won't listen is a direct result of your inability to get them to hear you.

Bottom Line: You are not a victim. You are creating the situations you are in; you are creating the emotions that flow from those situations. This is not theory; it is life. You must be willing to move your position, and, however difficult or unusual it may seem, embrace the fact that you own the problem. That is not all bad news. Accepting your role in your problems, acknowledging that you are accountable means that you get it. It means that you understand that the solutions lie within you. While everybody else is still out there blaming those who aren't responsible for the results in their life, you can be as on target as a laser-guided missile, and therefore, work only on those things that will truly change your life. That gives you a tremendous head start in the solution category. Let today be a huge wake-up call for you. Quit looking in the wrong place for answers.

Failing to accept this law is a "deal-breaker." Please don't say, "Okay, Phil, I now accept the law, and I will start creating my own experience." That's thinking in the right direction, but it isn't right yet. You've got to realize that you *have already and always have been* creating your experience in this life. The significance of this realization is that as you think back through your life history, you'll have to reframe reality, make it accurate, by reassigning responsibilities for the results. You need to understand what choices led to what results. *How did you behave and choose your way to where you are?*

Assignment #4: If you are going to begin to view your life from a position of accountability, a good place to practice is by re-evaluating the history that may have previously had you cast, at least in your mind, as a victim. It would be very useful for you to open your journal at this point and, thinking back through the various stages in your life, identify the five most significant times in your life when, before now, you felt that you had been victimized, mistreated, or in some way unfairly dealt with. Describe these situations with enough detail that you can capture the emotion of each. As you do this, leave space under each of the five situations to write some other things.

In the spaces that you have left, I want you to now identify how, in each of those situations, you were, in fact, accountable for your bad result. Maybe it's something you did, maybe it's something you failed to do, maybe it is some way in which you set yourself up for the result, or failed to recognize certain warning signs. Whatever it is, practice your new position by re-evaluating the top five times in your life that you were certain that you had been victimized by a world that was unfair or did not understand. Don't treat this as a superficial exercise or as busy work. Beginning to live as an accountable person means that you are beginning to think as an accountable person. This exercise will be important in formulating strategies for your future life that put you in the driver's seat, rather than back in the passenger compartment.

The immediate impact that I want this law to have is that it causes you to look in the one right place, not a million wrong ones, for the solutions to your problems. You need to stop saying, "Why are they doing this to me?" and start saying, "Why am *I* doing this to myself? What thoughts, behavior, and choices can *I* change to get a different result?'' As the preceding series of questions suggests, you are not just now creating your experience in life. You have already been creating your experience; you have already been accountable for your results, good or bad. Now that you know that, now that you have consciously admitted that, you can actively, purposefully choose to change what results and experiences you create.

As we move forward in this book, we will be creating and preparing your life by design; we are creating your strategic approach to living the life and getting the results that you want. Recognizing your own accountability is a crucial building block in that strategy. Absorb this awareness into the core of your soul, starting right now. Express that resolve in the way you analyze the events of your life. Then, looking ahead, express it in the choices that you make.

Keep the focus where it belongs: on your own choices and behaviors in the *here and now*. If you do, you won't ask yourself why your life is the way it is; you'll ask yourself, ''Why not? How could it be otherwise?'' Once you understand the Life Laws that control your life and make it what it is, you'll tell yourself, ''I have no reason to expect that my life would be anywhere else than where it is. Based on what I now understand, I can *see* why I'm depressed; I can *see* why I'm an alcoholic; I can *see* why I've been married three times; I can *see* why I'm stuck in a lousy job. I did not know the principles that were sealing my fate, but now that I do, I can adapt to them and work the system. I've been programming myself for failure, not for success. But no more.''

I know that this train of thought is at odds with conventional thinking. Certainly it contradicts almost every behavioral explanation that society currently offers. After all, it's easier to tell yourself that things are your parents' fault, your teachers' fault, the result of bad luck, or some kind of cosmic backlash. When I say that it's easier if it is someone else's fault, I simply mean that it's easier not to be responsible. It's easier if someone else is accountable—that way, you don't have to require anything new of yourself, because you are a victim.

Books abound about toxic families, dysfunctional families, and the crippling aftermath of childhood abuse, whether sexual, verbal, or physical. The books tell you that your childhood was stolen and your inner child is locked up and wants out. When we read things that, however they are disguised, send the message that you are not accountable, we feel relieved—for the moment. We desperately want to believe these books, because they seem to lighten our load. They seem to make at least superficial sense, because to say, "I am accountable" is confusing. Certainly you wouldn't purposely sabotage yourself, so someone besides you must be to blame. And when you assert that the other people involved were in the wrong, no one can argue with you. You're hurting; somebody caused it; it has to be them and not you. After all, you would never hurt yourself. That may sound like common sense, but it simply isn't the case. If you are an adult, and you live independently, free from dementia, a brain tumor, or some other involuntary disruption of thinking, then you *are* accountable.

If you find this hard to really accept, you're not alone. The vast majority of patients I have ever treated, seminar participants I have ever trained, and friends who have ever cried on my shoulder or otherwise sought my counsel, all blamed something or someone else for their misfortune. But you must not lose sight of the goal. No matter how scary or unpleasant it gets, if you truly want an edge, if you truly want to accommodate yourself to the reality of this law, you have to be a steely-eyed realist who calls it like it is, not like you want it to be. To do otherwise cripples your effectiveness; you'll be misguided in your quest for answers or solutions.

The problem is that it is at the very core of human nature to blame other people; it is fundamental self-preservation to try to escape accountability. You don't want things to be your responsibility, so you will go to any extreme of rationalization and justification to explain why they are not. This is particularly true if we are talking about an emotionally charged area of your life. Think about it. How many times have you heard someone who was going through a divorce describe his or her mate as the vile, unfair, vicious perpetrator of all the misery? Once anger or hurt enters the mix, your objectivity will give way to self-preservation. While you're passionately blaming someone else, your self-diagnostic skills simply fall apart. Your best chance to get real control of your life is to stop that thinking right now. Don't try to place accountability somewhere else, or you are going to continue to cripple any efforts you are making toward becoming a winner.

Imagine losing your keys and looking all over the house to find them. You look in every drawer, pocket, nook and cranny, high and low. You go to heroic lengths to find those keys—you transform yourself into an expert key hunter. Now suppose that the keys are actually in the ignition of your car, not in the house. No matter how thoroughly, no matter how hard or how long you look, you will never find those keys in the house, because they aren't there. Likewise, when you set out to find the causes to your problems in other people, you'll never find them, because *they aren't there.* They're in you.

In a competitive world, accepting accountability alone can be the difference. Once you decide that no one but you is going to get you out of the mess, you stop kissing frogs, looking for that one magic one, and you start working the problems.

You will never, ever fix your problems blaming someone else. That is for losers. Don't be a sucker just because it hurts to admit the truth. You're the one screwing up, if anybody is. The sooner you accept that, the sooner your life gets better. Let's face it. No matter who you might want to blame:

You made the choice.
You said the words.
You settled too cheap.
You got mad.
You wanted kids.
You treat yourself like dirt.
You let the little tramp hang around.
You wanted the damn dog.
You trusted the jerk.
You got in the backseat that night.
You let him in.
You married him.
You scratched it.
You invited her.
You chose the feelings.

You decided you weren't worth it.
You quit.
You let them come back.
You sold out your dreams.
You chose the job.
You let them treat you like dirt.
You wanted to move.
You left it in the refrigerator.
You bought the damn thing.
You ate it.
You let them talk you into it.
You asked her.
You believed him.

I am not just being dogmatic or repetitive, but I do understand the vise grip this attitude can have on you. To accept and acknowledge this law is to strip yourself of what may well be your number-one "coping" strategy in life. If being forced to do that seems harsh and unfair, you need to understand an important point about this law: I didn't say you are to blame. I said you are accountable, as in "responsible." There's a huge difference between blame and responsibility. To deserve blame, you must have intended your actions, or recklessly disregarded their consequences. By contrast, responsibility simply means that you were in control. Accountability or responsibility does not imply intent or recklessness; it says only that you did, or allowed to be done, whatever led to the outcome.

If I am roughhousing with my friends, jump on a chair with both feet, and break it, I have at best shown a reckless disregard for the property. I am responsible for the damage, and I can justly be blamed for it. Now suppose I simply sit down on the chair and it breaks. I am responsible for the damage. I was using the chair properly and had no intent to destroy it, so I am not to be blamed as though I had maliciously destroyed it. But I'm still responsible.

So I'm not saying that the unsuccessful behaviors or unsuccessful choices you've made in your life make you blameworthy. I'm just challenging you to recognize that you did make the choices and you did engage in the behaviors, and that therefore you and only you are responsible for the results.

Recall Maya Angelou's comment on past behaviors: "You did what you knew how to do, and when you knew better, you did better." That is where I want you to be in your self-assessment at this point. Whatever you've done in the past, you did what you knew how to do: You did it, you are accountable for it, you are responsible for it. I hope that as we work together through this book, you will know better and you will do better. Either way, you are and will be accountable.

What about things that happened to me as a child? I realize that certain realities, some of them horribly sick realities, are visited upon us when we are children. I am not suggesting that, as children, we choose all of the events and circumstances in our lives. We don't pick our parents. We are neither responsible nor accountable for being raped, abused, or molested. That is not what I'm saying. What I *am* saying to you is that while you may not have had the knowledge or power, as a child, to make certain choices, and are therefore not accountable for those events, as an *adult*, you *do* have the ability to choose your reaction to those childhood events and circumstances. You must accept the premise that the only time is now. The past is over and the future hasn't happened yet. Sitting there at this specific moment as an adult, you and only you can choose your reaction to the events of your earlier life.

If, tragically, you were violated or mistreated as a child,

statistics tell us that it was probably by a family member or a trusted friend. That means that multiple violations—physical, mental, and emotional—have simultaneously occurred. If in the current timeframe, you choose to feel dirty because of those events, not to trust anyone, and to run from adult intimacy and healthy sexuality, then you own that choice and are responsible for the results in your adult life. Is it fair that it happened to you? No. Is it fair that you have to deal with that? No. Is it fair that you have to live with it and manage it for the rest of your life? No. *Are you nevertheless accountable for how you live with it and manage it?* Absolutely.

I suppose that your accountability is both good news and bad news. The bad news is that the burden is on you. The good news is that the choice is yours.

We have talked, at some length, about epidemic behavior. Life accountability in general, and accountability for epidemic behavior in particular, arrives in one of two ways. Dreams, plans, opportunities, and self-dignity can vanish in the blink of an eye, or fall away, one fragment at a time. I've witnessed the first kind of accountability in the courtroom as well as in life.

In the courtroom, in the space of time that it takes to read a verdict, the results of all of those bad choices are finally realized. Accountability comes crashing down in a single, undeniable hammerstroke, and freedom is lost or fortunes change hands. It's often dramatic, even spectacular. Headlines scream; it's on the six o'clock news; the whole world seems to be watching.

After we've gobbled up the headlines, the rest of us shake our heads and turn away and return to our own lives. But for those accountable for those bad choices, for the lack of a good strategy, their lives are never the same. I've seen it in life, too, where destinies are changed seemingly in a flash. A trigger is pulled by an angry lover; a poor decision is made by an airline pilot; a young man loads his fiancée in a death wagon as they leave a party drunk and incapacitated. Accountability is swift, harsh, and inescapable.

But there's a second kind of accountability, the kind you will probably recognize. It's much slower and quieter than the first, insidious in its subtlety, and just as catastrophic. It's the prolonged, day-by-day draining away of a life. No TV cameras are there to catch the details; there are no tabloid reporters jotting it all down. No single event in the chain is dramatic enough to be a wake-up call. The only witness is you, looking back over a lifetime of bad choices, recognizing that you have compromised and stagnated, watching your dreams erode or grow stale. Over weeks, months, and years, the questions gnaw: "How could I have done this to myself?" "How did I end up with a life like this one?" "What happened to my life and my plans?" "Why am I in such a rut?" Sneaking up on you like a silent but violent storm, this second kind of accountability is devastating.

Because this law of accountability is so fundamental, and so outcome-determinative, let's examine the actual method by which you create your own experience. You create your own experience by and through the choices you make every day. This choice-making creates your own experience, because with every choice you make comes a certain consequence. Specifically:

—When you choose the behavior, you choose the consequences.
—When you choose the thoughts, you choose the consequences.
—When you choose the thoughts, you choose the physiology.

Simply put, when you play, you pay. Whatever choices you make in this world, those choices have results. Those results accumulate to define the experience that you have of this world. Those results *are* your experience. If you choose really stupid behavior, you are likely to experience severe, negative consequences. If you choose to live recklessly and without regard to personal safety, you choose the likely consequence of pain and injury. If you choose the behavior of staying with a sick and destructive partner, then you choose the consequence of pain and suffering in your emotional life. If you choose the behavior of drug and alcohol abuse, then you create an experience of a dark and sick world.

Your *thoughts* are behavior, too. Choosing thoughts contributes to your experiences, because when you choose your thoughts, you choose consequences that are associated with those thoughts. If you choose thoughts that demean and depreciate you, then you choose the consequences of low self-esteem and low self-confidence. If you choose thoughts contaminated with anger and bitterness, then you will create an experience of alienation, isolation, and hostility.

And we can't discuss consequences without mentioning

the mind-body connection. When you choose your thoughts, you also choose the physiological events that are associated with those thoughts. For every thought you have, a physiological event occurs in unison with that thought. Imagine biting into a crisp, vinegary, crunchy dill pickle. Smell the vinegar and dill seasoning. Hear the snap of that first bite. Taste the explosion of dill and vinegar flavors in your mouth. What happens? I suspect that you begin to salivate; that is, you experience a *physiological change* in your mouth.

Another example: Think back to a night when you may have been walking down a pitch-black street, or perhaps going to your car in a parking garage that was deserted and dark. Recall hearing a sudden noise behind you. Your body immediately reacted. The hair stood up on the back of your neck and on your arms, your heart rate increased dramatically, and you became hypervigilant, as if your entire body had become a single, twitching nerve. Nobody touched you, nobody did anything to you; you simply conceived a thought, and that thought was, "I am in danger." Abstract thoughts have the power to produce tangible and dramatic physiological events. It is naïve to deny that there are relevant physiological reactions to every thought.

There's a very powerful connection at work here. Your physiology determines your energy and action level. If your internal dialogue is negative and self-effacing, then the physiology that simultaneously occurs will be just as negative. Your depressed thoughts suppress energy and action. Your body will conform to that central computer message. You are mentally, behaviorally, and physiologically programming yourself to go through life in a particular way.

Think about how powerfully your thoughts program you. All of us engage in dialogues with other people throughout the day, but our most active and consistent dialogue is the conversation we have with ourselves. We may be with ten different people throughout a given day, but we're with ourselves, all day, every day. We talk to and program ourselves more than everybody else in our life combined. Some people have tapes that just play over and over in their heads. The tape plays from start to finish and then, as though in a continuous loop, starts over again. If that internal monologue—that self-programming monologue—is negative, is it any wonder that our performance is poor? If your internal dialogue contains "negative self-talk," you are creating obstacles for yourself that you don't need. Some typical negative statements include:

> I'm not smart enough.
> These other people are much more interesting and informed than I.
> I'm not as good as the rest of these people.
> I cannot and will not succeed.
> I always quit.
> No matter what I do, it won't make a difference.
> They've already got their minds made up, and I can't change them.
> I'm just going through the motions; nothing ever changes.
> They'll figure out how dumb I am.
> I'm a woman, and they won't listen to a woman.
> I'm too young to do this.
> I'm too old to do this.

Assignment #5: Right now, on a card and also in your journal, make a list of your top ten negative "tapes." Carry the card with you. Any time you hear yourself running another negative tape, write it on the card. You'll probably find it useful to update the card over several days. Check yourself to see how often you're running the tapes throughout your day. Once again, don't just read this and not do it. Writing it down is a key element of the learning experience.

We have spoken generally about the fact that when you choose the behavior or thought, you choose the consequences. Now let's examine some of the specific mechanisms of interaction that create results in your life. I want to focus on some of the most common choices you can make, and how those create results in your life. In other words, I don't want just to say, "When you choose the behavior, you choose the consequences," and leave it at a theoretical level. I want to talk about real-world choices.

> You choose where to be.
> You choose how to act.
> You choose what to say.
> You choose what to do.
> You choose whom to be with.
> You choose what to concentrate on.

You choose what to believe.
You choose when to go along.
You choose when to resist.
You choose whom to trust.
You choose whom to avoid.
You choose what behaviors to emit in reaction to
    what stimuli.
You choose what to say to yourself about:
    Self
    Others
    Risks
    Needs
    Rights.

One of the most important choices you make, and make daily, is how you present and define yourself to other people. Everybody has a certain way of "being in the world." Everybody has a look, everybody has an attitude; everybody has a certain role and demeanor that they choose when dealing with others. Some might call it your personality, and some might call it your style. This is particularly important for you to attend to, because when you engage other people in a certain way, they are most apt to respond in a certain related fashion. That means that every day, as you make these and hundreds of other choices, you contribute to your experience of the world. These choices define how the world, in turn, reacts to you. Let's look more closely at how this process works.

Reciprocity

The principle of reciprocity simply says that you "get what you give." The manner, style, and level you use to engage people will determine how they respond to you.

You experience reciprocity at the most basic level every day. You casually encounter someone you know, and that person says, "Hey, how are you doing?" And you respond, "Fine, and you?" And he or she very predictably responds, "Fine, just fine." No surprises there. Casual, superficial, polite exchanges. It is rare that such an interaction would include one or the other of these casual conversationalists bursting into tears and saying that the night before last they had caught their spouse in bed with some homewrecker. That kind of exchange would be entirely out of place when someone has just politely and superficially engaged another. Typically and predictably, you get what you give.

That same interaction could occur at a completely different level. You might begin the conversation by saying, "Gosh, you look upset. Is anything wrong?" You have now defined the interaction at a deeper level, and may well get a more genuine response. Because you have engaged the other person on a more intimate level, you can expect to participate in a more intimate exchange.

There are an infinite number of styles, ways, and levels with which we deal with others, and we may choose different ones in various situations. But there is invariably a pattern that defines who you are in the eyes of the world. The aggregate of those interactions is what defines other people's reactions to you, and therefore your experience of the world.

People do have a style—you have a style, a way of being. You hear people describe others by noting their persona: He's a real hard charger, or she's a cool customer. Some approach life as a combat: they're hostile, even explosive. Others are Milquetoasts who expect to get trampled, and do. Your attitude of approach dictates what you get back. You may complain about the way people react to you, but believe me, you create it, just as everyone else creates the reactions they get from the world.

Honestly evaluate your style of engagement, and you will begin to understand why the world responds to you as it does. To help you, here are some examples of engagement styles to which the world reciprocates very predictably. You may find yourself here, or you may have to create your own category.

The Porcupine
These people just seem to have a chip on their shoulder. They walk into every situation expecting to be offended. They're determined to find fault with anything and everything going on around them. No matter what the situation, they're quick to personalize any act or statement as offensive to their sensibilities. They're prickly. Trying to get close to them is like trying to hug a porcupine. As a result, people engage them, if at all, at arm's length. The world recognizes that interacting with the porcupine is a lose-lose proposition. Porcupines typically complain about how cold people are around them; they're baffled by other people's stand-offishness. Porcupines don't seem to understand that they act in that way, and that people are simply responding in kind.

Paws Up

We've all encountered dogs that have been so mistreated that when you approach them, they just lie down, flop over onto their backs, and put their paws in the air, in a totally defenseless posture. Some people act in the same way: "It's my fault. I screwed up. I deserve a whipping, so let me assume the position." They communicate to the world their understanding that, in every situation, there are whippers and whippees, and that they expect to be the whippee. These people invite the world to whale on them. Paws Up people have made it clear that there's a pecking order and they expect to be on the bottom. The world will gladly accommodate.

King or Queen of the Forest

This is the person who communicates to those around him that they are unwashed peasants who are fortunate to be in the presence of a truly big deal. They are legends in their own minds. These people discuss their own business, activities, and events as though these things are of cliffhanger interest to everyone around. To say these people are arrogant and self-important may not go far enough; Kings and Queens of the Forest are genuinely convinced that the entire universe revolves around them. In response, the world reacts to them with resentment. Family members and co-workers will often sabotage the King or Queen, using covert passive-aggressive behavior. For example, when it starts to rain, nobody bothers to tell the King or Queen that he or she has left his car windows down. Kings and Queens of the Forest have no inkling that they are creating an experience in which people glee-fully celebrate their demise.

The Poser

Posers might as well be mannequins in a department store display. They act in the most superficial manner imaginable. They behave as if stupidity were a virtue and superficiality divine. Their goal is to look better than you and make sure you know it. They spend most of their time striking poses and using phony self-criticisms to elicit compliments. Trying to make a Poser feel secure is like trying to fill a bottomless pit. Because they insist on engaging the world superficially, Posers create an experience devoid of genu-ineness and intimacy.

People-Eater

People-eaters have one elegantly simple goal: to control everyone and everything. They intend to manage your life, their lives, and anything and everything that you have the misfortune of sharing with them. They dominate all of their interactions. People-eaters will tell you what you think and how you feel. They will use you and everyone around them to get what they want. If you or anyone else becomes a casualty, that's a minor inconvenience; the People-eater will just get someone else. In this respect, People-eaters have an insatiable appetite. Because they engage the world in this fashion, People-eaters' relationships are entirely, painfully one-sided. Other people's responses to them are characterized by rebellion, rejection, or resentful passivity. Ultimately, the People-eater's experience of life is one of frustration and loneliness.

Drama Queen

For these hysterics, none of life's events, even the ordinary ones, are ordinary. Every sickness they have is the worst the doctor has ever seen. Every fender-bender becomes a fiery crash in their retelling of it. Every comment made to them is either the sweetest, warmest thing they have ever heard or the rudest, most vicious attack imaginable. These people could create drama from watching paint dry. They engage the world in such a way as to sacrifice all credibility. Those around them soon recognize their histrionics, and discount anything and everything they say. Nothing remains of the Drama Queen's ability to be taken seriously in any situation. Their experience is marked by ineffectiveness and lots of smiles and nods.

Victim

These people are accountable for nothing. Everything is done *to* them, not *by* them or *with* them or *for* them. They see themselves as captives on the evil train of life, and all the other passengers are out to get them. Victims are whiners, criers, and blamers. The world quickly tires of their hang-dog ways and has absolutely no respect for their competency as human beings. Their experience is marked by passivity, a lack of control, and the inability to overcome obstacles.

Einstein Analyzers

These know-it-alls epitomize the observation that "analysis is paralysis." Dissecting every situation to the point of complete tedium, they entirely miss the essence of any situation in which they participate, and therefore of life in general. They engage the world in such a way that they are seen as intelligent but impractical. Because their overanalysis bores people, Analyzers are typically avoided. They create an experience characterized by colorless living and an absence of bonding.

Conspirator Gossip

Conspirator Gossips are always looking over their shoulders and whispering to you some gripping "truth" that they alone know and will share only with you. They are viewed as untrustworthy busybodies. The world quickly recognizes that "if they'll tell it *to* you, they'll tell it *about* you." People treat them in the most guarded fashion; no one wants to provide them with the information that will become the topic of their next "top secret" meeting. Ultimately, Conspirator Gossips are shamed. They self-destruct by repeatedly trying to create a bond, trust, and intimacy at the expense of others.

Yeah, But

Of all the animals ever to walk vertically and use thumbs, these people may be the most frustrating. No matter what you say, no matter what solution you offer, no matter what you have to contribute, their response is always, "Yeah, but," followed by a myriad of reasons why your contributions cannot and will not work. Because an encounter with them can be so frustrating, people avoid them like sour milk. They *give* frustration and they *get* frustration. They create an experience that puts them at odds with the world and everyone in it.

Scarlett O'Hara

Faced with difficulties, these people choose not to address them. "I'll think about that tomorrow," they say. "Tomorrow is another day." The world disregards these Scarlett O'Haras with a shake of the head, perceiving them as unrealistic and asleep at the wheel. As soon as other people see that they are not going to deal with the issues in their lives, and that any effort to help them will be futile, those efforts quickly come to a halt.

The Mask

Ironically, the energy with which these people try to hide the "something" in their lives is, very often, what makes it obvious that they're hiding something. Yet efforts by the world to break through the mask are met with withdrawal and more overt deceit, and others justifiably conclude that what you see is not what you get at all. Other people's extreme distrust of Mask people prevents their success. For the Mask, meaningful relationships are virtually impossible.

Jekyll-and-Hyde

As the name implies, these people are totally unpredictable. The same person to whom you disclose your vulnerability on one day may prove, the next day, to be totally unworthy of emotional trust. People learn that the Jekyll-and-Hyde will blow up. The resulting barrier of fear and distrust creates unbelievable problems for the Jekyll-and-Hydes of the world.

Goody Two-Shoes

In the real world, some people have less than pure hearts and motives. But Goody Two-shoes types are unbelievably blind to this fact. It's as if they're determined to be innocent, without assuming any obligation to be wise. They squirm at the sound of off-color language like "Golly darn" or "Gee whiz." They behave in such a prudish manner that they're out of the mainstream of life. I'm not talking about people of genuine moral fiber, but about those who attempt to impose an extreme, unrealistic standard on themselves or others.

Perfecto

These people have taken it upon themselves to be perfect, unlike the rest of us. They present this objective as though it were a virtue. They *have* to be perfect. In fact, their "mission statement" is characterized by arrogance and condescension. They don't expect *you* to be perfect, only themselves. Ergo, they are way better than you: "You can be flawed, while I must be pristine perfect." But because there *is* no perfection, these people are constantly frustrated. They never, ever reach their standard. Although their days are characterized by constant, unrealistic self-degradation and little joy, they brag, "I am a perfectionist." The world says, "Get a life."

Chicken Little

The world is coming to an end and these people know it. Whether it's at work, at home, in their relationships, the economy, or the weather, a collapse is imminent, and as sure as God is in His heaven, it's going to be horrible. These people are anxious and urgent. They play the game of life with sweaty palms. They go from one imagined crisis to another. Others find their histrionics irritating and tiresome.

Whiners

For these people, nothing, I mean nothing, is okay. It's too hot or it's too cold. It's too far; they're too tired; it's too hard. As the saying goes, these people would "bitch if they were hung with a new rope." Nobody pays attention to or cares about them enough; life is not fair. They didn't get the same deal or the same treatment as everybody else. Whine, whine, whine. These people experience the world as an agonizing and very personal ordeal. In response, the people around them want to slap them and scream, "Shut up and deal with it! But mainly, just shut up!"

Guiltmongers

These folks have figured out that guilt is a prod, a weapon to be used in controlling and manipulating others. They use guilt to keep other people down. They may whine or be a martyr, but either way, you have hurt them tragically, and for your transgressions you get a life sentence of guilt and shame for who you are, or what you think and feel.

As you worked your way through this list, you may have found yourself, or at least found some images with which to describe your style of interacting with others. What I'm challenging you to recognize is that that style contributes to your experience of the world. I'll bet you found a lot of other people you know on that list, as well. I hope this gives you some insight about how and why they have the experience of the world that they do.

Once you acknowledge and embrace the second law, you stop being a victim. It's like sitting alone in a moving car; you can't *not* drive and expect anything besides a crash. Take the wheel. Begin to consciously, purposefully, and actively create experiences that you do want, instead of suffering through experiences that you don't want.

I pause here to remind you of something we discussed in chapter 1, which is that you cannot *not* choose. Even not choosing is a choice. Therefore, you can't say, "Phil, I don't want this responsibility of choosing consequences. I wish you weren't telling me this." Well, I am telling you. What's more, this law has been active in your life since long before I told you. I am simply making you aware of it, so you can use that awareness to create a different experience in life. The realization that you cannot *not* choose means that, each and every day, with each and every behavior and thought, you are going to make choices that will create your minute-to-minute and day-to-day experience. Do so with a conscious awareness of the influence that your thoughts and behavior have on your experience, both internally and externally. *Bottom line*: You are accountable for the life you have, and how you feel and react to it.

By definition, as you move into change, you are going to be doing things you haven't done before. That means the territory you're entering is new, it's unknown, it's not part of your life momentum; as a consequence, you probably aren't going to like it at first. It is a sad truth that it is human nature to judge and resist things that are new or that we don't understand. But by conscious resolve, you can overcome that human truth. Consciously assume the attitude of a "willing spirit." Be willing to experiment and try new things.

I cannot think of a single time in my life where my experience has been enriched or the quality of my life enhanced by my saying "no." I can think of dozens of times where my life has been enhanced simply because I said, "Okay, sure: I'll give it a try." Whether it was saying *yes* to a movie or play I didn't think I would like, or saying *yes* to going to college, I discovered those new heights only when I was willing. I never, ever got more of what I wanted by letting my judgmental, apathetic, tired nature win out.

Be a willing spirit. Lean forward. That doesn't mean that you are to suspend good judgment or take reckless risks in the name of willingness. If someone is saying, "Hey, try some cocaine; you'll love it," that's obviously not the time to be a willing spirit. Tell them to go blow their own nose! But you know what I'm talking about. Break out of your habitual doldrums. Climb up out of that rut and look around. You might be really surprised. The longer you have been trapped in an irrational and painful lifestyle, the harder it is to create a new one. Sometimes you do so a step at a time, and sometimes a window of distinct opportunity can be created as an escape hatch.

Jennie

Attending one of my seminars some years ago was a woman who had, throughout her childhood and early adolescence, been sexually molested and, ultimately, repeatedly raped by her grandfather. Fifty years old when we met, now more than thirty years into her marriage, Jennie confided to me that she felt dirty, damaged, and unworthy of her husband. Her eyes filled with tears as this strikingly beautiful woman told me that every time she looked in the mirror, she saw nothing but trash: her sexuality disgusted her and she hated her body. She confessed that she often became so filled with self-loathing that she would mutilate her arms and legs with razor blades or a red-hot knife or spoon.

Throughout her marriage, physical and emotional intimacy with her husband had been virtually impossible, since, as she readily acknowledged, she felt that sex was dirty and degrading. Her grandfather's hold on her was still so powerful that thinking of him, or any man, brought back all those emotions. Every time her husband approached her, the threat of closeness would cause her to shake and nearly vomit.

Despite the unending patience of her very loving husband, Jennie felt as though her grandfather had marked her with an indelible stain. At the intellectual level, she recognized that sexuality was a precious gift of love and trust that a man and woman share. However, in her soul, Jennie was convinced that her grandfather had cheated her of that gift. The more she tried to bury the pain and guilt, the more it festered, poisoning her marriage and her self-image. She could hardly bear to confront the problem, or even think about her grandfather, now dead, because it "just hurts me too much."

She recalled the time she had tried to tell her mother what was happening. Her mother's response had been outrage; Jennie was punished for thinking "dirty thoughts" about her "loving" grandfather. Scared, alone, with nowhere to turn, Jennie turned inward and suffered in silent shame—after all, "a bad girl should suffer." In Jennie's mind, she was filth, and always would be. Fearing that people could see, or sense, the evil in her, and convinced that she had done bad things, she felt judged, rightfully condemned.

Jennie told me she felt as if she were locked in a dark, cold room. She felt small, alone, and scared. Since she, and not her grandfather, had suffered, it was clear to her that she "must be the bad one.'' At his funeral, prominent ''men of God'' had stood up to testify to her grandfather's decency and righteousness. She remembered wanting to leap to her feet and scream, ''No, no it's not true! He hurt me!'' But on that occasion, and for the rest of her life, she had kept silent, alone with her pain and guilt.

If there was a bright spot in all of this, it was that Jennie admitted she desperately wanted out of that cold and dark place. She freely acknowledged that there were walls standing between her and her husband, and she hated them. During six days of difficult interactions in the seminar, I helped Jennie to understand that her grandfather, clearly a sick and vile man, still controlled her, even from the grave.

That direct confrontation was very difficult for Jennie to deal with. Over days of long, hard work, Jennie began to overcome some of the epidemic behaviors in her life. Her experiences of childhood had become the subject of blatant denial. Jennie refused to acknowledge it, even to herself. Because she had essentially eliminated sex from her marriage, the stimuli that brought up these horrible feelings were rarely, if ever, present. Emerging from that world of denial was scary and caused her to want more than anything to run away.

As a beautiful and vivacious woman, Jennie had defined herself in the world as a tower of strength. She was the one to whom friends came when emotions had gone wrong. She was the rock people turned to in difficult times. To reveal to the world, or even to herself, that she was in truth a ''wounded healer'' took away the comforting barrier of her social mask.

Overcoming her inertia was perhaps the most difficult task. As the subject of her childhood experiences became more and more the focus of her journey through the seminar, her fear and paralysis was devastating. But Jennie kept moving; she kept slogging her way through somehow, knowing that this was her time and her turn. The journey would take her through some dark passageways that contained not imaginary but real monsters. Even with all the love and help of those around her, these were passageways that Jennie would have to walk alone.

She began to realize that she had given her power away, allowing her grandfather to exert a poisonous control over both her marriage and her image of herself. She saw that her surrender of this control to him was tantamount to the rapes continuing. He continued, day after day, to rob her of her feelings of goodness and worth.

The awful challenge was that, for Jennie, pain had held her prisoner for so long that she had just about given up hope. Head down and crying, she seemed so small, so alone, that I wanted to put my arms around her and comfort her. I wanted to, but I held back—the realist in me knew that if she were ever going to escape that prison of emotion and regain her dignity and power, she would have to stand on her own two feet, fight her own way out, and declare that she would no longer be her grandfather's victim. At the end of one of our conversations, I challenged her with this line of questioning:

> "What if you deserved then, and deserve now, so much better?"
>
> "What if you're wrong, and it is *not* your fault?"
>
> "What if your mother was just too weak to believe and protect you?"
>
> "What if it is not too late? What if change is there for the taking?"
>
> "What if it is you, not he, who has been keeping you in that prison all of this time?"
>
> "What if the door to that cold, dark room locks from the *inside*, not from the outside?"
>
> "What if I could tell you right here and right now what you had to do to be free: Would you do it, no matter how scary or how threatening?"

These questions obviously disturbed her, but I could see that Jennie also felt a flicker of hope: "Maybe, just maybe. . . ." Reality was staring down her perceptions. She was having to face the possibility that *she* was the one keeping that prison door closed, and that she was going to have to be the one to open it. My strategy for her was to make her claim the right to her feelings, and from there, to reclaim her right to live with dignity and respect. Jennie had fought for herself tooth and nail for six long, difficult days. She had created a window in that prison wall; I prayed that she would not let it close.

My next question was very important: "Are you sick to death of this, sick to the point that you will stand up for yourself right now and declare your right to a better life? No matter who you have to face, no matter what you have to do? Will you grab on?"

Jennie trembled and sobbed, the tears streaming down her

face, but she looked at me squarely, for the first time, and said, "Yes, if this is my time, if it's my turn, then I want it and I want it right now."

The other seminar participants had witnessed this journey. Unbeknownst to Jennie, I had recruited a volunteer who matched the physical description she had given of her grandfather, right down to his black-framed spectacles. Also without Jennie's knowledge, I had positioned this man directly behind her. I now said to her, "If you're sick of this, if you are unwilling to be a prisoner another minute, then you tell him, right now, what he did to you." And without warning, I turned her around.

It would be hard for me to describe the intensity of the ensuing barrage. Thirty years of pain, hatred, and emotion erupted with the shriek of the words, "You son of a bitch. I was just a little girl. You killed my heart and took away my innocence. You are a disgusting, cowardly pig. I am taking me back from you. I spit on you. You cannot hurt me anymore. You will not affect me anymore. You will not hold me prisoner anymore. I will not feel dirty and degraded another day of my life. It is you who are bad, not me. It's not me. Do you hear me? It's not me. Do you hear me? I have paid for too long. My God, I've paid enough. I am a good and clean woman."

He had robbed her of happiness in her marriage. He had robbed her of her dignity. He had robbed her of herself. Now, at last, Jennie acknowledged those truths, and she placed the responsibility for them where it belonged. Yet she also recognized that it was she who had the final say about what influence her grandfather's actions would have on her life. She refused to continue creating for herself an experience of guilt and misery.

In those same critical few moments, I saw yet another testimony to strength and courage, because Jennie also forgave him. Not as a gift to him, but as a gift to herself. She forgave him in order to break her own bonds.

Jennie took the risk because she was truly, truly ready for change. She took the risk because she had nothing more to lose. She had brought herself to the point of readiness for change and she reached out, grabbed on, and claimed her place in this world: *I am a good and clean woman.*

This gripping encounter occurred just over ten years ago, but the story doesn't end there. Just a short time ago, Jennie called me. She told me that her husband had suddenly become terribly sick, and that he had died only days before her call. She told me that on the night he died, they had promised each other that she would call to thank me. Alone in his hospital room, the two of them had exchanged what they knew would be their last, most heartfelt words. He thanked her for sharing her life with him, then told her, "Thank you for having the courage to walk out of your cold, dark place and into my arms and my heart. The last ten years we shared together were worth the thirty years of waiting."

It had all started when Jennie decided that it was not too late, that she deserved so very much more, and that she would deny herself no longer. It was not me who needed thanking. It was Jennie, because she had become accountable. By embracing Law #2, *You Create Your Own Experience*, Jennie reclaimed her life. How about you?

CHAPTER FOUR

PEOPLE DO WHAT WORKS

*I do not understand my own actions. For I do not do
what I want, but I do the very thing I hate.*
—St. Paul

Life Law #3: People Do What Works
Your Strategy: Identify the payoffs that drive your behavior and
that of others. Control the payoffs to control your life.

Christopher, ten years old, loves the independence of using his bike as real transportation. Today he stops at the park to
play basketball on the way home from his piano lesson. He's done
it many times before. He knows he will be late, and he knows his
mother will worry greatly. He loves his mother and doesn't want
her to worry, but he stops nonetheless.

At twenty-six years old, Katelyn has already lost her
mother and two grandparents to cancer. It scares her to think that
she may be predisposed to the disease herself. She thinks about
this as she tears open her second package of cigarettes for the day.

Jason is on a second probation with the law and a third
probation with the NFL. He will make $3.26 million this year, but
only if he plays. The girl he's with wants to go home. He knows
he should let her, but he doesn't. He knows it's wrong to keep her
against her will. His mother will be as disappointed as anyone.
Even so, he locks the hotel room door and begins to unbutton his
shirt.

Barry and Kay know it hurts their children to see and hear them fight so violently. After nine-and-a-half years of marriage, they know that discussing money problems at home, after long days at work, will deteriorate into a knock-down, drag-out fight. Tonight you can cut the tension with a knife. Even so, neither disengages. Neither one suggests they should discuss it another time. The fight is on.

Kimberly would give anything to be petite again. She has gained seventy-five pounds. Her appearance is everything. She hates her body and desperately works to have makeup and hair perfect, as though it will compensate for the unwelcome pounds. She lies in bed in the dark and eats her fifth candy bar.

If you are at all like me or one of the people in the stories you just read, I know there have been hundreds, maybe thousands of times that you, too, have said or done things, perhaps repeatedly, only to shake your head in frustration and disbelief. You may have said to yourself, "What is wrong with me? Why in the world do I keep doing that? I hate that, and I hate myself when I do it, so why do I do it?" Good questions. Why do you do that? The answer is in the current law, and it is a law that, like the others, is highly reliable. You do those things because at some level they work. At some level, you perceive that the apparently unwanted behaviors serve a purpose.

As you read about Christopher, Katelyn, Jason, Barry and Kay, and Kimberly, did you notice a pattern in their lives that is present in your own? All were doing things that on some level they did not want to do. All were doing things with a conscious awareness that negative and unwanted consequences, for themselves and others, were sure to occur. Nonetheless, they persisted in their undesirable behavior, just as you persist in yours. Is it possible that at some level, their behavior was working, in that it was generating payoffs for them?

By now it should be exceedingly clear that the behavior you choose creates the results you get. If you repeat the behavior, then by definition, those results must be desirable, or you wouldn't behave that way over and over. Conversely, if you do not repeat the behavior, then the result is not desirable. In other words, there is nothing in it for you. Imagine touching a hot stove: definite undesirable result; thus, no repetition. It should be equally clear, then, that when you change behavior, you change the results. If you really do "get" that, you now know that if you can do different, you will have different. Thus, you've taken a huge step toward changing your life.

Knowing what you need to do and knowing how to do it are two very different things. Unfortunately, some behavior, often that which we most hate and want to eliminate, is the very one that stubbornly continues to occur. But how could that be? Why would you, as a free-thinking, rational human being, repeatedly do what you hate and that causes you such pain? It is an understatement to say that that defies logic. Surely, no rational person would do what they don't want to do. Surely, no rational person would behave in a way that generated results that they do not want or that keep them from getting results they do want. But no matter how rational and logical you may think you are, you know that that's exactly what you do.

I'll bet you could make a long list of examples. You eat when you don't want to eat; you eat when you're not at all hungry. You smoke when you don't want to smoke; you argue and lose your temper when you wish you wouldn't; you give in to the demands of others when it is the last thing you want to do. You choke when the pressure is on, and you consciously want to have peak performance. You feel guilty when you wish you didn't, and spend a huge amount of time doing activities you don't really want to do. You don't want to "veg" out and stare at the television every night, instead of exercising or reading or spending time with your spouse or children—but you do. And what's more, you do these things over and over again.

Understanding how to eliminate this seemingly illogical behavior is critical to improving your life. And you can do it through at least two important methods: You can start behaving in the positive ways necessary to have what you want—or just as importantly, stop behaving in ways that interfere with your having what you want. You cannot eliminate your negative behavior without understanding why you do it to begin with. Only then will you know what buttons to push to get the desired change in your own behavior or that of others.

So how does Life Law #3, *People Do What Works*, explain this mystery of human functioning? To really get it, you must add to your knowledge of human functioning. You already know that your behavior creates results. What you may not know is that those results, which affect you and the choices you make, occur at different levels of awareness and that the results can take many different forms, some subtle and powerful.

This is particularly relevant to pattern behavior. When behavior becomes almost automatic, you stop paying attention to or evaluating the cause-and-effect relationships in the conduct. You probably recognize situations in your life when you seem to go on automatic pilot, not really thinking through a given situation as you reactively go through it. The truth is, the behavior only seems illogical. The truth is, you don't and won't behave in ways that reap only negative, unwanted results.

You mindlessly do these things because at some level, you perceive that it works for you. By "works for you," I mean you get some kind of payoff for performing the seemingly undesirable acts. And as you will see, this formula holds true even if at some other, perhaps more conscious or apparent level, you recognize that the behavior in question *isn't* working for you; you may even see that it creates pain. Yet based on results, you are getting some sort of payoff, or you wouldn't do what you do or accept what you accept. A simple example is overeating. At a conscious, rational level, you know it is counterproductive, but at some other level, it is rewarding you enough to maintain the overeating. So, based on results, since people only do what works, overeating must work for you in some way.

That is literally what this Life Law says. If you did not perceive the behavior in question to serve some purpose, to generate some value to you, you would not do it, plain and simple. You must apply this truth at the most literal level. If you are engaging in some behavior or pattern of behavior, you must assume that no matter how strange or illogical it may seem, you are engaging in it in order to create some result that you want. Whether you *want* to want it or not, you do.

As you probably know, this concept of *payoff* is a crucial ingredient in shaping all sorts of behavior. It's a central concept in the way we train animals. For decades, psychologists have been training the proverbial rat in a maze. The rat can be trained to navigate the maze and ring a bell, *if* doing so will earn the rat a food pellet. The rat can be trained to turn around in circles, *if* those circles bring rewards. Even the lab rat learns what works and what doesn't. Understand that when I say it "works," I don't mean that behavior-reward connection is necessarily healthy. I only say that you are willing to work to get it, healthy or otherwise.

People are shaped by their world in exactly the same way. Reflect on your children's earliest years. You probably, inadvertently, shaped your child's behavior in ways you wish you had not.

For example, many parents, when they hear their child screaming bloody murder from his crib, race in and supply a reward to the screaming behavior by scooping up the child and comforting him. In the child's logic, screaming behavior brings about comfort and pleasure. Soon he uses that behavior to get that kind of results from his parents. It makes you wonder what behavior you are maintaining through inadvertent rewards in other relationships, doesn't it? For example, what behavior of your spouse or significant other are you rewarding?

There can be even more disturbing consequences to payoffs than rewarding your wife or husband for pouting. I have often been asked how anyone in his or her right mind ever becomes a masochist. It seems stranger than fiction: How could anyone derive pleasure from receiving pain? Aren't these people crazy? While their behavior may be incredibly sad, they probably learned the behavior in a sick but logical progression of behaviors and rewards. By applying this simple principle of behavioral shaping, it may not be so hard to comprehend.

The histories of masochistic adults often reveal that they were raised by physically abusive parents. Think about it. A child is young, and quite predictably, values attention and comfort from the parent. Just as with the crying baby in the previous scenario, this child will do whatever is necessary to get Mom or Dad's attention. But suppose that this particular parent, rather than responding to the cries with stroking and cooing, is easily frustrated, loses control, and lashes out at the child with vicious physical violence.

We know that most physically abusive parents act upon impulse. Typically, after they have vented their anger, they come to their senses and are overcome with guilt. At this point, the parent, understandably wanting to undo the horror that he or she has committed, comforts the child with physical touching, kind words, and loving closeness. It will not take many more incidents of this before that parent has unwittingly indoctrinated the child into masochism—the pairing of pain and pleasure. The child perceives, quite understandably, that the path to love, comfort, and gentleness is through pain. The sequence may be sick and tragic, but it's also perfectly logical. The power of the payoff in shaping human behavior is overwhelming and undeniable.

Thankfully, the converse is also true. In other words, when

a particular behavior is followed by results that are perceived to be negative or painful, that behavior is typically eliminated. Recall the example of the hot burner on your kitchen stove. That is usually one-trial learning. Touching the hot burner yields such a painful result that even the most hard-headed and inattentive person eliminates that behavior completely and forever. Also, withholding positive results following undesirable behavior can cause the bad behavior to be eliminated. If, for example, your baby (or your spouse) does not get attention for pouting or throwing a tantrum, the behavior will disappear, because it doesn't work.

The nuances of these behavioral dynamics are too numerous to cover here, but I trust that you get the idea. You probably knew a lot of what I'm telling you before now. This is the easy part. The harder part is identifying what the actual payoffs are in your own life, so that you can begin to understand and control the cause-and-effect connections in your behavior. If you want to stop behaving in a certain way, you must "stop paying yourself off" for doing it. If you want to influence the behavior of others, you must first understand what they perceive to be reward for this behavior, and then, if you can, control those rewards, making them contingent upon the performance of the desired behavior.

If that sounds like you would be gaining knowledge with which to manipulate and control others, you're right. If, for example, you learn that your egomaniacal boss would rather tell stories about his exploits as a high school football hero than eat when he's hungry, and further, that he loves those who are a good audience, you know at least one way to gain favor. I'm not saying that you should subject yourself to that cruel and unusual punishment, but recognize that it is a payoff you can control.

If you think you are different, that you are not controlled by receiving payoffs for some behaviors and not others, that you are an exception to this Life Law—you're wrong. If you can't identify the payoffs, you just haven't analyzed the situation thoroughly enough and haven't looked hard enough. You may not have realized what you or others perceive to be a reward. The challenge is to consider all the possible ways you could be getting paid off without being aware of it. The "currency" of life can be one of a number of different kinds of payoffs. You may or may not be aware of what form your payoffs are taking. It is possible, for example, that you are feeding off some kinds of payoffs that may be extremely unhealthy, such as self-punishment, distorted self-importance, vindictiveness, or some other emotionally unstable response.

The most obvious and easily measured payoffs are, predictably, monetary. That's the primary reason we go to work every day, when we would rather stay home with our children or sleep all morning. We value money, so we are willing to make certain sacrifices and do certain things in order to get it. But there are other, even more powerful payoffs that are nonmonetary. Psychological income, for example, can take the form of acceptance, approval, praise, love, companionship, greed, punishment, or fulfillment.

These payoffs act powerfully to condition you to repeat the behaviors that bring them about. Feelings of safety and security are the other, more general categories of psychological payoff that come from healthfully leading a stable life, or—not as healthfully—from sitting on the sidelines, dominated by fear and the desire to avoid risk. Spiritual income is a payoff that can manifest itself in terms of peace, a sense of connectedness with a higher power, or feelings of righteousness and morality. Physical income is the often-powerful sense of physical well-being that comes from good nutrition, exercise, proper weight management, and healthy sexual activity. In the less healthy vein, physical income can be derived from physically intimidating or dominating another, or from being preoccupied with one's own body, either negatively or positively, as with body weight or self-inflicted pain. These incomes, too, can be highly influential in driving behavior.

Achievement income has its currency, as well: a feeling of accomplishment; recognition from others within one's field of endeavor; or an inner awareness of a job well done. Less positive is the same income in the context of measuring one's self-worth solely as a function of work-related performance: the income of the "workaholic." Social income derives from feeling that you are a part of a group, and of course increases when you feel you not only belong, but are a contributor or leader. On the unhealthy end of the continuum is the insecure person who measures self-worth as a function of the approval of others, and whose constant craving for social acceptance is a bottomless pit.

All of these categories of payoffs are at work in almost everyone's lives. You may be more money driven, or you may be more motivated by achievement, but make no mistake, the behaviors that you exhibit, particularly those that you exhibit regularly, are elicited and maintained by these various types of incomes. As you seek to understand *why* you act in certain ways, look hard and honestly at *what you are getting out of what you are doing.* In some cases, the payoff will be obvious; in others, you'll have to do some digging. All of these categories, whether considered healthy or unhealthy, can become toxic in the extreme. If you work so hard for achievement income that you avoid family commitment, that's not good. If you are so dominated by family payoffs that you fail to meet financial needs, that's not good, either.

Be aware that you can be blind to the impact of your payoff system. As we've seen in the two scenarios of the crying child, parents can inadvertently reward unhealthy, destructive behavior, whether it's tantrum behavior or masochistic behavior. The unfortunate fact is that the power of a payoff can support even behavior that you do not *consciously* want. For example, you may consciously be lonely, and yearn for the social and psychological income that derives from participation and companionship with others. But the fear of rejection can be so powerful that the payoff of escaping that anxiety may override your desire to reach out. In this battle of the payoffs, the easier and more immediate payoff comes from simply staying at home and not participating. Sometimes, one payoff prevails only because it is the path of least resistance.

And as I've said, not all payoffs are obvious. With a female patient I treated some years ago, I witnessed a pattern of behavior that was seemingly illogical and seemingly unwanted. In fact, without the insight provided by this Life Law, her behavior might have seemed downright bizarre.

Karen was often 50 to 100 pounds overweight. She had the very frustrating pattern of losing weight, only to gain it back. Sound familiar? She would tell me that she wanted desperately to lose the weight and keep it off. She recognized that the effect of the obesity was to alter her appearance dramatically, and that it was just plain unhealthy. She could recite for me all the benefits and values of losing the weight, and was very articulate about the good feelings and rewards she got from doing so. Nevertheless, after very effectively and efficiently losing up to 80 percent of the unwanted weight, Karen would invariably, and seemingly without explanation, begin to fail in her efforts; she would eventually gain all of it back. It was as if she sabotaged herself every time she approached her goal.

I knew enough about payoffs to be convinced that Karen must be getting some kind of reward for this self-sabotage, so I began to dig as deeply as she would tolerate. Ultimately, I learned that Karen had been sexually molested as a child. As a consequence of that trauma and the unwanted attention and the feelings that her body had attracted, she had become uncomfortable and ashamed of her sexuality. The guilt and anxiety she felt when men took a sexual interest in her was profound.

Once we discovered this, Karen and I began to see that gaining weight provided her with the safety of sexual irrelevancy. In other words, since male attention brought guilt, fear, and anxiety, she took refuge in gaining enough weight so that she felt her sexual attractiveness had been neutralized. Reflecting on it, Karen described her own behavior as "zipping on a hundred-pound snowsuit" to hide her sexuality. Although that "suit" offered temporary comfort, Karen's guilt, anxiety, and fear would eventually diminish. When she had spent months without much attention, those feelings would be replaced by the loneliness and defeat she felt when she was morbidly obese. At that point, the vicious cycle of lose-gain, lose-gain would start all over. It was a war between the psychological income of feeling safe, free from the acute anxieties associated with male attention, and the transient, but powerful feeling of accomplishment she got during the early stages of weight loss. Once Karen identified the psychological income derived from her self-sabotage, she was able to start dealing with the true problem. She broke the vicious cycle.

Keep in mind that Karen's payoff system was rather subtle and complex. Payoffs can and often are much more simplistic. For example, there is a much larger group of obese people who overeat simply because of the pleasurable sensation of ingesting the food: it tastes good. For them, the sensory gratification of eating the food outweighs the enjoyment of being at their ideal body weight. And depending on the person, food serves a number of other purposes: celebration, medication, relief from loneliness, social "lubrication," or comfortable entertainment. In other words, the payoff may be not just the ingestion of food, but the secondary gain that comes from the event of eating the food.

The behavior you want to eliminate may be overeating, or it may be something entirely different. The point is that, to analyze *why* you act a certain way, you have to determine the payoffs that elicit and sustain the behavior. The payoffs may be apparent; they may not be apparent. The payoffs may be healthy results, or sick and even disgusting results, but people only sustain behavior if they are getting payoffs, and in some form that they perceive to be positive. So you've got to devote a lot of serious thought, first, to identifying those behaviors, thoughts, or choices that you want to eliminate. Then ask yourself, "What am I getting out of this? What is my payoff, healthy or otherwise?" Once you have identified the sustaining results, you can target those consequences for change.

Assignment #6: Let's call time out and deal with the specifics of your life. I'm going to ask you to open your confidential journal and write a list of the five most frustrating and persistent negative behavioral patterns or situations in your life. Be thorough in your description of each. For each one, identify the specific behavior; describe the pattern; and try to put in words the degree of its intensity. Then write down two or three sentences explaining why you find this behavior or situation negative. Next comes the hard part: For each of the five, make your best effort to analyze, identify, and write down the payoff that is feeding and maintaining this negative behavioral pattern.

To help you get started, let me outline perhaps the broadest categories of nonmonetary payoffs, since they are most likely at least contributing to your behavior. Remember, I said earlier that the number-one need in all people is acceptance. The number-one fear in all people is rejection. Don't get hung up on wordplay. For example, you might be tempted to disagree because you think that the number-one need is success, and the number-one fear is failure. But when you stop to think about it, being successful means that whatever you do is accepted and acknowledged by other people. If you're a failure, that can only mean that the world has in some way turned you down, rejecting you and what you have to offer. So as you begin to evaluate the payoffs in your life, know that your number-one need is for all of the people you encounter to accept whatever you offer at a given point in time.

Be alert to the possibility that your behavior is controlled by the fear of rejection. As we've seen, fear can be so strong that you'll do almost anything to avoid it. It's easier not to change. It's easier not to try something new. It's easier not to put yourself on the line and risk being turned away. So for every nonconstructive, nonchanging, nonreaching behavior you identify, ask yourself: "Is the payoff the comfort that comes from avoiding risk and the fear of rejection? Is the payoff simply that 'it's easier not to?' "

By taking the line of least resistance, you reward yourself with apparent comfort and relief from the anxiety that comes from reaching for something else. We will talk more about this self-sabotage when we discuss comfort zones in the next chapter. For now, recognize that your payoff is often that you feel safe when you don't attempt change, and threatened when you do.

Another element to consider in analyzing the payoffs in your life is the appeal of immediate versus delayed gratification. As a society, Americans are not very good at delaying their gratification. *Fast-food* restaurants, *convenience* stores, and *prepared foods* all testify to the fact that we have conditioned ourselves to want what we want, when we want it. Our demand for immediate gratification creates an appetite for a small payoff now rather than a large payoff later.

This explains why you will lie in bed on a Saturday morning instead of getting up to go jog. Lying in bed feels good right now, whereas jogging may extend your life twenty or thirty years from now. That's nice twenty or thirty years from now, but it feels good to lie in bed today.

I had friends in high school who, as soon as we graduated, wanted a new car, and they wanted it now. As a result, they took an unskilled job which allowed them to handle the payments on a new car, and they got immediate gratification. Others in our class chose to go to college rather than taking on a job and the debt that would force us to keep that job. Some chose the immediate reward of a new car; others chose the delayed gratification of a higher standard of living, long term. When you choose the behavior, you choose the consequences. "Right now" relief from pain, or "right now" reaping of a reward, is an extremely powerful influence.

These are things to consider as you go about identifying and writing down your payoffs. Don't get frustrated. Don't give up. You've got to be getting a significant payoff for your negative behavior, or you would not be doing it. The thought that a certain pattern of behavior could be working for you is so despicable that you will behave as if functionally blind to avoid seeing it. That of course, means it will never get solved. This is perhaps your greatest danger.

There's no question that the payoff systems we construct in our lives can be as intricate, sticky, and convoluted as a spider's web. But if you are stubbornly continuing some repeated pattern of self-destructive or frustrating behavior, unraveling that web is not only worthwhile, it is essential to your getting what you want and need. You cannot enjoy a peaceful and constructive life if you have competing agendas, with one part of you serving one master, and the other serving another. On the one hand, for example, you may want to participate fully in life, enjoying the camaraderie of others (social payoff); on the other hand, you may want to avoid the pain of possible rejection (psychological payoff). This tension between two sets of competing payoffs can make you crazy, or at a minimum, keep you in constant conflict and turmoil.

Payoffs, particularly those that relieve or allow you to avoid serious pain, or minimize the fear and anxiety of potential pain, can be as addictive as the most powerful narcotics. Thus, fear of the possible outcome becomes the most powerful agent of all. I say this to put you on serious alert. If you are being controlled in this way, such fear can imprison you and ruin your life. The payoff of escaping the pain of dealing with the problem can so seduce you, you can be so dominated by the fear of what might be, that you walk through your life in a zombielike state, grateful for the numbness. I want you to realize that you may be so controlled by payoffs that you're being overwhelmed by them.

As complex as the web of addictive payoffs can be, you do have a "North Star" to guide you, to keep you focused on what is really happening. The "North Star" that you must keep uppermost in your thinking is:

> Regardless of the logic, if I am repeatedly doing whatever it is that I am doing, I *am* getting a payoff. I will not delude myself by thinking it is not so. If I search, I will find the payoff, because it is there. I am not getting paid off for some of my patterns of behavior; I am getting paid off for all of them, every time. I am not an exception, because there is no exception.

If you never take your eye off of that truth, you can continue to close in on the answer. Find the payoff, and you can consciously unplug from it. Fail to identify it, and you are like a puppet on a string, being controlled by some unknown person or thing.

When I first met Bill and Denise in one of my seminars some ten years ago, they appeared to be the archetypal lucky young, affluent couple: energetic, intelligent, seemingly in control of their lives, with no confusion about who was in control. Both were attractive, healthy, athletic, and very much in love. They seemed to have it all. And then I met their daughter, Megan. Four years old, burdened with multiple birth defects, Megan could not walk, talk, or gesture with any proficiency at all.

It seemed impossible that a person so tiny could be afflicted with so many terrible infirmities. With severe neurological disease and cardiopulmonary deficiencies, this tiny spirit with a cleft lip and palate was a heart-rending child to behold. Her eyes were full of hope, her heart full of courage, but her body would not cooperate.

Over the next several years, as their daughter deteriorated daily, I watched these parents teach us all about love, commitment, and sacrifice. Never complaining, never tiring, they did their best to fashion a world for this fading little treasure. Bill and Denise were, to say the least, inspirational.

Choosing not to risk further genetic anomalies, they sought to adopt, rather than bear a second child. God smiled on them in record time with a healthy, vibrant son. Jeffrey had sandy hair, big green eyes, and a strong and flourishing constitution. He was a dream come true. Bill and Denise taught Jeffrey about his sister as soon as he was old enough to understand. Given Megan's extremely limited communication skills, the closeness between the two children was phenomenal. They bonded immediately and seemed to understand each other just fine.

By the time she was eight, Megan had had her share of chest colds. But this one did not look or sound good at all. It sapped her energy, seeming to wilt the little girl in her wheelchair. The doctor said that a turnaround was imminent, that the antibiotics and antiviral agents would soon take hold.

Denise knew better. Mothers seem to know about these things, and her maternal instincts told her that this was a crisis like none before. She told me that this time Megan seemed exhausted. It was as if she had tired of fighting the terrible uphill battle that was her life. While Dad and her grandparents remained hopeful and optimistic, Mom remained vigilant, silently watching, silently knowing.

Megan's decline began in the middle of a cold winter's night and, once it started, was unbelievably rapid: labored breathing prompted a dash to the hospital, where she soon lapsed into unconsciousness and was put on a respirator. Suddenly, it seemed, came the time for the decision. The machines that were doing the work of Megan's heart and lungs only delayed the inevitable. The anguished expression on the child's face made it clear that prolonging this precious and difficult life would have been selfish and cruel.

When the machines were switched off, the silence was deafening. Megan went quietly. No dramatic music played; there was no "scene cut-away" to a happier time; there were just the sterile room, a dead child, and two parents, very much alone.

Although I continued to have contact with Bill and Denise after Megan's death, I had not seen them for several months when I encountered them at a community support group for parents who had suffered the untimely death of a child. The two vibrant, alive, intelligent people I had known were gone; left behind were what appeared to be their hollow shells. Far from just grieving for the loss of their precious daughter, they were actively angry with themselves and each other for their "failures" as parents. Each criticized the other for being cold, distant, and emotionally unavailable for Jeffrey, who was now five. It seemed that after Megan's death, both Bill and Denise had pulled back from their son, physically and emotionally.

We were well into the Christmas season. While both parents acknowledged that Jeffrey was anticipating the holiday with the excitement and innocence that only a child can, they also confessed that in their home there were no tree, no decorations, no Christmas music, and no joy. Jeffrey was living in an emotionally barren world with two trusted parents who were causing him to wonder what he had done wrong.

Ultimately, both Bill and Denise confessed to keeping Jeffrey at arm's length. While they hated themselves for denying him their love and comfort, they admitted that they routinely were distant, cold, and totally emotionally absent. Both were nearly insane with guilt and confusion about how they could knowingly hurt their little boy. They recognized that they were cheating Jeffrey at a critical time in his life, making him pay for sins not committed. Both of them professed their willingness to give or do anything if they could just once again feel the freedom to love and care for their surviving child.

My question to them was predictable: "If you hate so badly what you're doing to Jeffrey, then why do you stubbornly persist in doing it?"

Their answers ran the gamut of rationalizations and justifications, but basically boiled down to, "I don't know." They sincerely wanted to break out of the pattern; they truly wanted to give to Jeffrey; but neither of them could seem to do it, or even explain their inability to do so. They were also angry at each other for no apparent reason, and were systematically denying each other the love, trust, and companionship that can only be shared by those intimately involved. They said they almost never spoke of Megan and resisted attempts by others to do so.

I suspect that you've analyzed Bill and Denise's situation in the same way I did. The answer was not so trite as that they resented Jeffrey for being alive, while poor Megan was not. It was much deeper and much more insidious. Applying this Life Law, you have to assume that these parents were getting powerful payoffs for withholding their affection from Jeffrey. You can also conclude that the payoffs must have been incredibly strong in order to overcome their natural inclinations to give him love and attention.

But how could anything reinforce such awful behavior? How could anyone say that withdrawing from an innocent child "worked" for these parents? That is, in fact, exactly what I'm saying. People only do what works. If the behavior was not generating a payoff at some level, Bill and Denise would not be doing it. Not until they "got it" were they going to overcome it.

As I stated earlier, there is a mesmerizing and addictive power in escaping pain. It has been said that "fatigue makes cowards of us all"; so, too, does a deep emotional pain.

Not surprisingly, Bill and Denise could not even begin to comprehend that they were behaving this way toward Jeffrey in order to get a reward. It made them almost physically ill to consider that they might be sacrificing this young boy's heart for their own gain. So at first, they argued with me. They loudly resisted feeling small and selfish for engaging in what was, essentially, child abuse through neglect. It was an ugly, ugly truth, the avoidance of which offered payoffs as well. But by staying focused on the truth, by moving forward on the assumption that however illogical it seemed there had to be a payoff for their behavior, we agreed that it had to be working, or they wouldn't be doing it. Eventually, they found the explanation for such hateful behavior.

Today, both Bill and Denise will tell you that the pain and hurt they suffered at the loss of Megan was so devastating as to have completely intimidated them. Perhaps as a product of her helplessness, these two loving parents had drawn even closer to their daughter than was normal. The urgency of their love, intensified by their awareness of Megan's dramatically shortened life expectancy, ran them headlong into an emotional brick wall. Losing her was an event that, though anticipated, was one for which they were unprepared.

During those bewildering days, they didn't know much, but they knew that the pain had to stop in order for them to survive. They will tell you today that they had a debilitating fear of ever investing so heavily in anything or anyone again, and thereby subjecting themselves to that kind of pain of loss. Without being aware, they withdrew from Jeffrey because they could not allow themselves to be vulnerable again, to be exposed to a pain that, if it occurred, would be beyond enduring. Loving Megan, then losing her, had depleted them. They could not imagine being able to feel or give again.

Whenever they allowed Jeffrey to get close, the same love, warmth, and giving that are at the heart of healthy families only horrified this young couple. After all, the last time they had felt those emotions, the most devastating result in the world had come to pass. So avoiding that kind of emotional connection, that giving and receiving, offered a feeling of protection. The payoff was safety and escape from hurt, fear, and anxiety. It was emotional anesthesia. Remember that our number-one fear is rejection. The departure of little Megan had been the most crippling rejection imaginable.

As is so often the case, from childhood forward, when you turn on the lights, the bogeymen disappear. When you confront the demons, they shrink and run away. Once they had the courage to acknowledge the subtle workings of their own self-preservation, Bill and Denise began to dissect their problem. What had been a sick payoff was now just sick. They found their way back to Jeffrey. They live today as a happy and thriving family, loving, giving, sharing, and trusting. Because their avoidance no longer worked for them, they abandoned it.

The obvious question for you is, "Are you addicted, invisibly, to the sense of security that comes from avoiding the pain and risk of intimacy, of failure, simply of living?" If what you want in your life is neither present nor being worked toward, it might be wise to put your eye on the "North Star" and figure out what's keeping you stranded.

Bottom Line: You are shaping your own behavior by the payoffs you are getting in life. Find and control the payoffs, and you control the behavior, whether it's your own or someone else's. If—but only if—you understand and embrace this concept, your personal control will dramatically increase.

CHAPTER FIVE

YOU CAN'T CHANGE WHAT YOU DON'T ACKNOWLEDGE

We've got them.

—Gen. George A. Custer,

on being attacked at the Little Bighorn, 1876.

Life Law #4: You Can't Change What You Don't Acknowledge

Your Strategy: Get real with yourself about your life and everybody in it. Be truthful about what isn't working in your life. Stop making excuses and start making results.

Perhaps this law, more than any other, seems self-evident. And to some degree, it is. If you're unwilling to acknowledge a thought, circumstance, problem, condition, behavior, or emotion—if you won't take ownership of your role in a situation—then you cannot and will not change it. If you refuse to acknowledge your own self-destructive behaviors, not only will they continue, they will actually gain momentum, become more deeply entrenched in the habitual patterns of your life, and grow more and more resistant to change.

Imagine your doctor asking you whether you've been having dizzy spells, and rather than admit it, you say, "Well, no, not really." What's going to happen? The doctor isn't going to address the problem, and you'll keep getting dizzy. He might treat your sore toe, or the ache in your elbow, but because you have lied to him, he may never deal with the real underlying problem.

Because the doctor assumes that you are motivated to get better, he trusts you to identify your problems for him so he'll know where to focus his efforts.

You very likely believe that you can rely on yourself in a similar fashion. Just as the doctor depends on you to be honest with him, you depend on yourself to shoot straight with yourself. But as we just saw with Life Law #3, you may have a competing agenda. If, by denying the existence of a problem, you reap apparent benefits for avoiding a painful subject, that makes you anything but a reliable informant.

If you hope to have a winning life strategy, you have to be honest about where your life is right now. The connection between knowing exactly, precisely where you are in your life right now and where you want your life to be should be obvious. Suppose you're out there, wandering around the United States, and you call me on the phone and ask, "How do I get to Toledo?" My first question is obviously going to be, "Well, where are you now?" Clearly, if you tell me that you are in California, I'm going to give you directions very different from those I would give you if I learned you were in South Carolina. The same holds true for the directions I might give to you for changing your life: if you reported, for example, that your marriage was absolutely wheels-off and in the ditch, I'd approach the situation differently than I would if you told me that your marriage was doing fine. If you told me that you are in a quagmire of poor self-management mentally, emotionally, and physically, I would give very different directions for change than I would if you told me that you were self-disciplined and on top of your personal matters. Likewise, if you lie to *yourself* about any dimension of your life, you can distort the entire picture so much that an otherwise sound strategy will be compromised.

You must be keenly aware that you can lie to yourself in two ways: You can affirmatively misrepresent the truth, or you can lie to yourself by omission. Failing to tell yourself what is, is just as dangerous as misrepresenting what is. So you have to have the strength and courage to ask yourself the hard questions, and to give yourself realistic answers.

Right now, you may be thinking, "Phil, I don't even know what *questions* to ask to get to the real deal, let alone the answers." That's okay; we will do this together, once you have some more tools you'll need in order to do it right. The point now is that you have to be willing to allow every belief, every position,

every pattern in your life to be questioned, examined, and challenged. When we discuss a truth, you have to be willing to honestly assess your beliefs, positions, and patterns against that truth.
You cannot afford the luxury of defensiveness, and you cannot
afford the luxury of lies and denial. Denial, after all, is what kills
dreams. It kills hope. It kills what might have been a real chance
to overcome a problem had the solution just been pursued in time.
Denial can, quite literally, kill you.

I don't say that to be dramatic; I say it because it's true.
In virtually every walk of life, I've seen the sad effects of denial,
and I'll bet you have, too. It's time to address the denial in your
own life. Let's begin by recognizing that, in all humans, there's a
seldom-discussed self-protective mechanism that behavioral sci-
entists commonly refer to as "perceptual defense."

Perceptual defense is a mechanism that protects us from
those things that our minds, at some level, determine we cannot
handle or which we do not want to face. You may have heard this
mechanism described as the "humane amnesia" or "selective amnesia" that takes effect during overwhelmingly traumatic situations. I've dealt professionally with a number of people over the
years who have witnessed the death or maiming of their children
or loved ones, only to find that event completely blocked from
their memory after the fact. I have worked, as well, with survivors
of terribly painful accidents, people who remained fully conscious
while being horribly burned, dismembered, or injured. They, too,
mercifully, had no conscious recollection of the agony that they
unquestionably experienced.

In circumstances like these, we can only regard the phenomenon of perceptual defense as a gift from God. But as in most
things in life, no matter how flat you make a pancake, it's still got
two sides. Perceptual defense does not always work to the good.
It's not confined to being just a self-protective mechanism in
highly traumatic situations. I'm calling your attention to this fact
because, as this law states, only if you acknowledge the presence
of a condition can you make a conscious effort to offset or control
that condition. If some natural human trait works against that self-
honesty, you need to know it.

Perceptual defense is active in your life every day. It can
and does keep you from seeing things you simply do not want to
be true. In a number of situations, it may prevent your picking up
warning signs that, if you acknowledged them, could prompt you
to take important and timely coping steps. Perhaps this mechanism

keeps you from recognizing that you are falling out of favor with your boss. Maybe it blinds you to the deterioration in your most important relationship, thus allowing further distance and damage to occur. Perceptual defense can keep you from recognizing the warning signs of a serious disease that, if detected and treated early, could be contained or cured. It can keep you from seeing the warning signs of any number of negative behaviors in your children, such as depression, drug or alcohol abuse, or a general alienation from the world.

As a graduate student, I replicated a perceptual-defense study designed some years earlier by a psychologist much more creative than I. In my version of the study, I used a very sophisticated slide projector to show certain stimulus words to a number of subjects. The slide projector had the capacity to display the words for precisely calibrated lengths of time. Members of my team could cause the words to appear for as little as a hundredth of a second, or keep them on the screen indefinitely.

In this case, my subjects were a delightful group of very conservative elderly women from a local Baptist church. Before asking the ladies to look at our slides, we attached to their temples and forearms sophisticated polygraph-type equipment, designed to measure even the slightest physiological changes. We then showed them a series of stimulus words that ranged from the totally benign, such as *oak tree* and *stagecoach*, to highly risqué words that good taste prevents me from including here.

When words like *oak tree* and *stagecoach* were presented, even at surprisingly brief exposure times, these women unerringly perceived and reported them. But their efficiency went way down when it came to the offensive words, even when those words were presented for intervals ten times longer than those of the benign words. Their perceptual defenses simply prevented them from seeing those words. However, even though they could not report seeing the words and they showed absolutely no signs of embarrassment, their physiological readings went off the charts: their skin temperatures, heart rates, and other stress indicators all went haywire. It was clear that at the subconscious level, they recognized, and their bodies saw and reacted to, what their conscious minds could or would not.

Thus, on the one hand, the perceptual defense mechanism protected these ladies' conscious values and beliefs; on the other hand, it also created a huge hole in their view of the world. Your perceptual defenses have the same effect on you. When you see the world like a censored letter, with 50 percent of the words cut out, you are living a fantasy. If that doesn't scare you into thinking about what you might be missing because it's upsetting to you, then I would suggest that your perceptual defense is at work as you're reading this. The things you're not seeing may not be a handful of vulgar words, but issues that are vastly more important. Your "blind spot" may be the very things in your life that you most need to see. A scary thought.

Denial, and the mechanism of perceptual defense that underlies it, touch your life in more ways than you could ever imagine. Problems don't get better with time. You cannot change what you do not acknowledge. And what you do not acknowledge is going to get worse until you do.

Throughout my career, I've had the privilege of being professionally involved in the field of aviation—a love of mine from an early age—as a human-factors consultant for several airlines. Just as a pathologist or coroner performs autopsies on the deceased to determine the physical cause of death, a human-factors expert is called upon, after the tragic loss of a flight, to conduct a psychological autopsy: that is, to reconstruct the psychological circumstances leading up to the disaster.

I have performed this function at crash sites the world over. The tools of my autopsy are the black box cockpit voice recorder, which yields an audio recording of the last thirty minutes of the flight, and the flight data recorder, which reflects critical instrument readings up to and including the moment of impact. I also create cross-sectional and longitudinal histories of the flight crew, to determine whether any prior events may have contributed to the accident, and I study eyewitness and survivor reports, as well. Although admittedly morbid and often disturbing work, it has provided me a unique opportunity to listen to and learn about human problem-solving, crisis management, leadership, and mental-emotional functioning in the most extreme psychological conditions. It has also taught me about the power of denial.

The time was one minute past midnight. The weather was clear, and visibility was about five miles. Flight 427, which carried over two hundred passengers, half of them Americans, was bound for an airport in an eastern European country that had not long been open to the free world. Captain Mallen and First Officer Holleman were flying together for the first time. They were using the customary radio beacons as navigational aids, but were also relying more than usual upon ground reference, since the navigational system in this backward nation could be unreliable. As they descended below 10,000 feet in preparation for landing, there was, as called for in the regulations, no nonessential conversation in the cockpit. It was all business.

The airport lay at the northern end of an elongated valley only nine miles wide. Snow-capped mountains towered more than 12,000 feet on both sides. With the plane properly positioned for the approach, the flight deck instruments should show the airport to be at the twelve o'clock position, or due north—directly in front of the aircraft. The autopilot can be set to fly the course, and in this case, the pilots had selected autopilot. But as the flight leveled off at 8,000 feet, and the crew awaited further clearance to descend, their instruments clearly indicated that the airport was off to the left, at about ten o'clock. What follows is a portion of the transcript generated by the cockpit voice recorder:

00:01:14 *F.O.: (referring to the instrument showing the airport to be left, rather than straight ahead.)* "What's wrong with this thing?"

00:01:20 Capt.: "I don't know, let's just continue on here and it will true up. Just continue."

00:01:32 F.O.: "I've recycled this thing, still not right. Didn't we come our initial fix with it working?"
(*Captain does not respond.*)
(*In background, sound of flight attendant giving passengers their final instructions before landing. She thanks them for flying her airline.*)

00:01:48 F.O.: "I don't get—This thing is all screwed up—says we are, says airport—this is not—says airport is over there. Why is our heading 060 degrees (northeast)? Is that messed up—is that not right either?"

00:01:54 Tower: "Flight 427, you're cleared to land runway 35R, wind 355 at ten knots. Altimeter 30.06."

00:02:00 F.O.: "Flight 427 cleared to land—umm—cleared 33R—uhh—35R."

00:02:05 Capt.: "There, I have it centered up. I don't, I don't know what—just come left right now, come left, we go direct to airport. Uhh, we're cleared to land. Start, start—no, hold that. This just doesn't—"

00:02:23 *F.O.: "Look right. Maybe we should—"*

00:02:26 *Ground proximity warning system:* "Beep, beep, pull up. Terrain. Pull up. Terrain. Beep, beep."

00:02:27 *Capt.:* "What the—Pull up! Climb right now. Cli—" (*sound of impact*)

The last recorded sound is that of Flight 427 slamming into the side of a 12,000-foot peak.

Unraveling the technical details of the tragedy was rather straightforward. Entering the valley, these pilots were very busy in the cockpit, because this destination was new to them. Preoccupied with communications radios, and with the broken English of the foreign air traffic controllers, they had not noticed a one-degree-per-second turn to the right, the result of their autopilot's being dialed to the wrong navigational aid. They were traversing the valley at approximately five miles per minute. Because the valley was only nine miles wide, it took only a minute for them to be flying substantially off course, and at an altitude below the tops of the mountains.

In my opinion, what killed this flight crew, and their two-hundred-plus passengers, was denial. Looking at their conversation, you can see that this crew had some indication of disorientation at 00:01:14, when the first officer said, "What's wrong with this thing?" Commercial pilot training is very clear and very precise. If you become lost or disoriented in mountainous terrain, you don't debate the matter. Rule #1 is "Climb, and climb now." Altitude is your friend.

Now, I've altered some of the details of the incident, out of respect for those involved, and what I offer here is my opinion. Others might emphasize other aspects of the event. But I submit to you that at the heart of this tragedy is the pilots' own denial.

In order for them to climb out of trouble—in order for that coping strategy to take effect—these pilots had to admit to themselves and to each other that they were, in fact, lost. For a professional pilot, that is an extremely distasteful admission. It's tantamount to telling yourself, "You're failing the standard; you don't know where you are." Rather than face facts, rather than come to terms with that embarrassing acknowledgment, they projected blame onto their instruments, and continued to resist the truth. And in this tragic situation, their window of opportunity was less than one minute. By denying the truth, by failing to acknowledge that they were indeed out of control, they continued at a rate of five miles per minute toward a headlong collision with a mountain. Put another way, in the fifty-odd seconds that they denied the troubling conflicts in their data, they consumed 100 percent of their margin of error. They suppressed their own acknowledgment of a problem long enough to deny themselves—and 250 other people— to death.

Such denial is, in my opinion, the number-one killer in the aviation industry. Flight crews fail to recognize problems and react to them in a timely fashion because they simply don't want the problems to be true. But I'm equally convinced that that is a human tendency found in every walk of life. We do not want problems to be true, we do not want bad news, and as a result, we become functionally blind to signals that are practically shouting at us.

A twice-married woman, determined that her second marriage will be nothing like the first, denies to herself that the identical patterns of conflict are beginning to occur in this one. A husband and father, proud of his standing in the community, and determined to maintain the appearance of a happy family, insists to himself that all is well, even though every other member of the family is in counseling. By refusing to acknowledge that you are out of control, that things are not as they should be, you let valuable time slip away, and with it, precious options to expire.

The pilots involved in this incident had less than sixty seconds to acknowledge and correct their problem. How much time do you have?

Your life is not too bad to fix, and it's not too late to fix it. *But be honest about what needs fixing.* Being honest means taking off the rose-colored glasses and seeing the world, and your life, clearly. That may mean recognizing critical and immediate threats that loom on your horizon like those in the cockpit, or identifying the slow leaks that may be draining away your hopes and dreams. Maybe the truth you must embrace pertains to others in your life, but maybe the truth has more to do with you. If at this point in your life you're living like a lazy slug, admit it. If you're bitter and hostile, admit it. If you're scared, admit it. Be honest, or you will cheat yourself out of what may be the best chance you've ever had to escape the shadows of your current life and to get what you really want.

Not surprisingly, we find it much easier to see this law at work in the lives of other people. Why can't they see how they are messing up, right? There's a useful illustration in alcoholism. Almost everyone in our society has knowledge of alcoholism. You may be an alcoholic, know an alcoholic, or have at some time had a relationship with an alcoholic, whether friend or family member. Based on that familiarity, how would you assess the chances of an alcoholic's ever overcoming his or her drinking problem, without first acknowledging that a problem did in fact exist? If you put those chances roughly at zero, I'd say your estimate may be a little too optimistic. If they don't face it, they will never replace it.

The same necessity for acknowledgment applies to you, as well. If you're unwilling or unable to identify and consciously acknowledge your negative behaviors, characteristics, or life patterns, then you will not change them, any more than will the alcoholic who lives in denial. Period, end of story. What is it that I want you to acknowledge? I want you to acknowledge whatever is *not* working in your life: self, marriage, career, attitude, anger, depression, fear—whatever is not working. As I've said, I don't care if you are absolutely, no doubt, drop-dead certain that what you are doing is right. If it is not working, then change it.

We need to talk very candidly about what I mean when I say *acknowledge*. I'm not talking about a simple nod of acknowledgment or lip service, lacking any real conviction or commitment to change. How many times have you heard someone say, "Boy, I really need to get busy on this," or "I know this is such a problem; what will I do?" or "You're right, and I really want to change that, *but . . .*"?

That is not acknowledging the problem. Acknowledgment is a no-kidding, unvarnished, bottom-line, truthful confrontation with yourself about what you are doing or not doing, or what you are putting up with in your life that is destructive. It's not some pious, phony-baloney, half-hearted rendition of what you think they want to hear. Nor is it a watered-down, politically correct "confession" that you think will buy you closure, at the expense of truth. I mean brutal reality: slapping yourself in the face and admitting what you are doing to screw up your life. This also means admitting that you are getting payoffs for what you're doing, however sick or subtle those payoffs may be. If you are not willing to rise to the level of being brutally, penetratingly honest with yourself about who you are and what is wrong, then you will never effect change. It's just that simple.

Recall the words of the Jack Nicholson character in the movie *A Few Good Men*: "You can't handle the truth!" In our most candid moments, most of us would have to acknowledge the accuracy of that statement. What most people want is not truth, but validation. They want reinforcements for their thinking, right or wrong. They seek out the people and the information that support the conclusions they've already reached, factual or otherwise. The only things they want to hear are things that make them feel good, that give them comfort about who or where they are, right now.

Test that observation on yourself. Reading about making real and lasting changes in your life, you may instantly be able to come up with fifty reasons why you can't change. And you know what? Keep it up, and once more in your life you'll be right. We make ourselves right, because that's what we treasure in life: being right. We make ourselves right by living according to our beliefs. In all the years that I worked with patients, and particularly the times I worked with couples, the most common goal of each patient was not to find out how to live and behave productively, but to convince me that what they were believing or doing was correct. Seldom did either partner in the marriage come to me and sincerely say, "Dr. McGraw, I want our marriage to work, no matter who is right." What both of them usually said, in effect, was, "I want you to recognize that I'm right, and convince my spouse that I'm right, so that we can do things my way."

This insistence on being right can have tragic outcomes. I saw couple after couple in which the individual parents held so strongly to their separate views of how to parent a child that they were willing to destroy the relationship and family, rather than give up their beliefs. And in most of these cases, *both parents* were wrong. Way wrong.

If you accept the premise that people are by nature hedonistic—that is, that we seek pleasure and avoid pain—then you will recognize that it's not easy to deal with the truth, and it's not easy to change it. In order to stay comfortable, you must maintain the status quo, since movement can be scary, risky, and demanding. There's something very threatening about acknowledging a problem. It can create a lot of pressure. It's a kind of self-indictment. As long as you never admit your life isn't working, you can just "go along getting along." But once you do admit something is not working, you're also forced to admit that you are selling out for what you don't want.

Once you have acknowledged the existence of a problem *and* your ownership of it, living with the status quo becomes much more difficult. You have broken through your delusional system;

now you have to consciously self-destruct, or change. Once you admit ownership of the problem, you cannot hide behind other people. Remember, there are no accidents; you create your own experience by what you choose and do. Lying to yourself by omission is not a good way to begin to change.

In order to incorporate this law into your life strategy, you need to come fully to grips with the concept of honesty in general, and with self-honesty in particular. Honesty means the truth; the whole truth; the unvarnished, ugly truth. It takes courage and commitment to be brutally, genuinely honest with yourself.

As you take up this opportunity to create a strategy for your life, make a deal with yourself right now: There will be no lies, no excuses, and no conning yourself about what is going on. This is not the time to cheat yourself with namby-pamby self-evaluation, telling yourself what you *want* to be true, as opposed to what *is*. You have to be willing to ask yourself the hard questions and give yourself brutally honest answers:

—*Am I living like a loser?* If so, then admit to yourself, "I am living like a loser. I've got no excuse. I'm just living like a loser."
—*Am I lazy? Am I simply not requiring enough of myself?* If so, admit it.
—*Is my life a dead-end journey, heading nowhere?* If so, admit it.
—*Am I scared? Am I playing this game with sweaty palms?* If so, admit it.
—*Is my marriage in the ditch and emotionally defunct?* If so, admit it.
—*Are my kids living like losers, and self-destructing in their own right?* If so, admit it.
—*Do I have no goals? Am I just going through the motions, day after day?* If so, admit it.
—*Am I continually making promises to myself that I never, ever keep?* If so, admit it.

I have long believed that 50 percent of the solution to any problem lies in defining the problem. Once you've had the courage and commitment to lay it out to yourself exactly as it is, then you cannot and will not spend another day in a fantasy. But it takes nothing short of that. For example, if you're trying to assess why you are failing to achieve a certain goal, you must not give yourself the benefit of the doubt. You mustn't allow yourself excuses. You must live and think by the Life Laws that we have covered so far. Specifically, you must *acknowledge* that whatever your circumstance is, it did not happen by accident. No excuses: you own it; you created it.

You must *acknowledge* that you have to gain knowledge if you want the power to change. You must *acknowledge* that you are getting some kind of payoff for living with what you don't want, and you must be willing honestly to *acknowledge* and label whatever personal characteristics are keeping you from success. If you are scared, then you must say, "I am scared." If you are confused, admit it. Consider how refreshing it would be to wake up tomorrow and honestly be able to say, "For the first time in my life, I am not lying to myself. For the first time in my life, I am facing the honest truth."

You cannot heal what you don't acknowledge. This means—as you have consistently heard throughout this book—that admitting to yourself what is wrong is a positive. Now, in the past, you may have treated this kind of admission as a negative. But that attitude is for suckers. It's choosing denial instead of reality, and it will leave you eating the dust of those who deal with the truth.

Consider what is to be gained by your acknowledging your problems. This opportunity can be compared to the parole board's making an offer to someone serving a life sentence: "We will give you amnesty—a free pass for every crime you've ever committed—if you will just confess each one in writing, right now. Write down every one of your crimes on this piece of paper, and you'll walk. If you don't name the crime on paper, you can still be prosecuted for it. But if you do write it down, it's a free pass."

If that criminal rejected the offer because he was too embarrassed, too lazy, or too far into denial about his crimes, wouldn't you think he was a moron? You would tell him: "Don't cheat yourself out of this chance! Have the courage to put it all down, right now; have the courage to seize the day and eradicate every ill in your life in one fell swoop." That's exactly what I'm saying to you now. Be brutally honest with yourself. Don't deny any of your "crimes of living," and don't mince words when you do it. If you're fat, you're fat. If you're lazy, you're lazy. If you're scared, you're scared. You don't have a glandular problem, an energy deficit, and a careful approach to life. You're fat, lazy, and scared. Be willing to tell it like it is, or it will stay like it is.

The price of poker is going way up when we start acknowledging the truth about ourselves. You can be halfhearted here and tell yourself part of the truth, but if you really want to change, don't do it halfway; "that dog won't hunt." Not even close. Part of the challenge here is accepting that there is something in each and every one of us that is not pretty, not courageous, and not appealing. It is that part of us that makes us compromise; it is that part that causes us to work at cross-purposes with our healthy goals. I'm not trying to drag you down; I'm trying to make you be real. Face it so you can replace it.

You have to give yourself permission to be less than perfect. You have to give yourself permission to have accumulated baggage—distorted thoughts, feelings, and emotions—along the way, without condemning yourself as a bad person.

If you're old enough to have driven to the bookstore to purchase this book, then you've been around long enough to have experienced events that have changed you dramatically. Maybe you have loved, only to have your heart broken. You may have gone away from that situation with bitterness, resentment, hurt, and fear. Maybe you have been falsely accused and condemned by others, and that has left you angry, resentful, and bitter. Maybe you have lost a child or a brother or sister, and that has left you questioning the fairness and justice of life, feeling distanced from God or generally fearful of life. Maybe you are living in a marriage or relationship that is marked by discord and hostility, and that has left you guarded and unwilling to be open and vulnerable. Maybe you doubt your self-worth, or question whether you have the qualities that other people have, leaving you feeling scared and alone.

These are meaningful aspects of who you are and what you create in this life. You have chosen ways to accommodate or incorporate these characteristics. If you ignore or deny the fact that these experiences have created characteristics in you that dictate how you interact with others, you are denying an important aspect of your life. You cannot change what you do not acknowledge. If you do not acknowledge the presence of the distorting characteristic or event, whatever that is, and you do not acknowledge that you really own it, then you cannot and will not ever escape that experience. When I say really own it, again, don't play blame games. Don't say, "Yeah, it's my fault because I wasn't born pretty or born smart." That's a cop-out. Acknowledge for real that you can make choices for change.

Effecting meaningful and lasting change in our lives, even under the best of circumstances, is difficult enough. Don't add to the difficulty by being naïve or gullible in assessing what's really happening in your life. You mustn't be duped by your own self-talk, any more than when you listen to other people. If this book is going to meet you where you are, then you'll have to be honest about where that is. You'll have to get real.

CHAPTER SIX

LIFE REWARDS ACTION

Well done is better than well said.
—Ben Franklin

Life Law #5: Life Rewards Action
Your Strategy: Make careful decisions and then pull the trigger. Learn that the world couldn't care less about thoughts without actions.

The responses and results that you receive from anyone, in any situation, are triggered by the stimuli you provide. The stimuli are your behaviors. This is the only way people can get to know you, and decide whether to reward or punish you. If you behave in a purposeless, meaningless, unconstructive way, you get inferior results. If you behave in purposeful, meaningful, constructive ways, you get superior results. That is how you create your own experience. When you choose the behavior (the action), you choose the consequences. The better the choices, the better the results; the better the behavior, the better the results. But the bottom line is that, if you do nothing, you get neither. Life rewards action.

People don't care about your intentions. They care about what you do. The IRS doesn't care if you "meant" to pay your taxes; your child doesn't care that you "meant" to fix dinner; the people in the crosswalk are not at all comforted that you "meant" to stop. What matters, what determines the script of your life, is what you do.

Assignment #7: Let's find out what sort of stimuli you are providing to the world. Do your behaviors have you in a rut? Have you stopped taking the kinds of actions that create quality results, and instead settled into a hum-drum, going-through-the-motions lifestyle? Take the Rut Test and see how you measure up. And don't lie; you'll just feel guilty if you do. Remember that you cannot change what you don't acknowledge.

Rut Test

1—Do you spend a high percentage of your free time as a "couch potato," watching ridiculous sitcoms or "blood and guts" dramas on television? **Admit Deny**

2—When you're at home, do you put on the same house dress, T-shirt, and baggy shorts or pajamas so often it's regarded as your "uniform"? **Admit Deny**

3—Do you stand at the refrigerator, staring into it, as if you really might discover something that wasn't there when you looked five minutes ago? **Admit Deny**

4—Do you treat life as though it is a spectator sport, and you are in the cheap seats? **Admit Deny**

5—Do you actually live vicariously through characters on TV, and discuss them as though they are real people? **Admit Deny**

6—Do you actually count and recount the items in your grocery cart before you venture into the express line? **Admit Deny**

7—Is your job or your kids all you ever talk about? **Admit Deny**

8—On the rare occasions you decide to go out, do you spend thirty minutes debating where to go? **Admit Deny**

9—Do you only eat out at places where you have to look up rather than down at the menu? **Admit Deny**

10—Do you have sex quarterly, and in less than four minutes, so you can time it with commercial breaks? **Admit Deny**

11—Do you fantasize about things you never **Admit Deny**
actually do?

12—Are you suspicious of people who look **Admit Deny**
really happy, because it just doesn't seem
possible?

13—Do you have a lesser standard of conduct **Admit Deny**
when you are alone than when you are with
others?

14—Is the most exciting thing that's ever likely **Admit Deny**
to occur in your life something that has
already happened?

15—When you awaken, do you dread starting **Admit Deny**
another day?

16—Do you feel alone, even when people are **Admit Deny**
around?

17—Do your appearance and your standards of **Admit Deny**
personal grooming seem to be on the
decline?

18—Is your goal in life simply to get by for **Admit Deny**
another week or month?

19—Do you say "no" a really high percentage **Admit Deny**
of the time, no matter what the question is?

20—In order for you to meet someone new, **Admit Deny**
would they have to throw themselves on
the hood of your car, or pull a chair up in
front of your TV set?

If you answered "admit" to eight or more of these items, you're in a rut. If it was twelve or more, we'd better send out a search party. But by progressing this far into the book, you've expressed a desire to lift yourself out of the rut. You're programming yourself to be receptive to the Life Laws, and to start functioning at a higher level. You recognize that it's time to begin translating your insights, understandings, and awareness into purposeful, meaningful, constructive actions. Right?

Start by committing to measure your life and its quality based on *results*, not intentions. It has been said that "the road to hell is paved with good intentions." I take that to mean that good intentions without actions will lead you nowhere but down. Yet your natural tendency, whether you want to admit it or not, is to make excuses. Your natural tendency is to give yourself permission to say what you want to do or intend to do, but then to fall far short of doing it. It is the human way. You didn't invent this method, but in a society of procrastinators, it's the norm. In a society overcrowded with "victims," it is typical. "It's not my fault. It's not my job." I've got news for you: You are your job.

I'm not interested in helping you develop a list of intentions. Nor do I care to provide you with "interesting insights" into your life that stop there, with no associative action. I am interested in creating *change* in your life. To know why you are failing at any endeavor is half the challenge, but only half. I want to influence you in a way that gets you out of your typical behavior and excuses. That means that you are going to have to measure yourself *based on results*.

Measuring success or failure purely as a function of results means that you are taking a hard-nosed, bottom-line approach to self-evaluation. You might as well do it that way, because *that's how the world is measuring you*. You can't make your own rules or laws: the world already has its own. More importantly, the world has the ability to enforce them.

It doesn't matter whether it's the Super Bowl scorekeeper, your boss figuring up your sales commissions, or the motorcycle cop who's watching you at the intersection. Not one of them cares what you intended to do; they only care what you did. As Plato observed, "You can learn more about a man in an hour of play than in a year of conversation." That's nothing more than a rather eloquent way of saying *talk is cheap*.

If you are going to start measuring your life based on results, that means you don't take excuses from other people, either. If you decide that you will require better treatment from those with whom you live, then measure that treatment by measuring their actions, not their words. You cannot spend the rest of your life letting somebody else tell you how you feel, or tell you that you just see things wrong. They need to either put up or shut up, and so do you. If this book is going to be of any value, no matter what we're talking about, no matter what problem we're attacking or what issue we're addressing, you must commit to measuring yourself and everyone else on the basis of outcomes. Hard, but true. Only with results can we be sure that the changes are real. You know as well as I do that what I'm saying is the way it is. You may choose to ignore the truth, but that won't change it.

Procrastination—mere intention—is the bane of human existence. Assigned to a geriatric rotation while serving my internship at a V.A. psychiatric hospital, I had the opportunity to do "therapy" with a number of elderly veterans whose life circumstances had led them to our hospital. I put the word *therapy* in quotation marks, because in most of these encounters the patient was the teacher, and, in all honesty, I was the student.

These men, from all walks of life and all levels of education and sophistication, taught this young doctor some important things in life. Paramount among those lessons was that every single one of them, approaching the end of his life, wished that he had done things that he had not. One regretted that he had never returned to the Philippines to visit the grave of an army buddy; another had dreamed of publishing his detective stories, but "never got up the guts" to send off any manuscripts; another wished that he had spent more time with his teenage granddaughter before her tragic death in a car accident.

Every one of them, in one way or another, said, "Doc, don't waste it, son. When it's over, it's over." With the wisdom of age and experience, each told me that he had intended so much more than he had ever done. They talked not only of actions not taken and opportunities lost, but of *timing*. It is true that life presents windows of opportunity. Very often, the window of opportunity will be open for a time, but then slam shut forever. As you evaluate your life in the areas and the categories in which you feel moved to take action, recognize that you have to seize the opportunities when they present themselves, and create them when they do not.

Do you ever seriously wonder: *How much time do I have left?* If you're forty years old, perhaps you have forty more years to do what you have to do. Then again, maybe not. Maybe you won't finish this chapter before your life is over. What then?

Remember Gray Dog's gospel: "This ain't no dress rehearsal." Time is relentless. It is the one resource that you cannot regenerate. The life you have now, the one you are living, is the only one that you have been awarded, at least in this world. And every moment in which you fail to take purposeful action is another moment wasted.

The time-honored formula for taking purposeful action goes like this:

Be
Do
Have

What the formula says is BE committed, DO what it takes, and you will HAVE what you want. With this Life Law #5, we're talking about the DO. You can know a hundredfold more today than you knew a week ago, but if you don't do anything about it, you aren't any more effective than you were last week, in your unenlightened state.

Until knowledge, awareness, insights, and understandings are translated into action, they are of no value. If a doctor knows why you are dying, yet does nothing about it, you are dead. If someone knows he is standing on your foot, yet does nothing about it, your foot is still bruised. If you know why your marriage is failing, yet you do nothing about it, the marriage still fails. If you know why you continue to be frustrated and depressed in your life, yet you do nothing about it, you continue to be frustrated and depressed. Life rewards action—not intention, not insight, not wisdom, not understanding.

The difference between winners and losers is that winners do things losers don't want to do. Notice the word *do* in that statement. People who win take purposeful, meaningful action; they don't just think about it. They don't plan themselves to death; they don't have a meeting to plan a meeting to set up a meeting to decide what to do. There comes a time when you have to pull the trigger. To have what you want, you have to do what it takes.

Recall the Biblical warning that faith without deeds is of no value. Without purposeful action, you're just a passenger, being pulled along without self-imposed direction or control. Some people prefer the passenger role, because it imposes no pressure to decide or stand accountable for their life results. If you are one of those people, you need to either wake up and take the controls, or prepare to become one of life's crash test dummies . . . and I emphasize *dummies.*

I put this Life Law in this position on the list because you now know enough about yourself to begin to *do.* Now is the time, even before we have designed a specific life strategy for you, for you to begin doing some things differently. Life Law #1, *You Either Get It, Or You Don't,* tells you that you must do what it takes to accumulate enough knowledge "to get it." Life Law #2, *You Create Your Own Experience,* puts you on notice that when you choose the behavior, you choose the consequences. You need to start affirmatively choosing the right behaviors in order to get the right consequences. You've got to discipline your behavior toward having what you want. Life Law #3 says *People Do What*

Works. Do you need to change what you're doing so that you're getting healthy results, instead of unhealthy ones? If you change what you do, and you change the payoffs you get, you are moving in the right direction.

Nothing in your life will change until you begin to *do* different things. The question you may need to ask yourself is, "If not now, when?"

We're going to devote plenty of time, later on, to a discussion of the priorities in your life, and of how you allocate your time and energy. As for now, recognize that if you don't *have*, it is because you don't act. And if you don't act, you won't have, of that there can be no doubt. It's your task to use your knowledge of this law, and of the other laws of life, to ensure that those actions you will take are purposeful, meaningful, and constructive. As you create your own experience through your actions, the choices will be yours; those choices will be different from mine or anyone else's. I subscribe to the old saying that "You'll never meet a man who, on his deathbed, says, 'I wish I had spent more time on my business.' " We all know what's important, but do we focus on it and work on it, or do we just react to what's in our face, intending to do the meaningful things soon?

Pull the trigger. Get up off your knowledge and do something different with your life. Lives move by trends and momentum. If you begin to do different things, whether that means exercising, giving your feelings a voice, going back to school, praying, or applying for a new job, your actions will gain momentum. You'll meet new people; new possibilities will occur to you. Soon enough, you'll discover that your life is no longer the same song, seven-thousandth verse. You'll realize that those old sayings have long lives because they're true: "You can't get a hit if you're not swinging"; "You don't catch a fish if you don't put your hook in the water." This law is about getting you to swing the bat, or cast your line. It's about putting some verbs in your sentences and action in your life.

Assignment #8: If you're like a lot of people, one of the things you need to take action on is "catching up" emotionally with someone you love. Wouldn't it be tragic if you—or they—ran out of time before you overcame the inertia of your life and said what you had in your heart?

This issue of intended but unexpressed feelings is so important, and presents such a meaningful opportunity to take action, that I want us to address it right now. As an exercise in living with action, make a list, right now, of the five to ten most important people in your life. Now, honestly—and from the heart—write down for each person everything that would be left unsaid if one or the other of you were to die at this very moment.

Don't cop out and say, "Well, I haven't said it, but they know." No: When you die or they die, it's forever. No second chances. If, for example, one of those people is your child, and, God forbid, you died today, you may have wished that you had said something like: "I love you. I am and always have been proud of you, even though I did not tell you very often, if ever. You are so very special. Please know every day of your life that you were loved by me. And now that I know I am not long for this world, I am truly sorry that I did not spend more time knowing you, being with you, and letting you know me. You are a good man and a good father. The world is blessed by you. Please be happy and well, and live and love in your life. And know that there was someone in this world who recognized your specialness, who believed in you and loved you. Be kind to you, for me. If I die tonight, I will be at peace knowing that you knew what was in my heart."

Perhaps these words, spoken to me by my father shortly before his untimely death, can help you begin to give a voice to feelings you have that, unspoken, *without the critical ingredient of action*, are of no importance. By contrast, those same feelings, expressed in a heartfelt way, are to be treasured forever. Take the action to create your own experience. I must tell you that had my father not spoken these words to me, I would not have "just known." I needed to hear those words. So do the people in your life.

That's not all I gleaned from that last encounter with my dad. I, too, made it a point to speak from my heart, and knowing that nothing had been left unsaid was very comforting to me when he died. At one point, I asked him how he felt physically. His answer, so typically "Dr. Joe" (as he was known) was, "Well, I wouldn't buy me any green bananas, I can tell you that. And by the way, I went to a funeral last week, and the preacher was saying that this was a 'passing to a better life' and that we should 'rejoice.' Well, that's bull—I want *everybody* at my funeral crying, or I'm coming back and causing big trouble!" It was clear that he had made his peace and was going to have some fun on the way out. He had faced the truth and dealt with it.

My dad's life was a lesson about action. At the age of

seventy-one, thirty years after earning his Ph.D. in psychology, he enrolled in the seminary with the intention of earning a Master of Divinity degree. The problem was exhaustion: his heart was so bad he could only walk fifty feet at a time, so he had to get to campus thirty minutes before class. Then, from the parking lot, he had mapped out a route as complicated as any pass pattern in the NFL: fifty steps to the park bench and rest; thirty-seven steps to the tree stump and rest, and so on, every day, all to go 150 yards. But he saw it through. Ultimately, after two years and I don't know how many rest breaks, my dad stepped onto the dais to receive his diploma, and the whole arena erupted in cheers. So don't tell me about how hard it is to do things.

Have you made your list? I hope that writing it down brings home to you the need for doing. What other areas of your life require purposeful, meaningful, constructive actions? As we move into the parts of this book concerned with developing your personal, specific life strategy, this kind of evaluation can be very useful.

The following is a chart that may help you get started.

	Personal	Relational	Professional	Familial	Spiritual
1.					
2.					
3.					
4.					
5.					

Assignment #9: In the column devoted to each category of your life, list the top four or five actions that you feel you need to take in that category. For example, if in the familial area, you recognize that you need to spend more time with your children, put that down. If you need to take action in the personal area of your life by devoting a few minutes every morning to organizing your day, then put that in writing, too. Don't approach this with the mind-set of a perfectionist, worrying too much about being specific, or thinking you've got to tackle these issues immediately. The point here is simply to identify some key areas of your life where action is needed, and to record them for future reference.

Making such a list should help you see that sometimes the key to meaningful change is skepticism about "the way things are." If you are going to measure your progress based on results, then you must be willing to question *every pattern* and *every structure* in your life. You must be willing to question how and where you spend your time, what you say to yourself, how and why you interact with those you do, and every other aspect of your being. And you must be willing to change it. Resolve to escape the insanity and do something different. Don't *intend* to do it, actually do it.

I am not saying it's easy. I am just telling you that this questioning and willingness to do things differently are essential steps. They are critical ingredients in the truthfulness that can and will help you succeed in changing your life, when everyone around you is making excuses, talking about good intentions, and returning to self-destructive behavior instead of embracing long-term change.

If you have been cheating yourself in life, it's quite possible that you're in pain. Believe it or not, that may now actually be a good thing, something that you can use to your benefit. Pain, if acknowledged, can be a powerful motivator. Whatever pain is present in your life right now may serve as the fuel in your quest for change. If your life is really awful, but you are in denial and totally numb to it, just mindlessly going through the motions, then you haven't got much incentive to change. On the other hand, if you're really hurting, then acknowledging that pain can force you out of the numbing doldrums. Don't deny, or mask, or mislabel the pain. Use the pain to reach for something different. Don't rationalize and decide that you deserve it, or that it is not that bad. Admit it to "center-stage" consciousness, and it can move you.

I grew up in Texas, where, like most kids in the summer, I used to run around barefoot. There's probably not a person alive who hasn't had the experience I remember so well: You run out on the blacktop road barefoot, and when you're about halfway across, it hits you: "Yikes! My feet are *melting*!" Now, at that point, you are going to do something. You might go backward, you might go forward, but you aren't just going to stand there, waiting for your feet to burst into flames and melt up to your ankles. You will not stand in the middle of the road. You're going to move, one way or the other.

Pain gets you to take a direction. Use it to propel yourself out of the situation you are in and get you where you want to be. The same pain that burdens you now could be turned to your advantage. It may be the very motivation you need to change your life.

Some people just seem to be natural risk-takers; they keep on reaching, they keep on doing, until they get what they've wanted and dreamed about. They have a mind-set that accepts risk as a way of life. They are unwilling to settle for the "bird in the hand" if it is not the right bird.

Other people, however, scramble for safety or withdraw from the game when things start to look scary or unknown or hard. These people settle for what they don't want, and for a very logical—if unproductive—reason. By settling, they remove themselves from the stress, pressure, and fear of reaching and possibly failing. By "taking a seat in the comfort zone," they avoid the risk of failing, and the pain that goes with it.

If you pretend that what you have is okay, and you rationalize why you don't want or deserve more, there is no fear or risk of failure. You take what you've got and play it safe. Comfort zones mean no stretching, no changing, no risking a journey into uncharted waters. The Catch-22 is this: If you continue to reach and do new things, the fear can become so debilitating that you stop and become inert; if you pull out before you start, you never reach.

Risk simply means that something of value is put in jeopardy. In most cases, that something is, at a minimum, your peace of mind, your lifestyle, your relationships, or maybe your financial stability. The very act of admitting that you want more puts the balance of your existence in jeopardy. You feel a tension between wanting to maintain the security of sameness, however mundane and boring it may be, and the hope and excitement of having what you really want. No matter what the circumstances of your life may be, even if it is painful, disrupting the sameness can be scary. A familiar pain is like a not-very-good friend: it's not a good friend, but it is an old friend. It is predictable, you know how bad it gets, and you know where the bottom is. These things aren't true of new risks. We fear the unknown, and when we try something new, the results are always in question. How bad can this get? Can I lose it all? Will I fail?

Remember, our number-one fear is rejection. Why? Because we measure the results of our efforts in terms of whether the world accepts or rejects us. That being true, the world's reaction is a barometer of our very worth and value, at least in our minds. Every form of failure is in essence a rejection. If you open a small business and wind up in bankruptcy, you might interpret this as the world saying to you, "You aren't worthy of our business, our money, our support. We reject you and your efforts or products."

If what you offer is your companionship or your love, then it can, of course, be much more personal and painful. Messages that can be read as "I don't want you; you aren't good enough," are no fun. Recall, for example, those moments in school when you admired from afar the apple of your eye. Remember the anxiety associated with asking for a date, or hoping you'd be asked. Sometimes it may have seemed inconceivable that you would risk the humiliation of a rejection, or let yourself hope. Starting an actual relationship was way too much to hope for. It was just easier not to do it, not to put yourself on the line.

So goes the logic of avoidance: no pressure, no pain, no fear; just don't do it, and the problem goes away. You didn't get the date you wanted, but the anxiety went away. We've all made such choices. Call it a cop-out, call it choking, or call it selling out your dreams, but in any event, you quit on yourself and your life before you had "arrived." Life doesn't reward quitting. You are the only one who does that. And you may reward yourself for quitting with a pseudopeace, a peace that comes at the price of your hopes and dreams.

What I'm challenging you to do is to take a hard look at your hesitancy. Is your unwillingness to step out into a new endeavor or pursuit really justified? Or is the blind, unreasoning impulse of fear paralyzing your actions? Consider this: The potential

of trying new things, reaching for more and suffering a setback or
a rejection, is something that, ultimately, you can deal with,
whereas the fear of that event is formless, elusive, and difficult to
fight. Fighting fear is like trying to sack fog; you just can't get a
handle on it. Giving your power away to fear is worse than suffering the consequence that you're afraid of. Choose to give yourself the chance. It's normal to be anxious and afraid, but you can't
be dominated by the fear.

People talk so much these days about fear that it has become, to my way of thinking, a too-convenient excuse just to sit
on the sidelines and not take action.

I was contacted once by a fellow professional who had
fallen on some difficult emotional times and sought treatment. Dr.
Jason Doherty was a talented and passionate psychiatrist in charge
of the adolescent unit at a large, private psychiatric hospital. He
also did excellent volunteer work in the community, particularly
with the junior high and high school populations. This fine professional and caring man was making a real difference in his town.
We needed more people like him.

I had agreed to go to see Jason and was flattered that he
had asked for my help. At the door of his home, Dr. Doherty
greeted me with an uncertain handshake and a forced smile. The
den where we sat was as dark as a cave; all the blinds were drawn.
In a halting voice, he confided to me that he had not seen a patient,
or taken an active role in directing his unit at the hospital, for
nearly two months. Then he shared with me the horrifying details
of the incident that had shaken him to the core of his soul.

One weekday afternoon in March, on the way to one of
his volunteer meetings at the high school, he had stopped at a new
branch bank to set up an account. As the doctor waited second in
line to speak to a teller, a gunman burst through the door. Dr.
Doherty was instantly in the midst of an armed robbery. It was to
be a robbery gone bad. In a matter of seconds, and before Jason's
eyes, three innocent people lay dead and he was standing, dazed,
in a pool of blood.

The robber climbed over the counter, smashing the glass
panels with the .357 Magnum in his hand. Behind the counter, as
paralyzed with fear as Dr. Doherty was, the young teller began
screaming. The robber instantly shoved the barrel of the pistol to
the back of her head and, without a moment's hesitation, pulled
the trigger. Dr. Doherty tearfully described to me the expression

on the young woman's face before it exploded. The gunman then turned, shot a customer, and turned again and shot a security guard. Both died instantly.

Relating the scene to me, Jason sobbed uncontrollably. His head and arms shook violently, as if an electric charge were passing through his body. He spoke of being utterly numb with fear, and blinded by the blood and tissue that had fallen into his eyes. Still hardly grasping what was happening, he had run out the front door, with the gunman in hot pursuit. He ran aimlessly, and the killer caught up with him as he stumbled and fell in a parking lot not far from the bank. Kneeling beside him, the gunman coldly and methodically placed the barrel of the pistol to Dr. Doherty's forehead, then pulled the trigger. Nothing happened. The man pulled the trigger three more times, but the gun never fired. Frustrated, confused, and fearing the arrival of others, the robber leaped to his feet and ran off. When Dr. Doherty was finally found, he was crawling in a weed-choked alleyway, trembling, bruised, and completely incoherent.

Since that harrowing experience, Dr. Doherty had been unable to sleep, had experienced severe body tremors at unpredictable times, could not concentrate, and simply did not trust anyone anymore. He said he couldn't bear to leave the house. Clearly, he was suffering from Post-Traumatic Stress Syndrome, a disorder that, had he observed it in a patient, he would have quickly diagnosed and treated. But of course, it's different when you're the patient.

Understanding how debilitating that syndrome in particular, and fear in general, can be, I worked with Dr. Doherty over the next several weeks, often meeting with him two or three times a week. Gradually, we began to see progress, as he successfully eliminated many of his symptoms. The nightmares stopped, and he no longer found himself seized with tremors. At the same time, however, he began to acclimate to an unproductive lifestyle. I began to see that, having not worked outside the home in months, he had gotten used to not having to deal with the demands of the fast-paced psychiatric world. He was not taking action, and his family, the adolescent unit, the high school, and all those who relied on him were suffering.

As we approached the appropriate time for terminating his therapy, it was apparent to me that Jason's fear had become a not-very-good old friend. Fear had become his excuse for not getting back in the game. Living in a comfort zone defined by fear and the four walls of his home, he had become a casualty of life.

It was clear to me that Jason was in danger of "dropping out" and cheating himself out of continuing his rewarding life and career. I also recognized that he was comfortable talking to me, his one safe contact with the outside world. Knowing that I occupied that role, I decided I could not let this talented man overcome this trauma on the one hand, yet fall short of a full return to productivity on the other. I could not let him hide behind his fear any longer.

What I told him at our next meeting went like this: "I don't understand this fear business. I want to know what gives you the right to sit on the sidelines because you're afraid. I know you went through a terrible ordeal, but that is no excuse to drop out. We're all afraid. None of us knows what's going to happen tomorrow. Not one of us in this profession knows with certainty that our next patient is not going to get agitated, come in armed, and blow us away. But what gives you the right, when you are so blessed with talent, training, a healthy body, and such a vibrant mind, to check out of the game?

"You don't have the right to hide behind fear. You don't have the right to waste your gifts. You don't have the right to be so concerned about yourself that you're not doing what you have been prepared to do. You are cheating yourself, and you are cheating everyone whose life you could be touching. So I'm telling you that the therapy is over. You can lie here and whine and let that scum of the earth own you for the rest of your life—or you can make your hospital rounds tomorrow morning at seven o'clock. I'll meet you at the hospital, if you'd like. You're needed out there, buddy. You are discharged."

It was clear to me that Jason's time for action had come. The fear was too handy; it had become too easy. I knew Jason could wake up and feel needed. Life rewards action, and he obviously needed to take some.

When I met him at the hospital at seven o'clock the next morning, I said, "How are you doing, Doc?" He looked at me, smiled, and said, "You don't want to know. I'm going to get to work." He may have been scared, but he was there because he needed to be and deserved to be. How about you?

When it comes to taking action in the face of fear, it probably doesn't require much reflection to know that you've done this kind of thing before. You took a chance when you went from crawling to walking; when you went from one grade in school to the next; when you swam for the first time; when you moved away from home; when you changed jobs, or quit or moved to a new job in a new town; when you asked for that date. In each of these situations, you left behind the nonthreatening sameness of your life to reach for something more. Most of this kind of reaching is a good thing, since it is what broadens your horizons and allows you to develop your own competency and worldliness. Think, for example, about what your life and career would be like if you had never gone from crawling to walking.

The point is that, whatever your habit and your pattern may be, you must recognize that you no longer need to live your life in that way. However illogical it may seem, you must decide that you are worth the risk. You must decide that your dreams are not to be sold out. You must decide that you, for one, are willing to let yourself want, let yourself reach, let yourself admit that you are living a "sold-out" existence. You must be willing to say, "I know it may hurt for a while; I know it may be scary for a while, but I am worth it. I'm going to stop denying myself even the chance of getting my goals and dreams. I am going to set goals, make a strategy, and take action."

The kind of decision I'm talking about here is a *life decision*. Life decisions define, in large part, who you are: they are the decisions you've made at a bedrock, foundational level, and serve as the psychological and behavioral anchors for your values. For example, haven't you made a life decision that you will not steal? Refusing to be a person who steals is a fundamental value that you have incorporated into the core of your soul. You don't need to revisit this issue on a day-to-day basis, nor do you maintain an active, open debate about it. It has already been determined. If you are short of cash on your way out of town, you don't debate, "Gee, do I stop by an ATM, or do I rob this convenience store?" You don't have that debate, because some things are just not open for discussion; you've made a life decision. It is part of who you are.

If it were not for your life decisions, you might have to revisit all kinds of issues on a daily basis. Some days you might make the right decision, and other days you might not. Clearly, a life decision is a serious matter. Taking such a self-defining position should only be done after careful and heartfelt deliberation.

We will talk more about life decisions in chapter 8, when our focus turns to life management.

I hope that you have made life decisions about your integrity, your commitment to God, and your role in your family. But you may need to make it part of your life strategy to incorporate some new ones into the heart of your value system.

Consider that in the interest of incorporating the law *Life Rewards Action* into your life, you may need to make a life decision to actually put yourself at risk, even though this goes against your primal instinct for self-preservation. It challenges your natural craving for safety and security. But I suspect that this is one of those times when you simply must call upon yourself to leave behind the comfortable and familiar. Decide that you're going to move onward and upward. Make a life decision to risk reasonably, risk responsibly, but risk. I'm not talking about skydiving here. I'm talking about letting yourself want more, and taking the action to get it.

Doing so, of course, means that you must have a conversation with yourself, something like the following:

—"There will be setbacks."
I know it, and I will deal with them.
—"You may not succeed."
I may not win immediate success, but I will stay the course. To try and to fail is not indicative of my worth.
—"People will reject you."
We don't always get what we want on the first try. But to continue asking, continue working until I get what I want, will be the ultimate acceptance.
—"You'll be a failure."
I will be a failure only if I stop trying in the face of my difficulties.
—"Are you really worth it and capable of it?"
Yes, I am. In any case, I guess I will find out, because I am going to do it.

Resolve now that you will take the risk, make the effort, and be persistent in the pursuit of your goals. Your life should be filled with victories and rewards. If you are losing, that means somebody else is winning, so you know that winning happens. It might as well happen to you, but it's not going to happen by accident. It will happen because you make it happen. It will happen because you know what you want and move toward it in a strategic, consistent, meaningful, purposeful manner. Take *action*, and insist on *results*. This is a supremely important law of life.

CHAPTER SEVEN

THERE IS NO REALITY; ONLY PERCEPTION

There is nothing either good or bad,
but thinking makes it so.
—William Shakespeare

Life Law #6: **There Is No Reality; Only Perception**
Your Strategy: Identify the filters through which you view the world. Acknowledge your history without being controlled by it.

This is a law so profound that it determines whether or not you are happy, satisfied, and at peace. Accepting this law means that you embrace the fact that, no matter what happens in your life, how you interpret that event is up to you. Whatever meaning or value a particular circumstance has for you will be *the meaning or value that you give it.*

To appreciate how this law works, you need to understand the difference between sensation and perception. When light waves are received by your eyes, or sound waves by your ears, that is sensation: the phenomenon of stimuli being received by your sense organs. Perception, on the other hand, is your organizing and interpreting of those sensations. Perception is the level at which you *assign meaning* to the sensations you receive from the world.

The observation that "beauty is in the eye of the beholder" recognizes that your perceptions may be vastly different from mine. Both of us can look at the same picture, and I might like it, while you might not. The same holds true with each and every event in your life. We can't talk about what happens in your life without taking into account your interpretation of what happens.

Because you are a unique individual, your perceptions are unique. No matter how much you think you are like another person, the meanings you assign to what takes place in your life are yours alone. The failure to recognize this principle has created more trouble than you could ever imagine.

We now know, for example, that in addition to the differences from one individual to the next in terms of perception and interpretation, there are also gender differences that distinguish the perceptions of men and women. Married couples have for centuries been plagued by this phenomenon.

It's no secret that a husband and wife, looking at the same situation, can come up with two totally different versions of what it means. This "incongruency of perceptions" can lead to frustration, confusion, and marital disharmony. Specifically, having tested this theory with literally thousands of couples over the years, I have found that women think of even mundane chores very differently than do men. There are wide disparities in how the partners interpret something as simple as taking out the garbage. Men tend to categorize taking out the trash as a duty. Most women, on the other hand, interpret it as an act of love. Women have explained their thinking to me in this way: "Taking out the garbage is a distasteful job, and if he loved me, he would do it, so I would not have to. If he doesn't do those things that he knows increase the quality of my life, then he must not care about the quality of my life, and therefore I conclude that he does not love me."

By contrast, men perceive taking out the garbage as merely one of many duties they have to perform in a given day. Their perception of it is such that, if they are unable to "get around to it" that day, they will just add it to the list for the next day. It never occurs to men that since the women in their lives see doing this chore as an act of love, their failure to do it will be viewed as unloving.

There's nothing to be gained by asking who is right and who is wrong in this scenario. Neither spouse is right or wrong. There is no reality; only perception. If she interprets the failure to perform this task as an indication of not being loved, then that interpretation is as real to her as the sun coming up in the morning. If he interprets it as simply another of the day's jobs, having absolutely no emotional meaning attached to it, then that is his perception, just as real to him as hers is to her. How you view the event is what determines its meaning to you. The key point is that where your perceptions are concerned, you have the ability to *choose differently* from what you are currently choosing, if you wish. When it comes to how you see things, you do have a choice.

One of the harshest imaginable tests of this truth occurred in the life of Dr. Victor Frankl, an Austrian psychiatrist who was captured by the Nazis during World War II and held prisoner at the Auschwitz concentration camp. The SS had murdered his wife and his parents, and now, subjecting him to every indignity imaginable, held his life in their hands. Writing afterward of his experiences in the camp, Dr. Frankl described the obsessive control that the guards exercised: each day, he and his fellow prisoners were told when to sit, when to stand, when to work, when to eat, and when to sleep—and they were told whether they would be allowed to live or die.

In his fascinating and inspiring book, *Man's Search for Meaning*, Dr. Frankl noted that in the face of these unending atrocities, he discovered one very important aspect of his existence that the SS guards could not control. They could not control what attitude he took about his suffering. They could not force upon him how he would interpret and react to his treatment.

At a particular moment in the midst of his imprisonment, Dr. Frankl made a life decision. He saw that if he were made to suffer these terrible events in his life for no meaning, he would go insane. He decided, instead, to live by the principle that "we only know and experience this life through the meaning or the relevance of perceptions that we assign to it."

I believe that the lesson in Victor Frankl's experience is twofold. The first is his realization that you can, in any situation, choose your reaction: No matter what your circumstances, your perception of those events is of your choosing. But just as importantly, having discovered that he had this choice, Dr. Frankl saw an opportunity to prove that even under the most extreme circumstances, that discovery would still hold true. If he died before he could share the realization, he would have endured it all for nothing. As a result, he chose to perceive his situation as a challenge. From his suffering came his commitment to survive, to deliver his discovery to the world.

I trust that it is safe to say that you have never had to endure such a challenge as Dr. Frankl's. Nevertheless, his message has immediate applications. The events in your daily life have only the meaning that you assign to them. Put another way, there is no good news and there is no bad news; there is only news. You have the power to choose your perceptions. And you exercise this power of choice in every circumstance, every day of your life.

When you consider the relevance of this observation to your own life—in fact, to everyone's life—I believe you'll appreciate why I think it's such a profound truth. Dr. Frankl's philosophy is as true today as in the horrible setting of the concentration camp. Think about it. When you pick up the newspaper and the headline says, "Democrats Win Control of Senate," is that good news or bad news? In fact, it's neither; it's just news. It is not good or bad until you assign a meaning to it. If you yourself are a Democrat, and are comfortable with what the Democrats are doing politically, then it may be good news. If you're a Republican who is not at all comfortable with what they're doing, then it is decidedly bad news. The crucial thing to notice is that your response to the headline is not a function of what happened, but of how you chose to *perceive* what happened.

I am not suggesting that one of your choices is to decide that anything that may happen in your life is a "good deal." Obviously, that is not always a rational reaction. Should some injury or tragedy befall one of your children or a loved one, it is not rational for you to perceive that in some way as being good, but you do have a choice about whether that event will be your absolute undoing, or whether it becomes something you deal with in a constructive manner.

If, for example, one of your children is injured, you may choose to learn from that event, and thereby protect him or her and your other children more effectively in the future. You may choose to see that the child learns to deal with and overcome adversity. You may choose to teach that health and well-being are not to be taken for granted. You may decide to take steps to change the situation in which the injury took place, thereby protecting other children.

Everywhere you look, you see examples of exactly this kind of creating value from adversity. Mothers Against Drunk Drivers (MADD) is a wonderful organization and a perfect example of how parents who have suffered the loss or injury of a child at the hands of an irresponsible element of society have chosen, through social action, to create meaning out of that suffering. Please don't think for a minute that I am suggesting that a single one of those parents would consider his or her social action worth the injury or death of their child. I'm only pointing out that their reaction to the fact that it did happen was a choice, and that they chose a constructive alternative. You do have a choice about how you perceive the world.

We all view the world through individual filters. Those filters—our personalities, attitudes, points of view, our "styles"— powerfully influence the interpretations that we give to the events in our lives; those interpretations, in turn, determine how we will respond, and therefore how we will ultimately be responded to. The presence of these filters is neither good nor bad; it just is. Some filters may be healthy and constructive, while others may be distorted and destructive. But to live effectively, you've got to recognize the presence of your filters, and take care that they don't distort your perceptions so as to mislead you in your decision making.

There's no question that the filters through which we view the world are, in large part, a by-product of our learning history. Someone who, tragically, has been raised in a hostile and violent setting is likely to process his experiences through a filter that causes him to interpret the world as a threatening place. By contrast, a person whose upbringing was loving, caring, and nurturing will very likely view the world through a filter that causes him or her to interpret it as wonderful.

But remember the lesson of Life Law #2: *You Create Your Own Experience*. You are accountable. That means you must not use past events to build excuses. Yes, we are products of our learning history. Children do learn what they live. But what you need to recognize is that it *doesn't have to matter* in the here and now whether your past has been good or bad, just that it *has been*. I won't debate with you whether the cards you were dealt were good or bad, whether you got a fair deal or an unfair deal, got treated right or not. Suppose for a moment that we're in the counseling setting. Certainly I want to know what your history is. More importantly, I want *you* to know that history. I want *you* to recognize that if you were raped or beaten when you were five years old, that episode may have understandably distorted your view of relationships.

I certainly would not debate with you whether it is fair or "just part of life" that you were raped or beaten; of course, I'd agree with you that it's not fair—in fact, that it is terrible. That's not the point of knowing the history. The value of the history lies in making you aware that someone has placed a filter over your eyes and mind that influences the way you see the world. Once you realize that, then you can make allowance for the filter.

If you continue to view the world through a filter created by *past events*, then you are allowing your past to control and dictate both your present and your future. Take my example of someone who was raped and beaten at the age of five. The only thing worse than the event itself would be allowing that event to destroy that person's entire life by coloring how they see the world thirty, forty, or fifty years later. In that scenario, the event never comes to an end; it lives forever. As you have already learned, you cannot change what you do not acknowledge. Once you acknowledge that the pain of a particular event has altered the way you view the world and the people in it, then you can choose to be no longer a prisoner of those perceptions.

So you've got to acknowledge "it," whatever your particular "it" is, and recognize that it has distorted your outlook, your perceptions, and your experience. But none of that makes you any less accountable. You certainly, unequivocally, are not accountable for having been raped or abused as a child. You are undeniably accountable for how you react to it *now*. Where your filters are concerned, that means that you must test your perceptions. You must maintain an active, ongoing awareness of your filters. Otherwise, you will dramatically mislead yourself.

If you are not now asking yourself, "What are the filters through which I view the world?" you should be. Identify those filters so you can compensate for them. Do you have a chip on your shoulder—do you see people in general as the enemy, when they are not? Do you resent members of the opposite sex? Are you incredibly naïve and blindly trusting? Whatever your filter is, you need to know it.

You've probably noticed that there are some people who, when confronted with stress and demand, are prone to panic, decompensate, or "fall apart." I'm sure you know others who actually seem to thrive on crisis and do their best work under pressure. Two very dissimilar reactions can occur in response to the very same set of stimuli. Why? Because one person runs the crisis through a filter that causes it to be perceived as overwhelming and impossible to handle, while the other person's filter says, "This is an opportunity for me to shine."

More often, when we become aware of someone else's filter, it's because the filter is contributing to behavior that we find peculiar, if not downright bizarre. People with "unusual filters" are often labeled crazy. While it's true that many of these folks are in mental hospitals, we encounter plenty of them in our daily lives, spicing things up for the rest of us. Now, a common misperception is that these people simply do not know how to reason. Nothing could be further from the truth. In fact, while they clearly have a different view of things, their actual reasoning may, in fact, be very much like yours. They just start from a different place, since their filter or filters are different.

You may recall that making faulty initial assumptions was one "epidemic behavior" identified in chapter 1. I'm sure you'd agree that—like everyone else—you have at times made faulty initial assumptions about someone or something, and these assumptions have led you down the wrong path. The same can be said about many of those who populate our mental institutions. The only difference may be that their initial assumptions fall further outside the mainstream than yours. But both you and the mental patient make an important mistake, which is that *you fail to test your assumptions before you begin to treat them as true.*

In the first week of my internship at the V.A. hospital in Waco, I met a patient who seemed entirely out of place. Most of the patients there were decidedly impoverished. They tended to be scraggly, unkempt, and poorly dressed. But this gentleman had all the polish and grace of a Cary Grant. Chatting quietly with me in the hallway, dressed in a three-piece suit, he could just as easily have been waiting for a corporate board meeting to start. His comments to me were as lucid and articulate as those of anyone I had ever met. In fact, I mistook him, at first, for a member of the staff. Then I got to know the staff, and realized he was way too polished to be one of us. After a few minutes, I approached my supervisor about this fellow. My supervisor smiled and murmured, "Not everything about Richard is as it appears. Just be patient."

At that point, I considered myself quite the psychologist, even though I had exactly no experience. I was certain I knew virtually everything there was to know. Convinced that my supervisor was mistaken, I renewed the conversation with Richard, who professed that he was a veteran and that from time to time, he came to the hospital to recover from exhaustion. This annoyed me; I remember thinking, as I walked away, that a V.A. facility was not a hotel or resort, and that Richard should go home.

About a week later, on an Indian summer afternoon in November, I was walking across the hospital campus, enjoying the sunshine. As I approached a bench, I could see someone huddled under it, his entire body wracked with tremors. It was Richard. I hurried to him, bent over, and asked, "Richard, what's going on?"

"Get down!" he cried. "Get down! They're shooting, they're shooting!"

It immediately occurred to me that, if someone were to begin randomly spraying other people with gunfire, a twelve-hundred-bed psychiatric hospital would not be an unlikely place for such a thing to happen. I hit the dirt. Crawling under the bench with Richard, then scanning the horizon in every direction, I asked him to tell me more. Richard anxiously explained that "they're shooting at me with their heat-ray guns." More than a little embarrassed, I dusted myself off, got out from under the bench, and, now sitting on the bench instead of cowering under it, tried to figure out what had just happened.

To make a long story short, Richard was wearing a black nylon shirt; he had sat down on the bench; the sunlight had struck the back of his shirt. The weather was such that, as long as the sun was blocked by clouds, it was quite chilly; but when the sun shone directly on you, it warmed up dramatically. And as soon as he had felt the heat on his back, Richard made the assumption that "they" were attacking him with heat-ray guns.

Faulty initial assumption, of course. Somewhat bizarre, yes. But had his assumption been true, wouldn't all of the rest of Richard's behavior have made perfect sense? If you believed you were being shot at, then you very logically would take cover, fear for your safety, warn others, and be most agitated. Richard was not illogical; he just made a faulty initial assumption, and failed to test it to find out if it were true.

Isn't that exactly what you do in your life? Don't you make assumptions that you fail to test, and then treat them as though they were the gospel truth? And isn't the consequence of this behavior that you construct a reality based not on fact, but on untested perception? Maybe the assumptions you make and fail to test are not as bizarre as Richard's, but they can be just as wrong.

Think about it. Maybe your faulty initial assumption goes something like, "Nobody likes me." If you treat that assumption as true, and fail to test it, you may never pick up on information to the contrary. In any kind of social encounter, your assumption will cause you to make wrong judgments about what you should or shouldn't do. Now someone of a more bizarre twist may believe that the world is actually conspiring to get him (which, after all, is just a more extreme version of "Nobody likes me"). Suppose that he, too, fails to test the initial assumption. Both of you have made faulty initial assumptions; neither of you has tested them for truth or reliability. I would suggest that, with the exception of these two initial defects in your thinking, both you and your more eccentric counterpart have shown good logic from that point forward. You don't have to be illogical to make huge mistakes. If you start wrong and then think right, you still miss the mark.

Unfortunately, our filters are never more profoundly distorted than when we view ourselves. As a matter of course, people simply do not see themselves in a realistic and objective light. We completely overlook the ways in which we ourselves contribute to our experience of the world. Think about how many times you've heard people narrate an incident in their lives without seeming to notice any of their own accountability for what happened. You hear them blame the other people involved, often in excruciating detail, and charge right past what is obvious to everyone listening—namely, their own contribution to the incident.

I work with a brilliant and sophisticated trial analyst whose name it would be indiscreet to reveal: Lyndon McLennan. Some years ago, at the age of forty, Lyndon had just moved and was staying temporarily in an apartment. As I walked past Lyndon's office one Monday morning, I overheard him telling colleagues about what had happened in the neighborhood over the weekend. It seems that another patron—a man, probably in his twenties—entered the laundromat and, without asking, removed Lyndon's clothes from a dryer, piled them on a table, and then put his own clothes in the dryer. Lyndon had stepped out for a moment, but returned during this apparently heinous transgression against his clothes. As Lyndon told us about the deed, it was clear that he was still appalled. Now, I admit to being a little unclear about laundromat protocol, but I did not yet grasp the direction of the story.

Lyndon said he confronted the young man for his insolence, and an argument ensued. In a matter of seconds, the conversation apparently kind of dried up, because Lyndon and the stranger now wrestled each other to the ground and rolled under a table, where Lyndon wound up on top of the young man, choking him. The next part of the story Lyndon told with great passion. While sitting on top of this young man, his knee in the man's chest, both hands around his throat, Lyndon yelled, "If you will grow up and act your age, I will let you up!" The story ended with Lyndon's asking us if we could *believe* how childish and immature this young man had been.

Now, it occurred to me that Lyndon—who at forty years old, was wrestling someone under a table in a laundromat in a dispute over a dryer—might have been acting a little less than mature himself, and I said so. The blank look with which Lyndon greeted this suggestion told us that it had never occurred to him. He was totally oblivious to his role in the incident, and was clearly shocked when everybody in the room began howling with laughter. His nickname since then has been "Laundromat." (He may eventually live this down, but not if I have anything to say about it.) The point is that it was almost impossible for Lyndon to be objective about his own complicity in what happened, to see his own behavior in a clear and rational light. How about you?

One of the greatest difficulties with filters, whether they pertain to your perception of yourself or of others, is that they are made up of *fixed beliefs*. A fixed belief can be thought of as a life decision gone bad: it's a negative belief so entrenched in your thinking as to be a fixed part of your perceptual system. Fixed beliefs are typically very dangerous, if for no other reason than their fixedness. Consciously or otherwise, you have stopped seeking or receiving and processing new information. You're treating the belief as fact, and will no longer subject it to debate or modification. In this condition, you will not only miss new information, you will overlook important changes in yourself or other people that would negate the fixed belief. One of the most dangerous categories of fixed beliefs is what I call your limiting beliefs. These are beliefs you have about your own shortcomings and limitations, either real or imagined.

As in all things, you cannot change what you do not acknowledge. Not acknowledging that you have limiting beliefs, and identifying what they are, means that they will stay active, threatening to undermine the life plan you're about to construct. Very often, it's when you are already facing a challenge that your limiting beliefs arise, creating doubt about your abilities to navigate through the crisis. So neglecting them and thus allowing them to persist could prove fatal to your efforts. You want to make sure that you confront those beliefs and eliminate them *now*. To do that, you will first have to identify and acknowledge each one.

Let's be clear about what you're hunting for. Beliefs are things you hold to be true and accurate. You treat them as fact:

you no longer test them, let alone challenge them, because you believe you have found the truth, end of story. A limiting belief, then, is some negative self-perception that you have decided is true and accurate about you. You "know" it is true, so you just accept it and live with it.

Our objective here is to reopen your data banks on every single limiting belief you have. You must challenge those limiting beliefs, rather than living in obedience to them, as though they were commandments etched in stone. Far from being etched in stone, many of them are probably the products of a distorting filter created by events long past.

Assignment #10: *You can probably predict that I am going to ask you to search your mind and heart for the limiting beliefs that you carry with you from day to day. We all have them. The danger is that you have carried them for so long that you may not even be conscious of their presence. But the only thing more dangerous than a negative influence in your life is a negative influence that you are not on guard about, an influence that quietly, insidiously, and almost imperceptibly undermines your efforts. That is the nature of limiting beliefs.*

Some of these limiting beliefs may be rooted as far back as your childhood. (You know that a shrink can't write an entire book without talking about your childhood!) Others may be much more recent. But all of them contribute to the filter through which you view yourself and the world. Understand how these limiting beliefs affect you. If you enter a competitive situation, whether for a job, a mate, or in quest of some feeling of worthiness, and you're dragging with you a set of beliefs that says you cannot and will not achieve your goal, then you are defeated before you begin. You may recall the old saying: "If you think you can or you think you cannot, you are probably right." It's essential that you identify your limiting beliefs, so that when one of them begins to rear its ugly head, you will recognize it and can react against it. Get to know your limiting beliefs so well that if one begins to show even a hint of its presence, alarms will go off and you will counteract it.

To help you get started on identifying your own limiting beliefs, here are some typical examples that I have either carried with me or which others shared with me:

—Poor people have poor ways; I might as well
   accept it.

—I'm really just not very smart.

—I'm just not as good as the people I'm competing with.

—I never come out on top.

—No matter how good things start out, something always ruins my efforts.

—I cannot really change; I just am who I am.

—I don't have the family background to be what I really want to be.

—I've never been able to do it before; why get my hopes up now?

—If I get too happy and relaxed, something will go wrong.

—If people really knew how much of the time I was "faking it," I would really be in trouble.

—If I tried to change, it would just upset other people.

—It's selfish of me to spend so much time and energy on me.

—I don't deserve a second chance.

Perhaps you spotted some of your own limiting beliefs on this list. In any event, it's time to sit down, open your notebook, and create your own list. An ideal starting reference is the card that you used in response to Life Law #2, *You Create Your Own Experience.* Use it to list the "tapes" you play throughout the day. Root out and record all of the self-perceptions that hold you back. As you do so, tell yourself that you'll probably add to this list across time, since as you encounter challenges down the road, you may recognize various other limiting beliefs. Go on alert, determined to unmask the scurrilous beliefs. Getting rid of them is a key step in a good, solid life strategy.

Maybe you're holding on to beliefs about yourself as being destined for less than a high-quality life. Maybe your limiting beliefs cause you to think of yourself as not being equal to life's challenges. Whatever the message is, such beliefs lead to rigid thinking and rigid behavior, both of which threaten your future and your ability to control it. The time is ripe for reopening these beliefs for confrontation and change. If you fail to address them, right now—if you allow yourself to continue being misguided by them—you will compromise your ability to adapt what you're learning in this book to change your life.

Take whatever time you need to thoroughly examine all of your belief systems. In addition to your personal limiting beliefs, you may have fixed beliefs about

Your mate
Your relationships with loved ones
Your career
Your future
Your friends
God
The world in general
People in general

If you will acknowledge that you've been holding on to certain fixed beliefs that cause you to think and behave in a rigid fashion, you can reopen those subject matters for more active evaluation. In any event, you control your perceptions. Therefore, you control your interpretations of and attitudes about your life. That is power.

Do what it takes to see that your perceptions are grounded in fact. Your perceptions should develop not just from your view of the world, but from your testing and verification of that view. If you will "shake up" your belief system, challenging in particular those views you hold about yourself, rather than blindly or habitually accepting them, the freshness of your perspective can be startling. An old world can suddenly look new. The freshness of your perspective can make an old *you* look new.

You are a dynamic organism. With every experience, you are changing and, if you use the experience properly, improving. You are changing and improving with every page of this book, if you use it properly. There is no reality; only perception. Let your perceptions be fresh and new and grounded in fact, not in history.

CHAPTER EIGHT

LIFE IS MANAGED; IT IS NOT CURED

It's not whether you get knocked down;
it's whether you get up.
—Vince Lombardi

Life Law #7: Life Is Managed; It Is Not Cured
Your Strategy: Learn to take charge of your life and hold on. This is a long ride, and you are the driver every single day.

Simply put, never in your life are you without problems and challenges. You know that if everything is calm and peaceful in one area, such as your home, there's likely to be challenge and turmoil in the workplace, or vice versa. We try to dress up this paradox in order to make it okay. Clichés abound about why problems are a good thing:

—Facing problems builds character.
—Without occasional pain, we wouldn't be able to recognize and appreciate pleasure.
—Problems are opportunities to distinguish yourself.

While there is probably some truth in each of these clichés, the fact remains that life has to be managed. That's how it is, that's how it has been, and that's how it always will be. If you acknowledge and accept this Life Law, you are less likely to label every problem as a crisis, or to conclude that you're not handling your life successfully. It is important that you come to grips with this law now, so you don't make that error in judgment.

A long-established fact of psychological functioning is that it is not so much the particular circumstance that upsets the person involved, as it is the violation of his or her expectations. If a young, starry-eyed couple enter into marriage with storybook expectations that everything's going to be "sweetness and light," they are likely to react very badly to the adjustment pains that typically accompany the merging of two lives into one. On the other hand, if a young couple, perhaps because of other life experiences, anticipate that there will be adjustment pain, if they expect to face problems in the marriage, then the occurrence of these routine challenges will only confirm what they expected, and their emotional reaction will be much, much less problematic.

You can help yourself as a life manager if your "expectancy set" about life is realistic rather than naïve. Understand that success is a moving target, and that in an ever-changing world, your life must be actively managed. If, after reading this book, you implement all of the teachings, truths, and principles that you care to accept, your life will very likely be in a great place, and of course I will be delighted for you. But know that how well your life is working five years from now will be a function of how well you are actively managing yourself from now until then.

You've probably noticed that I've referred to you as a "life manager," as though you were two distinct people, one of whom had a client to manage. It will be highly valuable for you, from this point forward, to think about yourself as the manager of your life, in the same way that you might think of and evaluate the manager of a store, or a supervisor in your workplace. Thinking about the manager of your life as if he or she were another person can give you some needed objectivity in stepping back and assessing how you're doing. If you think about the state of your life as a function of how well your life manager is doing, you'll have an objective yardstick for measuring your efficiency.

Suppose you were called upon today to give your life manager a performance evaluation. How would you rate that performance? Disregarding the fact that your life manager is you, do a results-based assessment that takes into account at least the following criteria:

    1—Is your life manager keeping you safe and secure from foolish risks?

2—Is your life manager putting you in situations where you can utilize all of your skills and abilities?

3—Is your life manager creating opportunities for you to get what you really want in this life?

4—Is your life manager taking care of your health and well-being, physically, mentally, emotionally, and spiritually?

5—Is your life manager selecting and pursuing relationships in which you can be healthy and flourish?

6—Is your life manager requiring you to reach and stretch for those things that will keep you fresh and young and alive?

7—Is your life manager designing your day-to-day flow so that you enjoy some peace and tranquillity?

8—Is your life manager arranging for some fun and recreation in your life?

9—Is your life manager structuring your world so that there is balance among those things you consider to be important?

What kind of marks do you give yourself as a life manager? As the evaluator, you may decide that your biggest problem is that you can't fire your life manager, the same way you might fire someone who was mismanaging your business or your employees. This is a life manager you have to work with, motivate, educate, and be patient with.

Make no mistake: You are a life manager, and your objective is to manage your life in a way that generates high-quality results. If you're not doing a very good job, then you need to wake up and get on the ball. You may not be the only client you have, particularly if your family includes children, or people who act like children. But you are your most important client.

As your own client, you must treat yourself with great care, and manage yourself with the understanding that you are a very important person. In fact, I can tell you that the most important person in my life is Phil McGraw. I do not apologize for that, nor do I believe that it is selfish. I am the only husband and father that my wife and children have. If I take care of myself, then I have something to give in those two important roles. If I choose, instead, to be a martyr—if I constantly self-sacrifice and do not take care of myself, then I may not be there, physically or emotionally, when they need me. If I do not make deposits to the "Phil account" along the way, I may find myself emotionally and physically bankrupt at some point in the future, when the people I love are most in need of me. My motive for taking care of myself is, admittedly, them. But I am not just playing word games. This belief affects how I treat myself day to day. To keep from cheating them, I must take care of myself.

Because I believe that your job as a life manager is so important, here is a pretty darn good job description:

First, accept, acknowledge, and apply *to you personally* every Life Law we have discussed and will discuss.

Second, commit to *resolve* rather than *endure* your personal problems. The old adage that "the cobbler has no shoes" is profoundly relevant here: If you're the kind of person who busily addresses everyone else's problems and needs, but you don't take care of your own, you are headed for emotional bankruptcy. Problems that you put up with can linger so long that you become almost numb to them. You must resolve to spend a substantial amount of your problem-solving energies on your *own* problems, not just everyone else's. Remember, you can't give away what you do not have. If you have a tortured spirit because you let problems forever plague you, you cannot give a strong, healthy, peaceful self to *those you love*.

Third, beware of unanswered questions. You may have heard people playing the "what if?" game with their life worries: "What if my spouse leaves me?" "What if there is a spot on my lung?" "What if I get fired?" It has been my experience that, when people allow these kinds of questions to gnaw at them, it's because they simply do not force themselves to answer the question. They turn the question over and over in their minds, but they never give themselves an answer.

A formless dread of the unknown can be debilitating and paralyzing. For that reason, questioning yourself is a good thing, but if you're going to ask these "why," "what," "how," and "what if?" questions, it is critically important that you take the time to give thoughtful answers. And in the vast majority of cases, the realistic answers to the "what if?" questions are not nearly as bad or overwhelming as the vague, imagined results.

Maybe you find yourself asking, "What if I am diagnosed with cancer?" A realistic and studied response to the question might take into account that, for certain types of cancer, the cure rate is 80 percent, and for other types it's 100 percent. A realistic response might also recognize that great strides are being made in research into treating the disease, so that, in fact, this diagnosis is not nearly as catastrophic as it might have been even a few years ago. In other words, the more comprehensive, realistic answer turns out to be manageable, while the indefinite "nonanswer" is so scary as to be debilitating. You can ask the questions, but you must be willing to answer them, as well. If you play the "what if?" game, play it all the way to the answer.

Your fourth responsibility as a life manager is to refuse to live with unfinished emotional business. How many times have you witnessed yourself or others overreacting to some apparently insignificant happening or event? What these people or you are actually doing by overreacting is "cumulatively reacting." When you go ballistic over the fact that your mate has left the top off of the toothpaste, you are not really overreacting to that single event; it's just the spark that ignites feelings you've accumulated from a variety of earlier situations and circumstances. It is so easy, in a busy and ever-changing life, to allow emotional pain and discord to accumulate. But heaps of unfinished emotional business can crush you, dominating your very spirit.

To be an effective life manager, you must identify when you are hurting, angry, frustrated, or confused. You have to call time out and deal with it. Address it with the person with whom you're interacting, or at least with yourself. That means that if emotional pain or problems have cropped up in your life, you must insist on getting closure. Closure means you don't carry the problem or the pain. You address the issue, then you close the book and put it away. Whatever that takes, do it. Maybe it means confronting yourself or the other person. Maybe it requires forgiveness or making an apology. Whatever it requires, you do it to get past it. Avoid piling up this kind of burden in your life; give yourself emotional closure.

Finally, honor your agreements, whether they're with yourself or others. Broken agreements can become so repetitive and seemingly insignificant as to go unnoticed by the person who is breaking them. But make no mistake: Broken agreements are boulders that you drop in front of and behind you on the road of life. Think about how you feel when someone makes a commitment to you and then breaks it. Take the time to ask your children, in a nonthreatening way, how they felt when you left unfulfilled your promises about spending more time with them, or being there for them on a particular occasion. Have the courage to ask yourself what agreements you have broken, in the last week, with the people you care about. It sends a painful message to someone when you make a commitment and then dishonor it. Whether you intend the message or not, it tells them that they are not important to you. It says to them that they have been rejected.

I suspect you'll be more than a little surprised at the obstacles you may be putting in your own way by being unreliable. This kind of behavior is particularly significant for your family relationships, since the damage affects your spouse and children, and splashes back on you. I have often said that parents are only as happy as their saddest child. Broken agreements with children, whether age four or forty-four, create pain and distance, and that affects you.

You are your number-one worldly resource. Manage it and manage it well. If you are going to start to require more of yourself as a life manager, step up and do it like you mean it. Work as hard as you would expect anyone you might hire for the job to work. If you were paying big money to a life manager, you would want that person to absolutely get after the job. It's time now to start managing your life with that kind of purpose. Managing your life with design and commitment will cause what you do to look, feel, and be different. You'll know you have a life with energy, a life that matters, because you treat your life that way.

Think about someone taking a leisurely stroll through the park on a sunny day. He's got no particular place to go and no particular time in which to do it. He walks slowly—meandering, really—hands in pockets, turning this way and that. He pauses frequently and may turn randomly, occasionally doubling back or staring into space. Now, if the point is simply to enjoy the sunshine and the scenery, there's nothing wrong with this kind of attitude and approach. We do need, on occasion, to have this kind of experience. But it's no model for a life manager with big change and big challenge as the order of the day.

Contrast such behavior with that of someone who is on point—determined to make it to an important meeting, perhaps. He's cutting through the park to save time; he walks with purpose, direction, and perhaps even urgency. There's a spring in his step. He's got a place to go; he has a limited time in which to get there; and he will not be distracted from his goal. Even the most casual observer could pick which of these two people was on a mission.

You will soon be putting together a highly personal, individualized strategy that will enable you to manage your life by design, rather than as if it were a meandering stroll through the park. You must approach this task with the most intense commitment, direction, and urgency you can muster. Your mission is to stop the momentum and direction you now have, and replace them with the momentum and direction you want. If you approach this mission with nothing more than a "heightened awareness," you will never get what you want. To change your life, you must *be* different. Really managing your life means that you will stop living reactively and put your life on *project status*.

Project status means that the matter at hand has taken on a special significance and a special urgency, lifting it above your other concerns. Think about painting your house, for example. If you just kind of decided, "You know, gee, it would be nice if this house got painted someday," how soon and how efficiently do you think it would get painted? Compare this attitude to your waking up one Saturday morning at 7:00 A.M. and declaring, "Project status: I'm going to paint this house, and I'm going to do it by midnight Sunday." The difference in your rate of progress would be astounding.

That's the difference between how you are now living and how you will be living if you start designing your life as if you meant it. Project status means you will approach your life with the conviction that you deserve what others have, and that you're worth the effort required to get it. Remember, the primary difference between you and those "lucky people" is simply this: that they did what they did, and you did what you did. You just settled too early and too cheaply.

The rest of this year will go by, whether you are doing something to improve your life or not. Don't start on this project tomorrow, or even later today. *Start now.* If you've made it this far into this book, you are serious about having something different in your life. Put your life on project status, and you will have it.

I am not suggesting that the world will just roll over and start giving you what you want because you now are willing to reach for it. If you allow it to be, life can be cruel. You have witnessed that cruelty and probably have experienced it in your own life. Unmanaged, your life may be lacking in important and painful ways. Things you value may be snatched away. Someone you love may be lost. More subtly, an unmanaged life, rather than being marred by losses, may fail to generate what you've wanted and dreamed about. If you don't have a plan, you'll be a stepping stone for those who do. Not a pretty picture, to be sure; not a fun way to view the world, but the truth nonetheless. But in contrast to the cruelty and harshness that are so much a part of a poorly managed or unmanaged life, if you have a clear-cut strategy, and the courage, commitment, and energy to execute that strategy at a project status level, you can flourish; you'll overcome the tough stuff.

The world is not evil; it is just the world. It is not to be feared, just managed; and the key to managing it is having this consciously designed strategy. Think about it: If you give yourself a turn here, you will finally get the attention and focus you not only deserve, but need, if you are to have any real chance of changing your life for the better. What if this is your chance? What if this is your turn?

As you focus on your life management, I think you'll find that many of the Life Laws we've already dealt with will take on an even greater significance. Understanding these earlier laws of life means that you'll be that much better equipped to manage this ever-changing life of yours.

So far, for example, if you've been doing your homework, you have already acquired some essential tools. You have begun to consciously identify the behavior you have chosen that creates key consequences in your life. You've also identified the payoffs you are deriving from some of these persistent types of behavior. This kind of knowledge is, of course, a vital tool in your effort to manage your life effectively. Having looked at your behavior, pay-offs, and categories, you may already be very focused on what your life would be like if you effectively minimized or eliminated some of these problems.

The other good news is that, while life is managed and not cured, you don't have to start fresh every day. You don't begin with a blank slate every morning. Your life already has a certain structure to it, whether you are single, married, living with family, or cohabiting with friends. Whatever your circumstances, there is a structure there that is known to you and within which you can function.

Consistent with that structure you have probably arrived at and adopted certain life decisions, which we discussed in the context of Life Law #5, *Life Rewards Action*. You'll recall that life decisions are your psychological and behavioral bedrock, the fundamental values that you've incorporated into the core of your soul. Typically, you don't consciously spend a lot of time thinking about them; nonetheless, they are there. For example, haven't you made a life decision that you will not be physically or verbally abusive toward your children or loved ones? (If you haven't, I highly recommend that you do so—now!) You may have made a life decision that you will train your children to treat themselves and others with dignity and respect. Life decisions like these serve as the cornerstones on which to build your life management strategy. They are thematic; they are totally about you; and if you will continue to examine them, I suspect that you will almost immediately see that you aren't starting from scratch. You already have the beginnings of a well-managed life. You just need project status.

So, what are your life decisions? You may think that you've never engaged in such deliberate choice making, but I have no doubt that you have, in fact, made those choices. I also suggest that by acknowledging and giving words to your life decisions, you will bring a much-needed order into your life. You'll perceive, much more clearly, the foundation on which you'll be building a strategy.

Assignment #11:*Write down any and all of the life decisions that you are conscious of, not taking anything for granted. For example, I'll wager that you have made a life decision that you will not kill. You may think that you don't give a decision like that much thought; nevertheless, it is a life decision that has defined you as a nonviolent person. To help you get started, here are some other examples of life decisions you may have made or want to make now:*

—I will live with God in my family.
—I will live my life with integrity—meaning,
   specifically, that I will not lie and I will not steal.
—I will not fight in front of my children.
—I will not ask children to deal with or be burdened
   by adult problems.
—I will not resort to physical violence.
—I will take care of myself, so that I can take care
   of others.

Understand that when we are discussing life decisions, we are not talking about passing fancies or casual commitments. A life decision is one that has been made from the heart. It is beyond thought; it is a conviction that you live by, not some of the time, but all of the time. List yours. Once you've made a complete inventory of your life decisions, you may be pleased at the number and quality of important issues that, for you, are already resolved. At the same time, you may also discover some glaring holes that call for a life-decision level of commitment now. What are the holes? What are the problems?

A key element of life management, and a life decision that you may have overlooked, is your own standard of acceptability. I would think you'd agree with my initial observation that life is anything but a success-only journey. I have never encountered a person whose life did not have serious flaws, problems, and challenges. Those things are a given. The real issue is how you will manage those problems, and the level of effort you'll apply to managing them. If the standard you've set for yourself in managing your life is too high or too low, then you're adding to your difficulties. Obviously, if you don't require much of yourself, your life will be of poor quality. But if you are a "perfectionist," you have set up such an unrealistic standard that you are living in a dream world. It is important to be realistic about what you expect of yourself, and to be patient in building from one level to the next.

It should be clear to you why this issue of self-requirement rises to the level of a life decision. Resolving that you will not be a passenger in life, and that you will require excellence from yourself in all areas, is a defining moment in your life. Unfortunately, you may not have thought to conduct this heart-to-heart conversation with yourself before now. But there can be no better time than right now for deciding, as a matter of principle, what you will *demand* from yourself, as contrasted with what you are willing to *accept* from yourself. This standard you adopt should be one that you do not have to re-create every day. For that reason, this is a matter of great concern and relevance, worthy of the most careful and attentive self-conversation.

In thinking about your self-requirement, you may discover that you're living in a comfort zone: You're avoiding reaching for a level of achievement or accomplishment that is not already comfortable. You are complacently going through the motions of your life because you have adapted to the level of demand. You are living a risk-aversive life.

While comfortable, that sort of life can be more than stagnant. Staying in your comfort zone can be hazardous to your genuine well-being. Remember that you are the most important, if not the sole agent of change in your life. If you want change, you're the one who's got to take action. If events in your life begin to flow differently, it will be because you have changed what you think, feel, and do. Remember these simple truths:

> If you continue to do what you've always done,
> you will continue to have what you've always had.
> If you do different,
> you will have different.

Step out of your comfort zone. Behave differently by resolving to work harder and work smarter. That means demanding more of yourself, in every area, across the board.

If you are honest, I wager you will admit that you are "life lazy." For example, you never take the mental and emotional energy to sit down and write out a goal and a plan to get that goal. You may intend to, but you let yourself slide.

Effective life management means you've got to "ramp up." You've simply got to require more of yourself in every category of behavior, even the mundane: your grooming, self-control, emotional management, interaction with others, your work performance, your dealing with fear, and in every other category you can think of. Starting now, begin each and every day of your life with the question: "What can I do today to make my life better?" Ask it, answer it, and then do it, every day.

If the people around you cannot observe, from their external vantage point, that you are behaving differently, then you're falling short of what I am trying to describe to you. You must be willing to change the direction in your life. In order to do that, you must reorganize yourself and your day in a way that moves you up the performance ladder. Believe me, performance is contagious. If you begin to do some things differently, this will stimulate additional changes.

Maybe you've wanted for years to get in shape, but every day you come home tired and crawl onto your couch like a lizard on a rock and just sit there. Don't do that. Beginning today, don't do that. As someone who exercises virtually every day, I can tell you that at least a third of the time, I'm "sure" I am too tired, too exhausted to exercise. But fifteen minutes into my workout, I am feeling better, I'm energized, and I have a better frame of mind and outlook on what lies ahead. Don't give in to your negative momentum. Require more of yourself physically, mentally, emotionally, and behaviorally.

If you are in a relationship where you invariably lose your temper and get into an argument or shouting match, require more of yourself. The next time there's a conflict brewing, resolve either to walk away, or to respond in a calmer fashion. Stop going with the flow. Start your own river instead.

I could give you a thousand examples, but you know where your behavior falls below the bar of excellence. Consciously resolve to require more of yourself in the pursuit of your life goals and the solving of your problems, and you will have put in place a cornerstone for the foundation of your life strategy.

The essence of this Life Law is that *you* are your own most important resource for making your life work. How well you handle your overall life will be a direct reflection of how well you're managing your personal life. Although it may sound politically incorrect, my strongly held belief is that you do have to make *you* the most important person in your life. People are quick to react to that advice, in knee-jerk fashion, as encouraging behavior that is selfish and asocial. I submit to you that it is anything but.

I'm sure you are aware of times in your life when you made a decision and it just clicked. Everything worked. It felt right at the time, it worked subsequently, and it only looked more correct with the passage of time. But since life is imperfect, not every decision that you make or have made will naturally be a winner. Adopt it as part of your own philosophy of life management that sometimes you make the right decision, and *sometimes you have to make the decision right*.

Poor choices are the ones that test your maturity and resolve. These are the ones about which you have to say, "*I will make this decision right*," meaning, I will work to resolve the flaws, I will work to find a solution, and I will be committed to the end. I'm talking here about maturity. It is so easy, particularly early in life, to bail out on those things that don't work at first blush. But decisions such as marriage and children are not so easy to undo. Resolve that in your life, you will make a concerted effort to make right the wrong decisions you have made.

Never lose sight of the stakes involved. Poor life strategies can end in commonplace disappointments that can eventually break your spirit—or in a single disaster. It's not the behavior that determines which result is yours. When the issue you're addressing is trivial, so are the consequences of a poor strategy. When the issue is weighty, so is the outcome. But the reality is that the stakes are almost always tremendously high, if not immediate.

Your stakes are the quality of your life, your hopes and dreams and goals. Like it or not, you, too, are a life strategist; if you're a poor one, no one can save your client—you. The problem you're trying to solve is your whole life—your relationship with your family, your career, your physical health, and emotional well-being. You have substantial challenges, or you wouldn't be reading this book. The question is: Do you have the skills it will take, not just to survive, but to succeed? If you don't, you need to resolve to get those skills. Or are you going to be yet another casualty of that silent, life-wrecking epidemic?

The life you're managing is your own. The emotional life, the social life, the spiritual life, the physical life that you are managing: all of it is your own. Manage it with purpose, and manage it with knowledge. You make the choices that create your emotional state. Make them in an informed, purposeful way, and you will have what you want.

Remembering what you've learned from Life Law #4, that you cannot change what you do not acknowledge, you've got to identify the major challenges in your life. Take the time to identify those things that could and should be the focus of your management efforts. Once we begin building your personal, specific life strategy in chapter 12, knowing what these issues are will be critically important.

CHAPTER NINE

WE TEACH PEOPLE HOW TO TREAT US

No one can make you feel inferior
without your consent.
—Eleanor Roosevelt

Life Law #8: We Teach People How to Treat Us
Your Strategy: Own, rather than complain about, how people treat you. Learn to renegotiate your relationships to have what you want.

The life laws you have learned thus far have focused on how and why you get the results that you do as you go through your life. This law is no exception. It deals specifically with how you define your relationships and how you get results. But it has an important added dimension. This law takes into account the fact that in addition to getting results, you yourself are a result, and therefore you shape the behavior of those with whom you interact. Because people learn by results, whether or not you reward, accept, or validate their behavior impacts their conduct, and will influence their subsequent choices. How you interpret and react to their behavior determines whether or not they are likely to repeat it. You therefore actively participate in defining your relationships.

So if you ever wonder why people treat you the way they do, see Life Law # 3: *People Do What Works*. They do what they do because you have taught them, based on results, which behavior gets a payoff and which ones don't. If they get what they want, they keep that behavior in their repertoire. If they do not get the desired result, they drop that behavior and acquire a new one. Understand that here, as in all areas of your life, results, not intentions, influence the people with whom you interact. You may complain or cry or threaten to give them negative results, but if the bottom line is that you reward the behavior by providing a response that the other person values, then that person decides, "Hey, this works. I now know how to get what I want."

If the people in your life treat you in an undesirable way, you're going to want to figure out what you are doing to reinforce, elicit, or allow that treatment. If you're involved in a relationship in which someone is consistently abusive, exploitive, or insensitive toward you, find out what you're doing to encourage that behavior, so that you can realign the relationship in a more healthy direction.

Relationships are mutually defined: each participant contributes importantly to its definition. From the very outset, it is a give-and-take negotiation between the participants. Together, you and your partner hammer out the terms, rules, and guidelines. Therefore, if you don't like the deal, don't blame just your partner. You have ownership of that relationship just as much as he or she does. Here's how it works:

Person A starts out engaging Person B in some manner that sets a tone for the relationship. Person B then reacts to that original defining message by sending back a response either accepting or rejecting A's definition. If it is rejected, B may either totally withdraw, or modify it in some way. If B's response changes the definition, then A will in turn either accept or reject that new definition, and respond to B. This continues until a relationship has been worked out and adopted. Thus, you have been an active participant in creating the terms and conditions of every one of your relationships.

I once counseled a middle-aged couple who had been married twenty-seven years. John was an electrical contractor and Kay was a highly experienced medical receptionist. Both came from large families and had raised four children themselves, all grown and out on their own. While they professed to love each other very much, they acknowledged they had come to me because their communication was terrible.

They arrived at my office one day right after a holiday, saying that they had recently had their worst fight in all their years together. Kay fumed, but said nothing, as John described the events leading up to the fight. He said that he had developed an annual tradition of staying up all night on Thanksgiving Eve to cook the turkey for the large family gathering that was always held at their home. On this particular Thanksgiving, they were expecting twenty-six family members for dinner. While he only occasionally drank alcohol, John said that his traditional Thanksgiving ritual was as follows:

"Every Wednesday night before Thanksgiving, I get a jug of Jack Daniel's and wait until she and any of the company turn in, and then I start cooking.

"I like to cook it real slow. So usually about midnight, I stick the bird in the oven, knock the top off the jug of whiskey, and start an all-night ordeal. Usually after a quart of Jack Daniel's, me and the turkey get done about the same time."

Over the years, Kay had not seemed to mind this ritual. Unfortunately, however, this particular year John apparently got a little ahead of the turkey with regard to the whiskey drinking and forgot to light the oven. By the time he discovered the problem, it was six o'clock in the morning and he had a twenty-eight pound turkey still refrigerator-cold. With reasoning that could only spring from a mind pickled in Jack Daniel's, he made the only logical decision: fry the turkey, piece by piece. When Kay entered the kitchen and found grease stains decorating every wall, turkey parts being fried in eight or nine different skillets and pans, and John up to his eyebrows in flour, she was decidedly unhappy. And as the old saying goes, "When momma ain't happy, ain't nobody happy."

This crisis had strained John and Kay beyond all reason. For ten days, they had essentially not spoken. Each blamed the other for the disastrous state of their relationship. In John's view, the reason they didn't have much of a marriage was that Kay almost never spoke. Kay insisted that they had a poor relationship because John was always "running off at the mouth" and would never listen. Like most couples, they had not really come to me for help, but instead to have a referee or a judge who could declare which of them was right and which was wrong.

Not surprisingly, I couldn't fulfill that request, because neither John nor Kay was right or wrong. They had mutually defined their relationship. John had taught Kay that it was acceptable to treat him passively, with little or no communication, because for years and years he had accepted that behavior. Kay had taught John that he could dominate the relationship and do all of the talking, because she had allowed him to do so for twenty-seven years. By letting each other get away with the problem behavior, each had taught the other that his or her behavior was acceptable.

When they finally reached the point in their lives when only the two of them were left at home, and there were no children to act as buffers, their problems came to the forefront. At last, in the face of what they considered to be a major crisis—the Thanksgiving debacle—the foundation of their mutually defined relationship began to crack. It was time for them to recognize that each had taught the other how to treat him or her, and that in neither case was that treatment healthy. Once John and Kay stopped reinforcing each other's unacceptable behavior, they began to develop better communication skills and a greater degree of intimacy and trust (although I don't believe John ever got solo turkey duty again).

As John and Kay's history demonstrates, even a pattern of relating that is almost thirty years old can be redefined. If you can teach people how to treat you in the first place, you can reteach them how to treat you after that. It is in the give-and-take of relating, and of results, that relationships are successfully negotiated. You may not have known that you were negotiating and creating, but you were. Now you know: Being in a meaningful negotiation and not knowing it can be very dangerous.

The good news is that, because you are accountable, you can declare the relationship "reopened for negotiation" at any time you choose, and for as long as you choose. John and Kay did exactly that after almost thirty years. In any case, new relationships or old, you are responsible for whatever state your relationships are in. Please understand that I mean you are responsible in the most literal sense, and even in the most extreme, seemingly one-sided circumstances.

In a much more serious and tragic example of this law, I recall once, early in my career, being summoned to the emergency room of a local hospital by a neurosurgeon with whom I'd worked on a daily basis. Because I had developed a practice which included the diagnosis and treatment of brain trauma and disorders, he had asked me to help him develop a functional diagnosis of a woman with acute trauma to the brain and spinal cord, and a possible closed-head injury. I was only a few blocks from the hospital when I got the page, so I arrived even before attendants had finished cleaning up the patient and taking her history.

Dolores was semiconscious when I entered the room, but was anything but talkative. Her scalp had been lacerated at the hairline, and the flesh was laid back four to five inches across almost the entire width of her forehead. Her left ear dangled, and would have to be surgically reattached. Her bottom teeth protruded through her lower lip and chin, and her nose was severely broken, displaced and lacerated. This hospital was located not far from a major interstate highway, where serious wrecks had become commonplace. Dolores's injuries were consistent with having gone through the windshield of a car; it appeared that she might even have hit the pavement. More to determine her degree of orientation than to actually gather details, I began to ask her questions. My first question was, "Dolores, tell me where this happened." It would be of diagnostic, not to mention legal, significance whether or not she had amnesia, and whether she could report accurately as to person, place, and time. I also wanted to test her short-term memory by finding out if she could identify the highway or the intersection for me.

To say that Dolores's answer stunned me would be a huge understatement. In a soft, slurred voice, she answered, "It happened in my den and bedroom." She reluctantly confessed that her husband had beaten her. I was bewildered; I was appalled; and I was angry. All of the grotesque injuries I saw were the work of her life partner. In an effort to comfort her, I said, "I am so terribly sorry that this has happened to you. You must just be shocked."

Looking at me through bloodstained and swollen eyes, Dolores sort of shrugged her shoulders. Then she said, "Well, I was shocked the first time, but I guess I'm not anymore."

I confess to you that my attitude immediately changed. Granted, I was no less horrified by the scope and intensity of her suffering. Nothing could erase my conviction that her husband was vicious, wicked, and sick. But now I was confused. How could these people live like this? In my book, this was attempted murder. I instantly thought, "Dolores, whatever the deal, whatever his hold on you, you must escape. This is *not* okay."

Reviewing her chart, I learned the sad history of her previous trips to the emergency room: her husband had broken four of her ribs; had held her hands down on a hot kitchen burner; had knocked her unconscious twice; and over the last three years, she had needed stitches several times. Always, she covered for him; each time she lied, and ultimately, she always went home to him.

While there's no question that this was an extremely sad

situation, I maintain that Dolores's accountability in this relationship was undeniable. By remaining with him and failing to press charges against him, she had effectively and consistently taught him that "this is okay. You can get away with this. I will let you beat on me and even kill me."

Now you may say, "Dr. McGraw, you don't understand. It's hard for the woman in this situation, particularly if she's not employed outside the home, to have the wherewithal to escape." I know that is true, and that it is a helpless feeling to be trapped and have no ready option. It is difficult if leaving puts children in jeopardy. But you must first and foremost protect your life and body. You either teach people to treat you with dignity and respect, or you don't. If you remain, then they get away with it, and you are worth far more than that.

Dolores was not to blame; Dolores was the victim of a terrible crime—*but* she and only she could remove him or herself from the danger. In my opinion, her husband was too sick to trust, ever. She had to rely on herself. There is no in-between; there is no mitigation; there is no excuse; and there is no alternative. If you are getting beat on, you had better get out, reach for help, and reach now.[1] Our hospital system provided little help. My colleague and I did call the police. Ultimately, Dolores's husband received probation. But when I last heard about them, they were back together.

Whoever your relationship partners may be, you have taught them the rules and you have taught them the boundaries of the relationship. They have learned your response patterns and incorporated them into their actions. If you acknowledge your role in this ongoing transaction, then you are living and thinking in accordance with Life Law #2: being accountable. You are acknowledging that you have created your own experience, and that when you chose to accept certain conduct from your partner, you chose the consequence of living with that conduct. You are acknowledging that if your partner is doing certain things with, for, or to you, he or she is doing them because the two of you have worked it out that way. Your partner will have to be retrained about what works and what doesn't.

[1] The number of the National Domestic Violence Hotline is 1-800-799-SAFE (7233). This is a toll-free call. One call summons immediate help, twenty-four hours a day, seven days a week.

I fervently hope, if you happen to be in a negative relationship, that it is not nearly as sick and severe as Dolores's. But the rules are the same. You teach people what they can get away with and what they cannot. You teach them by either actively rewarding their destructive relationship behavior, or by passively allowing them to persist in that behavior. If and when you acknowledge this Life Law, you will begin to analyze your relationship behavior. You will ask not why your relationship is where it is, but why not? You will see that it is where it is because you programmed it that way. If *you* are the one who determines whether or not the things people do are working for you or not, then you can change the relationship, starting right now. I'm not saying it will be easy. You have to decide if you are worth the trouble.

It should be apparent that I am seeking to manipulate you here. I've said that the participants define a relationship, and I want you to have no doubt that they do. Obviously, I want to inspire and instruct you to define all of your relationships with a minimum standard of treatment, such that physically, mentally, and emotionally, both partners receive dignity and respect. But in order to make that standard prevail, you must be willing to control your responses. Since you cannot change what you do not acknowledge, let's focus on the specifics of how you have taught people how to treat you. Then you'll be able to target the response patterns that need change.

The fundamental issue, of course, is whether or not you are "paying off" your partner for unwanted behavior. I'm not suggesting that payoffs should not be part of any relationship. If your partner treats you with dignity and respect, then it's only appropriate that you pay him or her off for that desirable behavior. On the other hand, if your partner treats you with insensitivity or cruelty, and you are paying him or her off for it, then that needs to stop. When people are aggressive, bossy, or controlling, and it works—meaning they get their way—you have rewarded them for unacceptable behavior. Your challenge, then, is to identify what payoffs you may be giving your partner in response to any negative behavior.

This sort of pattern should be easy enough to spot. For example, if your partner pouts when you don't comply, and you give in: bingo, payoff for pouting. They now know how to treat you to get their way. But it may be that the payoffs you most need to identify are much less apparent. Sometimes we cheat ourselves by not requiring our partners to pull their own weight, thus allowing them to get by with lazy performance or poor-quality performance. Specific payoff: They get to coast. Perhaps you are constantly covering for your partner's inadequacies, or shouldering a mental, emotional, or financial load that is way more than reasonable. Specific payoff: He or she enjoys the fruits of your labor. Even more insidiously, perhaps you are holding yourself back in your level of performance, so as not to threaten your partner. Specific payoff: A false sense of equality and security.

Sometimes people parent their partners, supporting them and protecting them as if they were children. Specific payoff: No adult expectations. Perhaps you literally support your partner with money and a home. Specific payoff: A free ride. Perhaps your partner is threatened by genuine intimacy, and you allow the relationship to exist at a level comfortable for him or her, but unrewarding for you. Specific payoff: No emotional demands, and high-level self-absorption. Suffice it to say that, whatever you are allowing your partner to "get away with," the very act of that tolerance is a subtle but significant payoff.

Before you reopen the negotiation, you must commit to do so from a position of strength and power, not fear and self-doubt. Getting to that position requires the knowledge and the resolve we have discussed. The knowledge you have been accumulating since you opened this book, including the resolve to be treated with dignity and respect, must be uncompromising. You must make a life decision that you would rather be well by yourself than be sick with someone else. This means that you are not playing a game, you are not bluffing, and you are not taking positions for shock value. It means that you would rather be by yourself, treating yourself with dignity and respect, and living healthfully and happily, than be with a partner you cannot trust. You may be dependent on this person, and you may have a habit of being with him or her, but if he or she is not willing to treat you reasonably and properly, you say, "Change your way, or I am out of here."

As you evaluate your relationships, beware of the temptation to deceive yourself. It is hard to accept that you are even partly responsible for the mistreatment that you get at the hands of someone else. As we have seen, it is much more easy, natural, and convenient to be the victim, and to blame someone else. But I hope I've persuaded you, and you know in your heart, that you are in fact responsible. If you refuse to accept responsibility for the way people treat you, how much of a commitment will you make to change?

The worst thing you could do is make a lot of noise about changing things, only to revert to the old, familiar, destructive patterns. To talk about change and not do it is to teach your partner to treat your statements and declarations lightly. You will teach him or her to be patient, confident that you will soon give in. Your commitment to change needs to rise to the level of the life decisions we discussed earlier. Where your relationship standards are concerned, commit to yourself that, although it may be difficult to effect change, you must not compromise. To compromise in this area is to sell out your most precious commodity: you.

As is true of every element of your specific life strategy, it will be important to make these relationship changes in a meaningful, purposeful, and constructive manner. In order to do that, it is critically important that you first determine where you really are in a relationship in order to know what specific changes need to occur. In other words, you want to be careful that you don't "fix what ain't broke, and not fix what is." You'll need to have a heart-level conversation with yourself about the status of any relationship that you seek to change.

Assignment #12: *While the comments in this section are about teaching people how to treat you, and apply to all of the relationships in your life, the working example that is most natural to focus on is the one you have with your "significant other." The following list of questions may help you to diagnose not only the current status of your relationship, but the reasons for that status.*

Relationship Questionnaire:

1—In all honesty, do you feel that you give, while your partner takes?	**Yes No**
2—Is your relationship a parent/child relationship, rather than the interaction of two adults?	**Yes No**
3—Do you and your partner fight with increasing frequency and/or intensity?	**Yes No**
4—Do you find yourself frequently apologizing?	**Yes No**
5—Do you feel that you just need some space and time alone?	**Yes No**
6—Looking back over the last year of your relationship, do you feel that you have made most of the sacrifices and changes?	**Yes No**

7—Do you find that you frequently make excuses **Yes No**
for your mate, either to yourself or other people?

8—Do you feel that your emotional needs are not **Yes No**
being met?

9—If you answered "yes" to #8: Do you feel that **Yes No**
this has substantially cheated you out of a big
part of your life?

10—Are you physically frustrated in your **Yes No**
relationship?

11—Do you feel that your relationship plays second **Yes No**
fiddle to your mate's job, or the children, or
other priorities?

12—Do you keep significant secrets from your mate? **Yes No**

13—Do you feel that you are being used? **Yes No**

14—Do you feel that there has to be more to your **Yes No**
life than that which you are living in this
relationship?

15—Do you see patterns developing or being played **Yes No**
out in your relationship that mirror those in
either of your parents' marriages?

16—Do you find yourself too threatened to take the **Yes No**
risk of true intimacy in your relationship?

17—Do you feel that you are the only one who **Yes No**
legitimately works on your relationship?

18—Is guilt a major factor in your relationship? **Yes No**

19—Do you feel that you are just going through the **Yes No**
motions in your relationship?

20—Is your partner more like a roommate than a **Yes No**
partner?

21—Do you entertain fantasies about not being in **Yes No**
this relationship anymore?

22—Do you find that in order to have peace and **Yes No**
harmony with your mate, you have had to stop
being who you really are?

23—Have you and your partner stopped working at **Yes No**
your relationship, and just accepted it as is?

24—Are you in this relationship today simply **Yes No**
because you were in it yesterday, rather than
because you really want to be?

Highlight those questions to which you answered "yes."
Obviously, the more "yes" answers you've given, the more trou-

ble your relationship is in. Perhaps these "yes" answers will serve as talking points between you and your partner as you reopen the negotiation of the relationship.

By requiring more from yourself and your partner, you are, in essence, "changing the deal." And make no mistake: Those with whom you are currently in relationships won't like it. *They will resist your changing the status quo.* You taught them the rules, you've been rewarding their conduct, and they, like you, have gotten comfortable with the deal. If the price of poker is about to go up, it's only fair that you warn them about the changes before you begin to respond to their behavior in a different way. If you have taught someone to go on green and stop on red, but now change the rules, he or she is entitled to know about the change.

When I say your partner will resist change in general, and in particular any change that requires more of him or her, do not underestimate the vigor of that resistance. The resistance may range from allegations that "you just don't care anymore," all the way to emotional extortion. Emotional extortion may take the form of threats to leave if you don't cave in on your new position, or may even involve agitated threats of suicide. You may well hear a speech similar to this one:

"I can't believe you are doing this to me! . . . How long have you hated me? . . . I've tried to make you happy; I've given and given. . . . You know how to hurt me and you are doing it. . . . There's someone else, isn't there? . . . Those so-called friends of yours are jealous and are filling your head with all this crap, can't you see that? . . . What makes you so perfect? . . . You don't have any room to talk; do you remember what you did last year? . . . I'd rather die than lose you."

Let's take a closer look at this speech. First of all, it is totally manipulative and self-serving: "I can't believe you are doing this to me" is victim talk. It is full of attempts to put words in your mouth, in order to create guilt and put you on the defensive. It implies that you are being hurtful; that there is someone else; or that it's your friends. It is also full of attacks: "You are doing this"; "I've tried, but no . . ."; "You aren't perfect"; "You don't care." Finally, it contains the ultimate threat: "I'll just kill myself."

This speech may be followed by your partner's pretending nothing ever happened, and attempting just to resume "business as usual"; or by a flurry of short-term "sweetness and light." Your partner may also contact your friends and family members, to recruit them to help dissuade you from this "craziness." In any event, the primary thrust of this and almost any attack within a relationship will be based on guilt.

Guilt is a powerful and destructive weapon in relationships, and you must steel yourself against being manipulated by it. Guilt paralyzes you and shuts you down. No progress is made if you are whipping yourself with shame. The healthy alternative is to acknowledge any problem behavior; figure out why the problem behavior happens; and make a plan for change. The universe rewards action; guilt is paralysis.

Stay the course. Do not be diverted from your resolve. If your partner threatens to leave or commit suicide, that's a bluff you must call. If you think the threat to harm him or herself is genuine, your relationship and your partner were much more unstable than you thought. In any event, if you believe they are capable of hurting themselves, call the police or the county sheriff and let the professionals deal with it, *but do not cave in.* If you back off, you are teaching the partner that you can be "handled."

Finally, and in the interests of fairness and completeness, no discussion of Life Law #8 would be complete without your considering it from the outside looking in. What are the people in your life letting *you* get away with? Have they taught you that it is okay for *you* to treat them with less than dignity and respect? Have they taught you that *you* can coast in your relationships, functioning at less than a quality level?

Remember the principle of reciprocity: You get what you give. Do not ask people to do what you are not willing to do yourself. Take a focused and serious look at your behavior in relationships. What payoffs are you getting for unhealthy conduct? Are you willing not just to identify those payoffs, but to give them up? By being honest about your own behavior, you can win tremendous credibility, and foster an environment conducive to change. Don't ever take someone else's inventory if you're not willing to take your own.

CHAPTER TEN

THERE IS POWER IN FORGIVENESS

Whatever is begun in anger ends in shame.
—Ben Franklin

Life Law #9: There Is Power In Forgiveness
Your Strategy: Open your eyes to what anger and resentment are doing to you. Take your power back from those who have hurt you.

Of all of the emotions in the human repertoire, hate, anger, and resentment are among the most powerful and self-destructive. They are awakened in you by the actions of those you perceive to have hurt you or those you love. You may think that you want and are justified to hate, or harbor rage against, someone who has hurt you deeply enough to create these emotions. You may believe that they deserve it and are made to suffer by your hatred of them. You may sometimes treat your hatred as though it were a mythical curse on the target of your disdain. But to do so, to carry and feel that hatred, is to pay an unbelievably high price, for the reality is that those feelings change who you are. They change your heart and mind.

Like fire raging through a dry forest, these intense emotions can become so pervasive as to crowd every other feeling out of your heart, consuming you with behavior that is either external—vicious aggression; or internal—deep bitterness. Think about it. When you encounter someone who's in the grip of these emotions and see the outward expression of their inner turmoil, it takes little imagination to guess what that person must be experiencing inside. Hatred, anger, and resentment eat away at the heart and soul of the person who carries them.

I mean this in its most literal sense. Remember my telling you that for every thought and for every feeling, there is a physiological reaction: Simply thinking about eating the dill pickle triggers very real physical reactions. These kinds of reactions are never more evident than when you are feeling these powerful negative emotions. When you harbor hatred, anger, and resentment, your body's chemical balance is dramatically disrupted. Your "fight-or-flight" responses stay aroused twenty-four hours a day, seven days a week. That means that hatred, anger, and resentment are absolutely incompatible with your peace, joy, and relaxation.

If you are carrying around these ugly emotions, it's likely that your body is almost constantly in a condition called *heterostasis*, a condition of physiological imbalance; put simply, it's a state of having too much of this, in terms of your natural chemistry, and not enough of that. People who stay in this powerfully aroused state often experience sleep disturbance, nightmares, poor concentration, and fatigue. It's not uncommon for them to develop tension headaches, migraine headaches, ulcers, back spasms, and even heart attacks. People are not built to be happy and sad at the same time. It is impossible for us to feel simultaneously peaceful and agitated. So to the extent that these powerful emotions crowd their more positive counterparts out of your experience, your physical state is going to be miserable.

I have told you what the effects of these emotions are on your body. You also need to recognize that these feelings are the stuff of which emotional prisons are made. When you choose to bear hate, anger, or resentment toward others, you build walls around yourself. You become trapped in an emotional complex of such pain and agony that negative energy begins to dominate your entire life.

And in addition to imprisoning you, these emotions have a spillover effect: They do not remain specific to the relationship in which you were damaged. Recall that you bring your thoughts, feelings, and beliefs into every relationship you have. To assume that you can turn your feelings on and off like a light switch is naïve. I suspect you already know that it doesn't work that way. Bitterness and anger are such powerful influences that once they enter your heart, they are present in all of your relationships. They truly do make you become a different person. Who you were goes away, and now you are defined by the hatred and bitterness. Ultimately, what makes these emotions so powerful is that they change who you are. They change what you do and contaminate what you have to give.

Think about that. It means that those who love you don't get you—they get the bitter shell of who you once were. Smoldering anger or bitterness completely disfigures your perceptions, and therefore, the manner in which you engage, receive, and filter the world. There is no reality, only perception—and yours is altered by these ugly emotions. Don't assume that they can be concealed behind a mask. The stimulus you provide, namely the face you wear, is unmistakably one of bitterness, rage, or withdrawal. You give people, in turn, little choice in how to react to you.

You've heard me say that you either contribute to or contaminate every relationship in your life. If you're dragging the chains of hatred, anger, and resentment into your other relationships, then, clearly, you are contaminating them. Clearly, you are eroding the quality of your emotional and relational life. Your task is to undo those chains so that you do not take those emotions with you into these other relationships. For the sake of your spouse, your children, other loved ones, and *yourself,* you must have the courage to break these bonds and cleanse your heart and mind of the poison of hatred. You must learn that you do not have to be angry just because you have the right to be.

If you still insist on "being right" with respect to your own anger, there's something else you must consider: *You cannot give away what you do not have.* Think about that in its most literal sense. No matter how much you might like to, you can't give someone a million dollars if you don't have it. Similarly, you cannot give pure and accepting love from a pure and accepting heart if you have neither. That would mean giving away what you do not have. If the love in your heart is contaminated, if growing within it is the cancer of hatred, anger, and resentment, then that is the only love that you have to give. If your heart has turned cold and hard because of hatred, anger, and resentment, then that is the heart from which all of your emotions spring. That is the love and that is the heart that you have to offer to your children, to your mate, to your parents, to your brothers and sisters, and to your fellow human beings. Hatred, anger, and resentment truly change who you are. They truly prevent you from being able to give to those you love that which you want them to have.

The feelings we're talking about here are the open wounds of unfinished emotional business with somebody, somewhere: whoever is the target of all that negative emotion. People who carry around the burden of anger invariably say they do so because they could never get emotional closure on the treatment they got at the hands of that other person. They tell me that they hold on to the emotion because the person who did this to them is not sorry, and may not even admit or understand that he or she has done such terrible things. Speaking to me about those hated others, people have said to me, "I can't forgive, because they aren't sorry and they don't deserve or even want my forgiveness." If that's the standard, there are many people in this world who, clearly, will never be entitled to forgiveness. There are people who do lifelong damage to others, without the slightest concern about the impact of their actions. There are people who couldn't care less if they have wounded, let alone destroyed, the life and heart of another person.

Recall that the second great Life Law, *You Create Your Own Experience,* expressed the reality that when you choose the behavior, you choose the consequences. You've got to apply this truth to whatever anger and bitterness you may be carrying, right now. Recognize that *you* are the one who chooses the behavior, thereby creating the consequences. Further, a *thought is a behavior*, to be treated the same as any other behavior.

To this principle, add Life Law #6: You know and experience this world only through the perceptions that you create. Your perceptions consist of your interpretations of the world. These two laws work in powerful combination to determine the quality of your emotional life. You, and only you, choose how you feel. Others can provide an event or behavior for you to react to, but *it is up to you to choose how you feel* about them. If you choose to carry the hatred, then know that you choose to see the world through a dark filter that, in turn, dictates a dark perception of the world.

Ultimately—and this may be extremely difficult for you to accept—forgiveness of those who have transgressed against you, or those you love, is not about *them*; it is about *you*. Recall the story of Jennie, in chapter 3, who by forgiving her grandfather freed herself. Forgiveness is about doing whatever it takes to preserve the power to create your own emotional state. It is about being able to say: "You cannot hurt me and then control me, even in your absence, by turning my heart cold and changing who I am and what I value. I am the one who makes those choices. You cannot choose for me how I feel, and I will not give you that power."

Most importantly, you must be willing to say, from your heart: "You cannot lock me into a bond with you, where you become part of my very being and part of what I think, feel, and do every day. I will not bond with you through hatred, anger, or resentment. I will not bond with you through fear. I will not allow you to drag me into your dark world. By forgiving you, I am releasing me, not you. You must live with yourself every day. You must live with the darkness in your heart. But *I do not*, and I will not."

Some of the most tragic lives I have encountered have been those of people who allowed hate, anger, and resentment to consume them, whereas on the inside, behind the brittle layers of pain and hostility, they were kind and loving.

David Kelly was such a person. The oldest son of a very harsh and stern father, David had struggled constantly to please, but nothing he ever did was good enough. No matter how long or how hard David worked on their ranch, it was not good enough. No matter how efficiently he handled his responsibilities, no matter how often he volunteered to help beyond those tasks assigned him, he could never win the favor of his father.

Not once in David's life did his father ever tell him that he was doing a good job, or that he was a good person. At no time did he ever tell him that he loved him. At no time did he ever touch him physically, unless it was to strike him, push him, or yank him. And no matter what happened, even in his earliest years, David was not allowed to cry; he was not permitted so much as a whimper.

He recalled the day when, at the age of seven, he had inadvertently leaned against an exhaust stack on a large tractor, severely burning the back of his right arm and shoulder. The burn was such that ultimately, David would need hospitalization and a skin graft. Yet standing there before his father, in agony, he was ordered to stop crying; his father mocked him as a baby, a "little girl" who ought to be ashamed of his tears. When David could no longer stand it, he fell to his knees, sobbing. His father jerked him to his feet and whipped him with a field rope.

David learned to be stoic, and he learned to be hard. It became his goal in life to prove to his father that he was a man, that he was strong enough and tough enough for anything. He threw himself into his work, often taking unbelievable chances in the course of the workday, all to impress his father.

On an autumn afternoon, not long after David got married, his father was working the fields with a disk plow. When he stopped to find out why the tractor had stalled, it suddenly lurched into gear, pinning him underneath. The plow rolled over him, severing one arm and leaving him to bleed to death, alone in the field.

David was absolutely outraged. It frustrated him that his father had gotten himself killed, cheating David out of the chance to prove himself. His hatred, anger, and confusion were all-consuming.

When I met David, it was at the behest of his wife, who was concerned about his treatment of their four-year-old son. She reported that David was treating their child the same way as David's father had treated David. He would not permit the boy to cry, and he would not permit him to be a child.

When I finally was able to get David to give a voice to his feelings, he spoke of the rage he felt toward his father for cheating him out of the chance to prove himself and be vindicated. Through tears of frustration and teeth-grinding anger, he said that the SOB had died without ever telling him that he was a man or that he loved him. David professed that he would hate his father until the absolute day he died for the way he had treated him, and for cheating him out of the chance to get even. The ugliness of his emotions left little to the imagination. This was a man racked with pain and bent on self-destruction.

It was apparent to me that David had to set himself free. If he did not forgive his father and get emotional closure on his feelings, not only would he continue to pay the price for the rest of his life, but his young son and loving wife would pay, as well.

Quite predictably, I told David everything that you have read in this chapter, but in his case, it had to go even beyond that. David had to take action to get emotional closure on his feelings. He felt trapped, with no way out, because his father's death had deprived him of any chance to make peace. Once he came to understand that his father had him locked in a bond of hatred and resentment that dominated his current life, David became highly motivated: It was terribly distasteful for him to think he was giving his power away. The thought of that man controlling him from the grave was sickening to David. He wanted his power back. He wanted it for himself and his family.

What ultimately turned the corner for David was that he came to understand that you don't have to have the other person's cooperation in order to forgive them. That other person doesn't even have to know. They do not have to be sorry. They do not have to admit the error of their ways. Forgiveness is about you, not them.

It also helped David to learn that in self-management, sometimes we have to give ourselves what we wish we could get from others. David's father could not tell him that he loved him. He could not tell him that he was, in fact, a good man worthy of good things in life. He couldn't tell him because he was dead. David could wait however long he wanted—he could pout and rage for years—but it would do no good.

I convinced David that he had to give himself that which he wished he could have from his father. He had to be willing to look at himself in the mirror and say the things to himself that he wished he could have heard from his father. He literally had to say, "You are a good man. You have always been good. You are entitled to the feelings and rewards of a healthy and balanced life. And you shall have them because you deserve them. Because your father did not choose to see these qualities does not mean they are not there. He did not see them because of his filter, not because of your deficiencies."

When David could honestly look himself in the mirror and give himself that which he wished he could have had from his father, he found the strength and courage to forgive his father. He knew if he was truly a man, he would have to "rise above his raising." He knew how torturous it was to feel the way he had felt, and he was able to appreciate that that may well have been the same tortured existence that his father lived throughout his life. He forgave his father for himself and for his young son and wife. He forgave his father because he did not want to live in his image and suffer the pain and hurt that had been so much a part of that relationship.

Once David gave all of this to himself and then forgave his father, he was free to choose his own way of being in the world. He decided that he would not be a prisoner of that parental legacy. In one of our last sessions, he looked me in the eye and said: "This cannot go on. It has to stop here; it has to stop now, or my son will pay the same price I had to pay." By having that insight, and following it with the actions I have described, David was able to break the bond and have the freedom that only forgiveness can bring.

Assignment #13: I challenge you to identify these same feelings in your life. I challenge you to identify and list in your journal those people who have you locked in this bond of hatred, anger, and resentment. I challenge you to care enough about yourself and those you love to break that bond and be free of the tortured existence that comes from harboring those terrible emotions.

By taking this approach and rethinking the meaning of forgiveness, you can, and will, set yourself free from the pain that has been caused by others in your life. Otherwise, your hatred, anger, and resentment will be so all-consuming that they'll become part of your every waking hour. They will make you cynical, they will make you suspicious. They will cause you to put walls up around yourself, and exact a toll from those who have done nothing but love you. If you allow people who have transgressed against you to lock you into that role, *they win*. Understand that. If you allow them to make you hate them, rage against them, and resent them, *they win*.

Trust me when I say that the only escape is forgiveness. The only way to rise above the negatives of that relationship in which you were hurt is to take the moral high ground, and forgive the person who hurt you. Everything they have done to you, they have already done to themselves. Their judgment will come from a higher power, not from you.

A final note. The only thing worse than being hurt by someone in your life is keeping that hurt alive after they have gone. Think about it. Very often, the people who have hurt you are no longer available for you to deal with assertively, constructively, or otherwise. Perhaps, as in David's case, it's a father, long since dead. Perhaps it's a friend who has moved away, never to be seen again. Are you really going to accept the role of being caretaker of that hatred, anger, and resentment for the rest of your life?

Don't do it another day. You have the ability to forgive those people—not as a gift to them, but as a gift to yourself. You are worth whatever it takes to rise above that pain and hurt. But remember, you create your own experience. You must have the resolve to create what you want, and get rid of what you don't want. If that person gets a windfall through your forgiveness, then so be it. The one to save is you. The one to release from the emotional prison is you.

The power of forgiveness is the power to set yourself free from the bonds of hatred, anger, and resentment. Seize the power and rise above the pain. You are worth it, and everyone you love deserves it.

CHAPTER ELEVEN

You Have to Name It to Claim It

I always wanted to be somebody,
but I should have been more specific.
—Lily Tomlin and Jane Wagner

Life Law #10: You Have to Name It to Claim It
Your Strategy: Get clear about what you want, and take your turn.

Common sense might suggest that one of the easiest steps in getting what you want from life is to "place your order": to stand up and declare what it is that you desire. Nothing could be further from the truth. I'm convinced that if the mythical genie ever did pop out of the bottle and say, "Tell me your wish," most people would stutter, stammer, and be in terrible conflict about what to ask for.

Not knowing precisely what you want is not okay. This Life Law means what it says in the most basic sense. If you cannot name, and name with great specificity, what it is that you want, then you will never be able to step up and claim it. The purpose of this chapter is to impress upon you the need for focusing on what you want and teaching you how to describe it and name it so that you can recognize it and claim it. If you've been folding the other nine Life Laws into your thinking—in other words, amassing the knowledge necessary to start having what you want—learning about this Life Law should be exciting and fun.

Being able to name and claim it is probably of greater

relevancy to you now than at any other time in your life. It may not have been critically important before now, since you may not have had a legitimate chance of getting what you wanted even if you had known what it was. That is no longer true. Nevertheless, if you find it hard to articulate and recognize what you truly want, you are not alone.

Most people do not know how to describe what they want, because they don't have a clue what it really is. Think about those times in your life when you have been brought to a standstill by a simple choice. If you can't decide which movie to see, what to order in a restaurant, or what to wear, is it any wonder you find it hard to identify goals? Indecision creates inaction. Inaction leads to results that you do not want. This makes your journey through life like that of an unguided missile, an approach that simply will not work.

What you probably can say with great confidence is what you *don't* want. Having lived in unpleasant circumstances, perhaps for years, gives you an unwelcome familiarity with and ability to recognize them. But having had little or no experience with the flip side makes it much harder to describe what you truly do want.

Not knowing exactly what you want is a major problem for a number of reasons. You live in a world where the most you will ever get is what you ask for. That's true about your major goals as well as your day-to-day desires. Suppose you put an ad in the newspaper, offering to sell your used car for $7,000. What do you think are the chances that somebody will look at it and say, "Gosh! This is a really great car. I don't think you're asking enough! Let me pay you nine thousand dollars"? Sounds pretty ridiculous, doesn't it? It sounds ridiculous because it *is* ridiculous. Likewise, where your life goals are concerned, the *most* you'll ever get is what you ask for. After identifying what you want, mapping out how to get it, and working hard, you may get something at least *close* to what you want. On the other hand, if you don't even know what it is that you truly want, then it is pretty obvious that you cannot ask for it. Whether it's you or someone else who can give you what you want, you have to be able to name it. If I am in charge of the world, I can't give you what you want if you can't tell me what it is.

If you've ever been in the same room with a baby who is obviously hurting and crying, you know how frustrating and help-less a feeling that can be. You want to help the baby; you want to give him what he wants and needs, but the baby can't tell you what it is. If you don't know what it is that you want, you're no better off than the baby who can't say it. The difference is that the world is not your mother, and won't put in nearly the same effort as she would to figure out what you want. If you can't name it, you are destined to go through life kicking and screaming.

If you're frustrated because you never seem to get the brass ring, consider this: That brass ring could be right under your nose, but you won't know it if you can't name what that brass ring *is* for you.

There's another harsh truth to take into account here. Since naming what you truly want is so basic to having it, you must proceed with great care in deciding the answer. Being wrong or misguided about what you want is even worse than not knowing at all. I can't tell you how many times I have encountered people professionally (and personally, for that matter) who spent years or a lifetime working toward something they were certain was what they wanted. They worked hard, they worked long, and they made sacrifices. Nothing was sadder than seeing them ultimately reach their goal, only to be disappointed by the arrival. They hadn't just been inert; they had gone down the wrong road, diligently moving in the wrong direction, and now were far, far from home.

Growing up, I was cautioned to ''be careful what you pray for, because you just might get it.'' If what you are going to get is exactly, precisely what you name, then you want to be very careful about naming it. You obviously don't want to end up like the people I just described, who in addition to suffering much frustration in the pursuit of what they didn't really want, discovered that the thing they truly valued most was within easy reach— yet they let it slip through their fingers because they chose the wrong goal. What they really wanted was probably much more attainable than the goal they pursued with such frustrated vigor. That's one of the ironies that results from neglecting this Life Law. And you'd have to agree that that would be a problem that you created yourself. So don't be deceived by the simplicity of this life law. Naming what you want deserves your utmost attention.

You must also pay attention to the time element associated with what you want. Opportunities for getting what you want are time-limited. They have a shelf life that can and will expire.

For example, suppose that you decide that what you really want is to have a meaningful and intimate relationship with your children; you want to have the opportunity to know them and influence them as they develop and define themselves as people.

But now suppose that you decide this long after that window of opportunity has passed: maybe they have filled that role with other people, or moved on to a point where they are no longer interested or receptive to your playing this role in their lives. Discovering that you had missed your chance would be heartbreaking. That's why I suggest you bring an element of urgency to your thinking and planning about what you want. I am not suggesting that you panic. I am not suggesting that you behave imprudently, in the pursuit of some poorly thought-out goal. But you should move with specificity and project status urgency toward naming and claiming what you want.

Your thinking needs to stay focused but flexible. One of my greatest fears in life is that I will miss the early-warning signs that tell me when I am getting sidetracked from what is really meaningful and important. I do my best to stay alert to these early signals, because I fear living in such a hard-headed way that I will be surprised by a big-time wake-up call. I keep in mind that *you either get it or you don't,* and I want to be one of those who get it, before I get thumped on the head big-time. Keep that thought in mind as you learn how to name and claim what you really want.

The need for specificity applies to every goal you will ever set. You need to know so much about what you want that whenever you are heading toward it, you know it, you feel it, and you sense it. Similarly, when you are off track, you need to know, feel, and sense that, as well. When you know your goals, you will recognize which types of behavior and choices support them and which do not. When you know a goal intimately, you'll feel it when you get close, and at the right time, you'll jump on it like a duck on a june bug—but only if you know it when you see it. When I say that you must have intimate knowledge of what you want, I mean that you must be able to describe it with a variety of terms and from different points of view. If you want to succeed, you have to be able to answer the following questions:

What is success for you? In other words, where is the goal line? What, specifically, do you have to create in your life in order for you to say, "Bingo, that is *it!*"?

—What is the it that you want?
—What will it look like when you have it?
—What will it feel like when you have it?
—What will you be doing behaviorally when you have it?

—Who are you doing it with?

—Where will you be doing it?

—How will your life be different from the way it is now when you have it?

What aspects of your life do you have to overcome or change in order to get it? In other words, what are you doing or not doing right now that will impede your efforts to get it?

If you can't answer all of those questions in some detail, you are not ready. One of the most common mistakes people make in declaring what they want is to be too general or abstract. How often, for example, have you said or heard someone else say, "All I really want in this life is to be happy"? It sounds like a commonsense answer, but as a life goal, it is destined for failure. My dog, Barkley, wants to be happy. Does that mean that the two of you want the same things? I don't think so. I'll bet everything I own that you and Barkley define happiness very differently. So unless you're willing to settle for someone scratching your belly and letting you sleep under the coffee table, you might want to be a little more precise about what you as a unique individual really want.

Consider a life that is focused upon, energized by, and defined in relation to goals; then contrast it with the life of a person who doesn't even know what's missing, or what it is that he or she needs. Naming what you truly want means that you can begin to guide your life like a ship toward the harbor light, because you now have a goal that is exactly, precisely, and specifically identified. One of the greatest frustrations in life is reflected in the old saying, "You can never get enough of what you don't want." The wisdom of that observation should be clear. When you're hungry for something sweet, all of the potato chips in the world just won't hit the spot. It's like trying a dozen keys in a lock, all of them wrong. Only the right key will do the trick. When you know what you want—how it looks, how it feels, and what experiences it contains—then you're holding the right key.

The following suggestions may help you get started on properly identifying and naming what you truly want:

Be bold, yet realistic. Don't be shy about admitting that you want some special things, some special feelings and experiences. As I've said, the most you'll ever get is what you ask for. Don't aim too low, because if you do you could spend your life working for what you don't want. On the other hand, be realistic. Take stock of who you are and where you are. A favorite observation about the United States is that here anybody can grow up to be president. That may be true, but you probably need to have started taking preparatory steps long before you wake up at fifty years old with no political experience, no formal education, and a background in yardwork. If what you want is to play in the NBA, and you're forty-five years old with a vertical leap of about two inches, the chances are pretty good that you need to want something else.

So as you prepare to name what you want, be bold enough to reach for what will truly fill you up, without being unrealistic. If that sounds a little disheartening, just stand by, because I'll bet you don't have to be president or play in the NBA to get what you really want anyway, as we will see.

Secondly, be careful not to confuse the means with the end. Almost invariably, people will focus on an object or an event, without following through to the next important step, which is identifying how that object or event would make them feel. For example, your first attempt to name what you want might be, "I want a fancy car and a high-paying job." I would suggest to you that the fancy car and the high-paying job are means to an end, rather than being the end in themselves. You need to go further. You must be willing to ask yourself, "*Why* do I want a fancy car and a high-paying job?"

The answer is very likely that you want them because of how you think you will feel when you have them. In this example, the car and the job probably represent for you a sense of security and quality in your life, things to which you respond very strongly. Your true goal, then, is not the car or the high-paying job, but the specific feeling that you associate with having those things. Cars get old, beat up, and rusty. High-paying jobs can go away, through layoffs or your getting fired. If you really think it's a car you want, then just go to the junkyard and find the make and model you would have died for five or ten years ago. If that's truly your goal, you need to rethink it.

This is an important distinction. If you can recognize that it's not the thing or the event that you really want but instead the *feelings* that you associate with it, then your goal shifts from the thing or event to the emotions that are connected with them. If you can come to realize that what you really want is how that car and job would make you feel, then your goal becomes the feeling, not the car or job.

Put another way, if what you really want is to feel proud of yourself and secure in your life, it would be unfair to restrict yourself to just those two methods—car and job—of getting it. Maybe there are ten different ways for you to arrive at the same desired destination, and any one of the ten would work. Your chances of getting what you want, when you have ten avenues of pursuit, are clearly greater than when you've limited those means to just one or two. And it may turn out that when you determine why you want the car and job, you decide that those two things wouldn't do the trick anyway. You then avoid wasting precious time and energy working for what you don't want.

Having conducted life skills and life strategy seminars for thousands of participants over a number of years, I have had a front-row seat from which to observe the confusion shared by people from every walk of life when it comes to identifying what they really want. Because I consider this naming process to be perhaps the number-one outcome-determinative factor in a successful life strategy, I always included in the seminars a participative exercise that guided the attendees through a number of steps to help them identify what they wanted.

The following is a transcript of a dialogue from just such an exercise. The participant, Linda Williams, was a forty-four-year-old married woman from Los Angeles. Linda reported that she had enrolled in the seminar because she felt that her marriage, her family, and her personal life were all disintegrating. She lived near the inner city, and feared that crime and violence were spreading to her neighborhood and that her children, three boys, were losing their way. She said that while she and her husband still inhabited the same home, they had been living in what she called an "emotional divorce" for several years. Our conversation went like this:

PCM: So, Linda, tell me what you want—and tell me from your heart, not from your head. Don't screen everything; just say it.

LINDA: I want to move from L.A. I want to get out of that horrible, horrible place before something really bad happens. It scares me and I don't want to be there anymore.

PCM: So, what would you have to do to make that happen?

LINDA: I don't know. We can't move. Roger and I both have jobs and we're barely getting by as it is. We can't move. We are trapped there and there's not anything I can do about it. There's no point in even talking about this. I . . . , I don't want to do this, I don't want to talk about these things, because I can't have them. This is just a waste of time.

PCM: So how would you feel if you did have what you wanted; how would you feel if you were able to escape from the fear and threats of your current situation?

LINDA: Oh, my God, I would feel so safe and happy and I would have, I don't know, hope. I would have some hope again, some hope for me and my boys. I used to be so optimistic—I knew they would grow up and do well. Now, I don't even know if they will grow up at all. I can't even take a deep breath anymore, I'm almost hyperventilating all the time.

It was this last answer that I believe was Linda's actual first step down the road to identifying what she truly wanted. I interpreted her initial statement about wanting to leave L.A. as nothing more than a safe and superficial way of saying she wanted to escape her current pain and fear. I also knew how upset she was, not to be able to catch her breath. I concluded that her internal dialogue must be very disturbing, and I recognized that I would have to listen carefully for her true feelings. When she said, "I would feel safe, happy, and have hope again," I knew that she was, for the first time, speaking from her heart.

PCM: So, what you really want is to feel safe and happy and to find some hope again for your future and that of *your husband* and boys.

LINDA: (*beginning to cry*) Yes, yes, that's right. I am so tired of being afraid, I am so tired of feeling trapped. I just don't know what to do and I don't know where to turn. I know that I am letting my family down. I am so ashamed that I can't make a better life for our family.

PCM: So, what would you have to do to create that? What would you have to do to create some quality back in your family life and what would you have to do to not be ashamed of what you are now creating as a mother?

What would you have to do to not feel lost and scared anymore?

LINDA: I don't know, I just don't know.

PCM: Well, if you did know, what would it be?

LINDA: I don't know; I guess I would have to get close to my boys again. I would have to feel that they wanted the same things that I want. And I would have to have Roger back. We just aren't together anymore. We don't talk, we don't share, we don't support one another. I am so tired of being alone. I would have to have my Roger back.

Clearly, this woman was still in love with her husband. She had very likely been the one who had pulled back due to fear and frustration.

PCM: How would it make you feel if you were connected with your boys again? How would it make you feel if, as you say, you had *your* Roger back again?

LINDA: I wouldn't feel so ashamed. I wouldn't feel that I was such a lousy mother and wife that I couldn't keep my family together and I couldn't guide my boys. I wouldn't be ashamed of not being able to make my husband want me. I want to give to him so bad. He is a good man and he looks so tired and so alone and I just can't help him.

PCM: Don't tell me how you wouldn't feel, don't tell me that you wouldn't be ashamed. Tell me how you would feel if you could put those things back in your family and marriage.

LINDA: I don't know, I just don't know. I guess . . . I guess I would feel proud of myself as a woman again, I would feel whole and complete again. I used to be such a rock. I made our family warm and close, same as my mother did.

PCM: So, what you really want is to feel proud of yourself again. What you really want is to feel whole and fulfilled in your role as a woman and a wife and a mother.

LINDA: Yes, yes, that's exactly what I want. That's how I used to feel. If I could be those things again, if I could be who I used to be, then we could deal with everything else. We could deal with L.A. together. I just can't do it alone. I don't even have me now. You're right. I want to feel proud and fulfilled and whole again. That's what I want. I'm a good mother, I really am, I would die for my boys. I would do anything for Roger if he would let me.

PCM: So, what do you have to do to put those things back into your family?

LINDA: I have to make it happen. I have to quit feeling sorry for myself and quit being so alone. I have to go home and take Roger's hands and say, "We are not going to live like this anymore." I've got to do something to change where we are headed before it's too late. I have to sit down with my boys and take their precious faces in my hands and say, "Help me to help you." I have to do something instead of just hurting and crying at night. I have to do it and I have to do it now.

PCM: And how would that make you feel?

LINDA: That would make me feel proud and whole and fulfilled again. Because that's my job. That's what God put me in this family to do and I have not been doing it. That's what I want, that's what I want. It's not L.A., it's me and my family. We have to get right.

Obviously, Linda had a lot of work and a lot of planning still to do, but I trust you can see how far she had come in focusing on what she really wanted in her life. I could tell that she was now speaking from the heart. I could tell that she knew from the inside out what she wanted. I knew that she could now make plans, and could evaluate each and every option in her life against the standard and priority of this goal. I knew that she wouldn't go off on a tangent. I knew that she wouldn't be distracted or deterred from her goal, because she so intimately knew what it was.

Assignment #14: *Take note of the questions that I was asking Linda. These questions are the very ones that you need to ask yourself. You may have noticed that the questions seemed circular in nature. There is a definite pattern to this dialogue. Ask yourself those same questions, and write down your answers. If you continue to follow the repeating pattern, you will get down to precisely what you want in this life. Once again, the key questions are:*

1—What do you want?
2—What must you do to have it?
3—How would you feel when you had it?
4—So, what you really want is . . . (what you
   described in question 3).
5—What must you do to have it?
6—How would that make you feel?
7—So, what you really want is . . . (what you
   described in question 6).

And the cycle repeats. Be honest, be sincere, and above all, be precise. Like Linda, if you will devote the necessary effort, you'll be able to name with great precision what you want, and to claim it once you have created it.

What you want can probably be described in a number of ways, and you need to be as specific as possible in describing each one. Your "want" can be described in terms of how it will look to people other than yourself; how it will make you feel inside; the kinds of reactions and feelings it would generate in other people; and what behavior it involves.

By being specific and defining your goal in as many different ways as you can, you'll develop a more intimate understanding of what you want. As a result, the choices you make along the way will be more goal-directed. You'll be more likely to recognize your goal when you get there, since you'll have so many criteria by which to measure it.

Now for the second part of Life Law #10: *Claim It.* This half of the law can present as big a challenge, and be just as difficult a task, as naming what you want. Claiming it takes resolve and commitment. You've heard the joke, "The meek may inherit the earth, but none of them will step up to claim the deed." You must be willing to make yourself step up when the time is right and claim what you want and deserve. You must be willing to step up and say, "Stop the world. It's my time, it's my turn, and I claim this for *me*."

Understand that this is a competitive world in which we live. As we say in Texas, "There's a lot of dogs out there after them bones." Nothing could be more true. There are a lot of people who are ready, willing, and able to take from you that which is rightfully yours. It might be your property; it might be your space; it might be your very right to think, feel and believe in a certain way. Why would you want to make it easier for them? Why leave your windows open for thieves? Once you have strength and resolve enough to believe that you deserve what it is that you want, then and only then will you be bold enough to say, "It is my time, it is my turn; this is for me, and I claim it, here and now."

You know from personal experience that there is nothing more frustrating than seeing someone run the race and fight the battles, and then simply decline to stand up and claim the victory. Don't you be one of those people. You may have to overcome timidity, guilt, feelings of inadequacy, or self-consciousness. You deserve more; you can have more. Claim what it is that you want and deserve, because no one will do it for you. No one can step up and claim your place for you. If you don't, then it doesn't get done.

Having the willingness and courage to claim what you want is a major element in successfully applying this Life Law. It may be an especially important issue to you, since it may very well be out of character for you. If you have spent most of your life settling for what you don't want, or settling too cheaply, then enforcing a standard of excellence and noncompromise will feel like an unnatural act. That means that taking this step from mediocrity to quality in your life will require conscious resolve. You must, in effect, sit down with yourself and have a conversation that leads to a life decision. Life decisions, remember, are those we make at the level of heartfelt conviction, such that they are no longer subject to day-to-day debate.

As I said earlier, managers have to produce results in a competitive world. You must require of yourself what you would require of someone you would hire as a life manager. Assuming I took the job as your life manager, I wonder how long I would remain employed if, in our quest for attaining what you want in your life, I began to waver in my conviction about your right to have it. I wonder how long I would stay employed as your life manager if I came to you and said: "I've been thinking about your list of life goals, and I'm not really so sure that you deserve what you want. I mean, think about it: you're really nothing special. These are the kinds of things that *other* people get. Why don't you quit making waves and just settle for where you are? For *you* to get these feelings and experiences is going to be a lot of trouble, and in fact, may very well inconvenience some other people, and

I just think you're being kind of selfish. Not everybody can have what he or she wants. You just need to calm down and be happy that your life isn't worse than it is.''

Now, if I said that to you, you would probably fire me, and the problem would be solved. *But you can't fire you.* That means the solution is not so easy. Be the most effective life manager you can imagine. Make the resolve, now, that your wants are worth having, and that when the time comes, you will claim your right to have them.

CHAPTER TWELVE

A GUIDED TOUR
OF YOUR LIFE

Facing it, always facing it,
that's the way to get through.
Face it.
—Joseph Conrad

Creating a Life Strategy

You must admit that you've never had a better shot at genuine change than right now. I haven't romanticized things. I have not told you how wonderful you are, or explained the world in Goody Two-shoes, love-and-light terms. I have told you the real deal; I've shown you where the rubber meets the road in this life. I am going to assume that you, in turn, are ready to get behind the wheel.

Creating a life strategy is a learned skill, but you've already acquired the fundamentals by working through the previous chapters. You now have a general understanding of where your life is and where it's going as a result of your current self-management. You've also become intimately acquainted with the ten Life Laws that determine the results you get, whether you live with a strategy or not. Building on those cornerstones, this chapter and the next will equip you with a life strategy that is unique to you. The knowledge that you still need is a very precise awareness of your current situation, and—in keeping with the specificity that we have agreed is an essential element of goals—a thorough understanding of where you want to go.

A Guided Tour of Your Life

Remember, half of the solution to any problem lies in defining it. You can't really make progress against the problem until you understand what it is. The same holds true here, as we set out to build life strategies for you. The first thing we need to do is *diagnose* your life.

To be effective, a diagnosis must be specific. We discussed the issue of specificity extensively in Life Law #10, and I will not repeat those concepts here. However, it is important that you understand that the term *life* can be just as broad and ambiguous as the term *happy*. Thus, for you to say, "I want to be happy in my life" is so broad as to be completely meaningless. You must be specific in determining where you are *and* where you want to go.

Fortunately, you are not restricted to focusing only on one dimension. In making your diagnosis, you're going to be helped along by the fact that life is not one-dimensional. Also, remember Life Law #7: *Life Is Managed; It Is Not Cured*; therefore, success is a moving target that must be tracked and continually pursued.

One of the most effective ways to diagnose and manage life is to approach both challenges in terms of narrower categories. Some life categories overlap, while some stand alone, but your life needs to be looked at in terms of its separate strands. A minimum set of categories for evaluating your life would include the following:

—Personal
—Professional
—Relationships
—Family
—Spiritual

While each of these aspects of your life may certainly influence the others, each one also has certain distinct life dimensions that are worthy of separate consideration. The following table may help you break your thinking down into more manageable pieces.

What we have here is essentially a snapshot of the twenty-five or thirty dimensions that, together, make a representative profile of your life. These are the issues that are of greatest concern to each of us. You'll notice that the table makes reference to some writings you've already done. Your List of Five to Ten People, for example, identifies those to whom you most need to express your heartfelt emotions (*Assignment #8, p. 105*), and the Relationship Questionnaire is what you worked through in chapter 9 (*Assignment #12, p. 151*). You can see, too, that in all five categories, you're asked to consider your Life-decision list (*Assignment #11, p. 138*), which you developed in chapter 6 in order to identify the core values that, for you, are no longer subject to debate. As you work through each of the categories, being reminded to look at your life-decision list may alert you to areas where you really want to see some positive change.

You may have goals and objectives in every category and every Life Dimension, or in just some. Either way, examine each one and ask yourself, "Where am I currently, and what is it I truly want in this life?" You'll need to consider each category, and Life Dimension, even if you believe you are on solid ground in that area of your life. If in fact you are satisfied with your current status on that dimension, verifying such will be important and then you can move on to other areas.

Locating Your Life

By working through this chart, you begin the very important task of truly meeting yourself for perhaps the first time. In just a moment, you'll be given a seven-step process for assessing where you are on each Life Dimension in the table, and how your life would be if you had what you wanted. I cannot overemphasize the importance of your thoroughly and carefully progressing through *each and every one* of the seven steps for *each* Life Dimension. Whether you have been in individual therapy and counseling or not, I will wager that no one has ever invested in you the time, energy and thought that this guided tour involves. It will be the most organized assessment your life will ever get—if you will take the time. If you will truly take the time required for this tour, you will gain an insight, understanding, and focus that I believe will absolutely change your life. You will know yourself with an intimacy that few people ever experience.

Sadly, as things stand now, you may be the person you know the least about. I say sadly, because I believe that to not know yourself is a tragic loss. Failing to get to know yourself means that you cannot understand your own wants and needs. It means that you

Life Dimensions

Categories				
Personal	**Relational**	**Professional**	**Familial**	**Spiritual**
Self-esteem	Significant Other Friends New Relationships	Job Performance	Parents	Personal Relationship with Your Higher Power
Education	Repair of Existing Relationships	Business	Children	Your Spiritual Walk
Finance	Re-establishing Lost Relationships	Objectives	Siblings	Personal Study and Communion
Health	See List of five to ten People (Assignment #8, p. 105)	Promotions	Extended Family	Prayer Life
See Life-decision List (Assignment #11, p. 138)	See Life-decision List (Assignment #11, p. 138)	Career Change	See Life-decision List (Assignment #11, p. 138)	Life Focus
	See Relationship Questionnaire (Assignment #12, p. 151)	See Life-decision List (Assignment #11, p. 138)		See Life-decision List (Assignment #11, p. 138)

can't understand what is most important to and valued by you. Yet you are the person with whom you spend the most time; you are the person in whom you have the most invested. So you must not underestimate the gravity and importance of getting to know *you*.

You may never have thought about it this way, but you are the only *you* that will ever exist in the history of the world. There is no other, there has been no other, and there will be no other you. You were born, you are living, you will die, and there will never ever be another you. You are a unique individual, different from every other person who has walked on the face of this earth. For you to allow that life to come and go, without ever establishing an intimate relationship with that person, is wrong.

You allow it to happen because no one ever taught you any differently or raised the issue with you. Many cultures and societies emphasize this very important aspect of living, but ours is not one of them. Eastern civilizations, for example, train their populace in meditation and self-discovery. Ours does not. Believe me, I'm not trying to get you to hum or chant a mantra (although that can certainly be productive), but I do want you to give yourself the time to meet you.

You have heard me say that everyone wears a social mask. Perhaps not surprisingly, we often wear that mask even with ourselves. That is why the first condition I listed as a prerequisite to making this endeavor productive was total self-honesty. If you are going to meet you, meet the *real* you. Don't meet some phony fiction. It is only through the honesty of this self-appraisal that you will get where you want to be.

Underlying this entire process is Life Law #1: *You Either Get It, or You Don't*. The "it" here is you. As we saw in the context of that law, there can be no more powerful knowledge than that which you gain about yourself. You are the common denominator to every situation, circumstance, challenge, and relationship in your life. You are either contributing to or contaminating every situation and circumstance in which you are involved. It is time to find out which of these you're doing, and how and why you're doing it. Do this honestly, and it can be one of the most exciting and constructive things you have ever done for you. Look for the answers to such questions as:

—What characteristics am I carrying with me, from one situation to the next?

—Do I go into situations expecting a negative outcome?

—Do I go into situations with a chip on my shoulder?

—Am I so judgmental that I condemn people in situations the moment I arrive?

—Am I so angry and embittered that I spew ugliness on everyone I engage?

—Am I so insecure that I look for and find examples of how I am mistreated in every situation?

—Am I so passive and unwilling to claim my space that I invite people to overlook and disrespect me?

—Do I hide insecurity behind a wall of false superiority and arrogance?

—Do I try so hard that I wear people out with my overreaching?

—Do I spend all of my time comparing myself to others?

—Do I cheat myself out of genuinely experiencing situations by worrying the entire time about how people are viewing me?

—Have I doomed key relationships in my life by judging and condemning myself and others?

Don't be concerned with how to make changes; that comes next. Right now, just tell yourself that you're going to get to know yourself with more clarity and honesty than you've ever had before. The edge that knowledge will create is an awesome advantage. Knowing yourself is critical and learning about yourself will be exciting, even if you don't like everything you learn.

Thinking through these issues, rather than writing them down, will not work. Writing it down adds important objectivity to your self-appraisal. The written word is like a mirror. Just as it would be impossible to study your own face without a mirror, it is impossible to study your own life without writing it down. Doing so allows you to create some objectivity and distance from it. So here again, you will need your notebook, a regular pen, and a red pen. Write it down!

You're going to be answering some very basic but important questions. In order not to overlook any important category or Life Dimension, make it a habit to refer periodically to the chart that follows. As you refer to the chart, and as you address each question, make this a new beginning of "telling it like it is."

Assignment #15: If you'll look at pages 188–189, you'll see that each page asks you for a self-assessment on a Life Dimension. These pages are examples of outlines you can follow to evaluate and compare your life on a given Life Dimension as it actually is now, versus how it would be if it was ideal or perfect on that particular dimension. Using facing pages in your notebook, re-create the format of this spreadsheet, so that you'll have plenty of space to fill in the answers to the bullet-point questions. On the left page of your journal (the "Ideal" page), write "Life Dimension" at the top left, just as on the example page; then write "A. Behaviors" on the second line. Leave the next five or so lines blank; then write "B. Inner Feelings," leaving the same number of lines blank underneath it, and so on, until you've got the four bold-faced subtopics (Behavior, Inner Feelings, Negatives, and Positives) listed down the left page, with space underneath each one. You'll create the same format on the right-hand page (the "Actual" page) of your notebook again, simply re-creating the example pages.

On the line next to Life Dimensions at the top left of the "Ideal" page, write the name of the first specific Life Dimension that you have chosen to begin working through. Notice, too, that the upper-right corner of the facing "Actual" page calls for a self-rating, on a scale of 1 to 10, of this particular Life Dimension. How are you actually doing in this aspect of your life? If you see your life as perfect in this area, you'll give yourself a 10. If your life is a complete and total disaster on this dimension, it gets a 1. A rating of 5 would mean that your life on this dimension is comfortable, but not particularly rewarding. Numbers above and below 5 would, of course, be gradations above or below that "lukewarm" life experience. Be completely honest here, because where you rate yourself on this dimension is important now and will be very important later. Now we have often heard it said that "there aren't any 10s." I understand and acknowledge that we are seeking excellence rather than perfection, and that for that reason, a 10 is a fiction. But 10 is at least useful as our topmost reference point.

Now let's compare the "Ideal" and "Actual" pages of your spreadsheet. The purpose of this arrangement is to give you a side-by-side comparison of how your life would be on this Life

Dimension if you successfully transformed it into what you truly want, as compared to your life as it actually is.

Look at Step 1 on your left-hand "Ideal" page (in this book, page 188). It asks you to complete some thoughts:
If I were living my life as a "10" on this dimension:

A—My behavior would be characterized by:
B—My inner feelings would be characterized by:
C—The negatives that would disappear are:
D—The positives that would be present are:

The bullet-point questions under each sentence are designed to stimulate some very specific thinking about that area.

Compare this step to Step 2, on your right-hand "Actual" page (in this book, page 189). It, too, requires the completion of some key sentences, together with some bullet-point questions to encourage very focused answers: Since I am actually living this Life Dimension at level ____ :

A— My actual relevant behavior is:
B— My actual inner feelings are:
C— The negatives that are present are:
D— The positives that are absent, but needed are:

To be sure there's no misunderstanding, let's say for example that I have looked at the chart on page 180 and decided that the first Life Dimension I'm going to evaluate is Self-esteem. I would fill in the Life Dimension blank with "Self-Esteem." For all of Steps 1 ("Ideal" page) and 2 ("Actual" page), I will complete sentences A through D, including the specific questions associated with each, with a particular focus on Self-esteem.

Now actually look at the Life Dimension chart; identify which Life Dimension you're going to tackle first and complete Steps 1 and 2 for that dimension.

Step 3: Once you have filled out both sides of the spreadsheet for the Life Dimension under consideration, go back and read through every response you gave for Step 2 ("Actual" page), specifically looking at those places where you were judgmental of yourself, or expressed a limiting belief. Remember that limiting beliefs are negative characteristics that you've convinced yourself are a part of you: for example, "I'm just dull by nature," or "I can't finish anything I start." Whenever you spot one of these judgments or limiting beliefs, circle it in red. You're going to refer to those statements again later, so make sure you have captured every one of them in a red circle.

Step 4: Now you're ready to list the obstacles you must overcome in order to move from Actual to Ideal on this Life Dimension. You're going to take note of every obstacle that stands in your path from where you are to where you want to go. To develop that inventory, you'll want to look back through your notebook at your:

—List of negative tapes and limiting beliefs
   (Assignment #5, p. 55)
—List of negative behaviors (Assignment #6, p. 78)
—List of unhealthy payoffs (Assignment #6, p. 78)
—Responses to the Rut Test (Assignment #7, p. 100)

You'll also want to think about, and write down, every life circumstance that obstructs your path. Examples might be:

—Lack of money
—A spouse who may undermine your confidence
—Your living arrangements
—Your lack of education

Create a single, comprehensive list of all of the things that may be obstructing your path, whether they are internal or external.

Step 5: In contrast to Step 4, this step challenges you to consider what "helps" you've got for moving from Actual to Ideal on this Life Dimension. What are your resources? What things in your life can you best draw on in order to move from reality to your goal? Examples might include:

—A supportive family
—A good job
—Intelligence
—A clear resolve
—Pain in the current situation
—A realization that I have nothing left to lose

Step 6: The SUDS scale, referring to Subjective Units of Discomfort (page 190), is a familiar tool in psychology that allows you to quantify the degree of pain you associate with a particular Life Dimension's current status. Let's say that your spreadsheet shows you that your actual level of self-esteem is a 6, versus the ideal 10. The question is, *how much* does this disparity bother you? What degree of pain do you associate with this difference between your actual and your ideal self-esteem? Express that discomfort in terms of a number between 0 (no discomfort) and 10 (pain so intense that you cannot endure it one more day). Write the number down.

Step 7: Decide which of the following four categories best describes your priority for change on this Life Dimension and write it down.

> 1—*Urgent*: The need or desire for a life change is of the utmost concern. It probably generates a high degree of pain for you, and is so predominant in your thinking that it leaves you little time, emotion, or energy to think about anything else. Creating change in this Dimension is of critical importance.

> 2—*High:* A high priority occupies your feelings, emotions, and energies, although not to the degree that an urgent priority does. It is a concern that rises above the general challenges and problems that you face in life. To put something in the high-priority category means that, while it may not be a source of intense pain for you, it is unquestionably disruptive of your life, and is therefore worthy of serious focus.

> 3—*Medium:* A medium-priority concern is one that is worthy of change, even if it does not dominate your thinking. You're aware of the problem and monitor it closely. While it calls for your attention, there are other things in your life that justify your efforts and energies before you pursue the medium priority. As you accomplish change in the areas listed as urgent or high priorities, you move items on this list up into those other categories.

4—*Low:* These are concerns you can live with. You are aware of them and would like to see them change, but at the moment, they may be of questionable relevance or import. They do not rise to Project Status.

Life Dimension: _____ Ideal = 10

Step 1: If I was living my life as a "10" on this dimension:

A: My behaviors would be characterized by:
• What would I be doing?
• Where would I be doing it?
• With whom?
• How would my actions and my attitude appear to other people?
• What words would they use to describe the way I would be living?

B. My inner feelings would be characterized by:
• How would I feel about myself?
• What kinds of messages would I be giving myself?
• In the morning, how would I be feeling about the day ahead?
• Even when facing the inevitable difficulty or challenge, what emotional cues inside me would tell me I was still living as a "10" on this dimension?

C. The negatives that would disappear are:
• What undesirable consequences would I no longer be getting?
• What kinds of frustrating, dangerous, irritating, or painful moments would simply stop happening for me? What parts of my daily routine would no longer occur?
• Of the reactions that I now consistently get from other people, which ones would no longer happen?
• How would I know that these negatives had ended? If the negative is being overweight, for example, then getting on the scale tells me that I'm no longer overweight—how will the disappearance of the negative be measured?

D. The positives that would be present are:
• What responses would I be getting from other people, such that I would know I was at a "10" in this area? What kinds of "strokes" would I be consistently getting from others?
• What improvements in my daily activities would I see?
• Which parts of my daily routine would I find especially enjoyable?
• What physical improvements would I notice? Are there changes in my body—my posture, my facial expression, my blood pressure, my breathing—that would tell me and other people that I'm at a "10"?
• What resources am I capitalizing on?

Actual Self-Rating _____ = (1–10) _____

Step 2: Since I am actually living this life dimension at level _____:

A: My actual relevant behavior is:
• What kinds of things do I do that, afterward, I regret?
• What are the specific details of my actions that tell me I'm at the level shown above? How do I know that I'm falling short in this area?
• What do I tell other people in order to "cover up" for my shortcomings in this life dimension? What excuses do I use? Besides verbal excuses, are there specific actions I use in order to "cover up"?
• If there are particular people who trigger the undesirable behavior, what do they do to "bring it out in me"? When they act in those ways, what sequence or pattern does my response take: what negative steps do I usually go through?
• Are the important people in my life doing or saying things that tell me I have a problem in this area?

B. My actual inner feelings are:
• What is my immediate emotional reaction to this life dimension? When I think about this area of my life, what is my instant, gut-level response?
• When I have to deal with a difficulty in this area, what emotional signals tell me that it is painful for me?
• How does a crisis in this dimension make me feel?
• What excuses do I give myself for falling short? How do I explain away the problems to myself?

C. The negatives that are present are:
• What are the physical signs that I have problems in this area? What is the nature of the suffering that this life dimension causes me?
• What kinds of undesirable reactions do I seem to be getting from people, almost all of the time?
• Do I feel as if I'm wearing a "mask" in this area of my life? What does the mask look like? Is this a life dimension in which I'm almost never "the real me"?
• How do I explain to myself *why* I'm at the level I've written above? What is it about me that I think may be contributing to the problem?
• What obstacles are blocking me?

D. The positives that are absent, but needed are:
• What am I missing that, if I had it, would significantly raise my level in this area?
• What do I need to hear or feel from other people, that so far I'm not hearing or feeling?
• What do I need other people to stop doing or saying?
• What would satisfaction and fulfillment consist of on this dimension?

Step 3: Circle all judgments and limiting beliefs from Step 2 in red.

Step 4: List obstacles you must overcome to move from Actual to Ideal on this Life Dimension.

Step 5: List your resources for moving from Actual to Ideal on this Life Dimension.

Step 6: Rate your Subjective Units of Discomfort (SUDS). (Why?)

Step 7: My motivation for change on this Dimension is (write one: Urgent, High, Medium, or Low):_____

You should now begin to progress through the chart of categories and Life Dimension, one by one. For each Life Dimension that you feel is worthy of change, create a two-page self-evaluation spreadsheet. Take the time to do this right. Don't feel that you have to accomplish the entire process in a single session. I suggest, instead, that you distribute this work across a number of days, if necessary. But do make a commitment to yourself about when you will have the evaluations completed. It's also a good idea to set aside a specific amount of time at a particular time of day for doing this important work.

Assignment #16: Once you have completed your evaluation on all the categories and Life Dimensions, look at the Summary Priorities chart on page 192. You'll see that it consists of four columns, each labeled according to the level of priority: urgent, high, medium, and low. This chart can help you arrange your priorities for change. Suppose that you view five of your Life Dimensions as being positioned such that the need for change is especially urgent: you should now list those Life Dimensions in descending order. That is, of the five Life Dimensions that you assigned to the urgent category, which is the most urgent? That Dimension would be Number One in the urgent column. Underneath it, you will list your second, third, fourth and fifth urgent Dimensions, in order. Please go through this process for each Life Dimension, so that every one of them will be shown somewhere on the Priorities chart.

Summary Priorities Chart

Urgent	High	Medium	Low

Now in the interest of creating an overview of all your hard work, create a set of five Life Dimension Summary Profile charts (one for each of the five categories), an example of which is on page 193. These are to be filled out only *after* you have completed the step-by-step self-analysis process for each of the Life Dimensions included in the five categories on the Life Dimensions chart. You will notice that the example Life Dimension Summary Profile sheet has a 1–10 continuum for each Life Dimension under the "Personal" category. On each continuum, indicate your self-rating as of the time you filled out the evaluation spreadsheet for each particular Life Dimension, under a given category. At the bottom of the sheet is an *overall* continuum, representing the general category heading. Mark this overall continuum to reflect the *average* of the specific ratings on the summary sheet. Thus, if you've circled 4 on both the Self-Esteem and Financial continuums, and an 8 on Education and Health, then you would add 4 + 4 + 8 + 8 and divide the total, 24, by the number of ratings, 4, to get the overall rating of 6 on this broad category.

Life Dimension Summary Profile

Category: Personal

Self-Esteem
Rating

| 1 | 2 | 3 | 4 | 5 | 6 | 7 | 8 | 9 | 10 |

Education
Rating

| 1 | 2 | 3 | 4 | 5 | 6 | 7 | 8 | 9 | 10 |

Financial
Rating

| 1 | 2 | 3 | 4 | 5 | 6 | 7 | 8 | 9 | 10 |

Health
Rating

| 1 | 2 | 3 | 4 | 5 | 6 | 7 | 8 | 9 | 10 |

Overall Category
Rating

| 1 | 2 | 3 | 4 | 5 | 6 | 7 | 8 | 9 | 10 |

This Life Dimension Summary Profile provides you with an overview of where you have rated yourself on each Life Dimension, and shows you how those ratings combine to define your overall level of adjustment in that category of your life. Do this for each of the five categories.

Now, at the top of a clean page in your notebook, write Judgments and Limiting Beliefs. Go back to your original evaluation spreadsheets, and find every judgment or limiting behavior that you originally circled. List each one on this new page. Once you've finished this list, what you'll have is an overview of all of those things that you are believing, and therefore being programmed by, in terms of negative internal dialogue.

As a final step, also in terms of programming, turn your

attention to the general priorities you have regarding your life as you now live it. I am talking about those things that you value and hold most near and dear to your heart. This is different from the specific changes you have prioritized earlier. Here you are to deal not with desired change, but with what you care about. In the space provided, you should list the top five priorities in your life. Begin by writing in space number one that which you hold to be the most important thing in your life. Then list that which you consider to be the second most important thing in your life, and so on, through number five. I understand that there may not be much separation between some of these values, but force yourself to order them one through five, nonetheless. Give it careful thought and truly search your heart for what is important to you.

Priorities

1.

2.

3.

4.

5.

You are not quite finished with this important exercise. Using the space below, now list in descending order what it is that you spend your time on. In space number one, list that activity or pursuit that you spend the highest percentage of your waking hours on. Be honest and accurate here. For example, there are twenty-four hours in a day. If you sleep eight hours, that leaves sixteen waking hours to be divided among different pursuits. If you spend ten hours per day associated with work—that is, driving to work, working, and driving home—then by simply doing the math, you see that work is your number-one time absorption. That would leave six hours. If you spend three of those six hours watching television, then television is probably number two. These are just examples; take a moment to fill out your own time allocations, honestly and accurately, in the space provided here.

Time Allocation Profile

Activity	Percent of Time
1.	1.
2.	2.
3.	3.
4.	4.
5.	5.

Having performed all of your assigned steps in this guided tour, consider what you have now accomplished. You have completed an organized and thorough evaluation of your life, broken down into categories of Life Dimensions. In all likelihood, what you now have in your notebook is the most objective and thorough evaluation of you that anyone has ever done. And just to make sure you don't get lost in the sheer volume of information that you have generated, your summary sheets can help you to see the "big picture."

So what do I do with all of this stuff? Your first use of this information should be to review it to see if you can identify certain themes in your life. For example:

—Ask yourself how wide the gap is between your actual adjustment and desired adjustment. Are these levels of adjustment hugely divergent, or only mildly or moderately so?
—Do your problem areas appear to be clustered in one or two categories of your life, or are they spread across the entire scope of your life?

—What are the themes to your judgments and
limiting behaviors? In other words, are there
consistencies in what you tend to say to yourself,
no matter what the circumstances?
—Are you riddled with self-doubt and/or self-
loathing?
—What emotions define you? Is it anger, fear, pain,
or some other?
—Are there major drains on your physical,
emotional, or spiritual energy?
—When you review your Summary Priorities chart,
do you detect any parallels among those things you
have put in the different categories? For example,
are those things that you have listed as most urgent
performance-oriented, or are they, perhaps, more
personal and private?
—Do your priorities tend to involve other people, or
are they largely or entirely focused on you?
—What about time frames? Are your urgent priorities
more short-term, or are they long-term?

Answer these questions, and any others that may come to
mind, so as to get a better feel for where you are in your life and
what kind of time frame you have for your goals. Having this kind
of insight and overview is going to be tremendously useful to you
in moving your life in the right direction.

*Assignment #17: Having now transferred the results of
your step-by-step analysis to your summary sheets, and having
attempted to identify some themes in your responses, you're ready
to take the last step in the diagnostic process. As in most, if not
all things, there is some good and there is some bad. The good
part of doing the step-by-step analysis that you have just completed is that it makes a difficult and overwhelming task, such as
assessing your whole life, manageable. The down side of such
analysis is that when you break things down into pieces, you may
lose the flavor of that which you are breaking down. Think about
eating a piece of cake versus ingesting the ingredients one at a
time. A piece of cake has a certain flavor and texture that would
be completely lost if you took a bite of sugar and then a bite of
butter and then a bite of flour. While breaking your life down into
pieces makes it manageable and understandable, it is important*

*that we maintain the texture and flavor of your life as we think
about your creating what you want.*

*As a result, your last but certainly not your least important
diagnostic assignment is to write your own desired character profile. Without getting bogged down in the details of how and why,
it is important for you to be intimately familiar with what you
want your life to look and feel like when you have achieved your
goals. This character profile can become your "North Star." It
can become an intimate image that can keep you moving in the
right direction. We have talked in some detail about how your life
would look and feel in a particular dimension when you have what
you want. I am now talking about your life on a larger scale; I
am talking about how your life would look from ten thousand feet
as opposed to down on the deck.*

*I suggest that you write this character profile as though
you were writing a part for someone playing the lead role in a
poignant play. The dramatic play in this case is your life, and the
star is you. If you were writing a part for the lead character, you
would have to do it in such a way that the person playing that
part could understand the tone, the mood, the attitude, the texture
of the character's personality and behaviors. You would have to
describe to the actor how the character felt inside, as well as how
they behaved externally. Again, at this point, you are not to concern yourself with how or why; only with what your character
would look like, feel like, and act like.*

This assignment requires some imagination and some fantasy thinking. In this limited assignment, this can be a constructive
way to think. When I say you need to describe, within this character profile, how you would feel when you achieved the things
you want, I know that requires some speculation. But that is exactly what you need to do. If, for example, you dreamed of running
and winning a marathon, I would want you to talk about how it
would feel as you came across the finish line, knowing that you
had conquered the race and all of the contestants. How would it
feel to hear the applause of the crowd and know that it was all for
you? This assignment requires you to put yourself in that position
in your imagination, so that you can identify those feelings and
use them as a part of your North Star. This is one of those rare
occasions when imaginary life and fantasy is constructive. Enjoy
it as you become familiar with where you are going.

A woman with whom I once worked extensively completed this assignment exceptionally well some years ago, and has

given me permission to include excerpts from her work here. Carol's example is not meant to suggest the content of your own character profile, but is instead offered as an example of the kind of issues you may want to address. Read it with that purpose in mind, and then have fun casting yourself in the drama that is your life. Here is Carol's work. Note that for descriptive purposes, she writes about herself as though she were another person.

"Me In the Future"

Carol is thirty-eight years old but looks younger because she smiles a lot and has bright eyes. She seems optimistic and excited about what is going on in her life. She takes care of herself mentally, physically, and emotionally, by daily attention to those dimensions of her existence. She doesn't gunny-sack hurt, anger, or resentment, but deals with it as it comes up. She exercises regularly but not obsessively, and enjoys it when she does it.

Carol gets up thirty minutes before anyone else in her household in order to have some alone time. She spends a few minutes in prayer, a few minutes reading the Bible, and then organizes her day so that she has somewhat of a plan. Carol awakens her husband and two children with hugs and pats every morning, whether they want her to or not. Carol begins her day with a freshness and optimism that is refreshing to her and to those around her. She greets people that she encounters in her workplace. Carol is relaxed and at ease around those that she encounters during the day. She makes contact, but she doesn't try too hard, and does not personalize it if others don't seem too eager to interact with her. She doesn't need to be the center of attention, nor does she blend into the woodwork. Carol is self-assured and at ease with herself and around others.

Carol has slipped out of the bonds of her past and the anger, hatred, and resentment that had built up over the years toward those who have hurt her in her life. Although she has not made peace with everyone in her life, her door is open and they know it. Should they choose to enter that door, she will greet them with receptivity and fairness. Should they fail to do so, she is at peace in knowing that it is they and not she who maintains that barrier.

Carol is actively involved with her friends and hobbies again. Although she is deeply committed to her marriage and family, she also has a life as an individual. As in all things in her life, she maintains an appropriate balance between family and friends, duties and recreation.

These excerpts were lifted from Carol's overall characterological profile and constituted roughly one-third of what she wrote. Topics that she addressed in addition to those included here were:

—Self-esteem
—Guilt
—Motivation
—Financial management
—Humor
—Assertiveness
—Tolerance
—Judgmentalism
—Commitment
—Self-discipline

Again, use this as a guide in describing how your life will look and feel when you have assembled it the way you want it. This is an important part of building your life strategy. Do it well.

Taking Charge

Now you are ready to begin creating step-by-step, purposeful change in your life. In taking up this challenge, you're going to be operating from a position of strength rather than weakness, because you'll occupy a state of knowledge instead of ignorance. You have relevant knowledge of the ten Life Laws and relevant knowledge of yourself.

If you have completed all of the work set out for you in the previous section, you should feel organized rather than confused; you should have a sense of being focused on what you most urgently want in your life. You may not like the truths you have discovered about yourself, but at least you do know them. And you can take comfort in the fact that Life Law #4—*You can't change what you don't acknowledge*—has a converse principle: You *can* change what you *do* acknowledge.

Dreams vs. Goals

Now let's take up the issue of goals. You need to understand, first and foremost, how your dreams differ from your goals. Once we've made that distinction, we can begin to turn your dreams into goals.

Everyone has, or at least at one time had, dreams about what his or her life would be like. Dreaming can be healthy: dreams can inspire, compelling us to look forward in our lives, rather than being stuck in the past. Dreaming is entirely a mental and emotional process, limited only by the imagination. Dreaming requires little energy and no action. It is unconstrained by truth and real-world limits. Some people dream to the point that in their rich fantasy lives, they create and enjoy all kinds of exciting, desirable, and even exotic events.

For everything dreaming is, consider what it is *not*: it is not the world you live in day to day, and it creates no tangible results beyond short-term escape. In fact, it may distract you, or relieve the pressure you might feel and use to change the way your life actually is.

Dreaming is easy, but translating those dreams into realities is not. Don't get me wrong. Dreaming about how you want your life to be, and constructing a vivid and detailed fantasy world, often is an important first step toward genuine change for the better. But if you want to dream, all you need is a creative mind and the willingness to fantasize. By contrast, in order to turn those dreams into realities, you need much more. You need energy, strategy, programming, and a very specific set of skills and knowledge. I call these multiple elements Strategic Life Planning (SLP).

It is now time for you to learn specifically how to turn your dreams into goals. For it is goals, and not dreams, that you can effectively pursue and capture. The pursuit of your realistic goals can be broken down into seven key steps. Learn these seven steps, and use them in pursuing your strategic goals, and you will have them.

CHAPTER THIRTEEN

THE SEVEN-STEP STRATEGY

The best parachute folders are those who jump themselves.

—Anonymous

The Seven Steps to Acquiring Your Goals

Step #1: *Express your goal in terms of specific events or behaviors.* Unlike dreams, which tend to gloss over important details, or omit them altogether, goals leave no room for confusion about that which is desired. In order for a goal to be attainable, it must be *operationally defined.* In other words, it must be expressed in terms of the events or behavior that constitute the goal.

For example, in the language of dreams, the desire to travel might be expressed simply as, "I want to see the world." By contrast, in the language of goals and realities, it would be necessary to express this desire by describing the operations or behavior that define what is meant by "see the world." A goal statement might be: "I intend to travel to three different states and one foreign country each year for five years." Now that the desire has been broken down into steps, it can be managed and pursued much more directly than can the ambiguous, "blue sky" dream.

Bottom Line: For a dream to become a goal, it has to be specifically defined in terms of operations, meaning *what will be done.* So decide what it is you want. Identify and define your goal with great specificity. Know the answers to the following:

—What are the specific behaviors or operations that make up the goal? What will you be doing or not doing when you are "living the goal"?

—How will you recognize the goal when you have it?

—How will you feel when you have it?

Your answers to these questions, expressed in concrete detail, will become essential signposts, telling you whether or not you are effectively moving toward your goal, or whether you need to make a midcourse correction. Remember, "being happy" won't cut it; that's neither an event nor a behavior. When you set out to identify a goal, you've got to stay away from that kind of ambiguity. If you want to be happy, you must *define* happy.

Step #2: *Express your goal in terms that can be measured.* Unlike dreams, goals must be expressed in terms of outcomes that are measurable, observable, and quantifiable. In order for something to rise to the level of a manageable goal, you've got to be able to determine your level of progress. You need to know how much of the goal you've attained. You have to have some way of knowing whether you have, in fact, successfully arrived at where you wanted to be. In the dreamworld, you might state, "I want a wonderful and rewarding life." In the world of goals and realities, you would define *wonderful* and *rewarding* with the same kind of specificity we stated in Step 1, but also in terms that are measurable. That is, you'd express them in such a way that you could determine how much "wonderful" you have, and how "rewarding" it is. Relevant questions might be:

—In order for your life to be wonderful, where would you live?

—In order for it to be wonderful, who would you spend your life with?

—How much money would you have?

—In what type of work or activities would you be involved?

—How would you behave?

—How much time would you spend doing certain activities?

Any number of other details might serve as examples of measurable outcomes, but I trust that you get the point.

Bottom Line: Express your goal in terms of the measurable outcomes that will let you know whether you are approaching it, how far you still have to go, and whether you have obtained your goal or not. Test your goal by asking the same kinds of questions about it as are shown above.

Step #3: *Assign a timeline to your goal.* Unlike dreams, which are vague in both definition *and* time, goals require a particular schedule or calendar for their achievement. A dreamworld statement might be, "I want to be rich some day." A statement in the world of goals and realities sounds like, "I want to have achieved an income of $100,000 per year by December 31 in the year 2000." By making a schedule or timeline, you impose project status on the goal: The deadline you've created fosters a sense of urgency or purpose, which in turn will serve as an important motivator. Goals involve time-sensitive requirements that do not allow for inertia or procrastination.

Whatever the period, create a date by which you will arrive at your goal. If your goal is to lose sixty pounds in twenty weeks, your date would be twenty weeks from the day you start. Working backward from that date, you can see where you have to be at the midpoint of ten weeks. Likewise, you can see where you have to be at the five-week mark and the fifteen-week mark. Thinking in terms of a calendar allows you to assess the realism of your plan, and to determine the intensity of what you must do to reach your goal.

Bottom Line: You will obtain your goal only if you are on a timeline and commit to a certain date. Once you have determined precisely what it is you want, you must decide on a timeframe for having it.

Step #4: *Choose a goal you can control.* Unlike dreams, which allow you to fantasize about events over which you have no control, goals have to do with aspects of your existence that you control and can therefore manipulate. A dreamworld statement might be, "My dream is to have a beautiful, 'white' Christmas." A more realistic statement might be, "I am going to create a nostalgic and traditional atmosphere for our family at Christmastime." Obviously, since you cannot control the weather, snowfall is not an appropriate goal. On the other hand, you *can* control such things as the decorations, the music, and the food you offer during the holidays. It's appropriate to make those circumstances part of your goal, because you can control them.

Bottom Line: In identifying your goal, strive for what you can create, not for what you can't.

Step #5: *Plan and program a strategy that will get you to your goal.* Unlike dreams, where the objective is merely longed for, goals involve a strategic plan for getting there. Figuring out a strategy to get from point A to point B can be outcome-determinative. To pursue a goal seriously requires that you realistically assess the obstacles and resources involved, and that you create a strategy for navigating that reality.

One of the great benefits of having a well-planned, well-programmed strategy is that it liberates you from a pointless and misguided reliance on willpower. Remember, the notion that you've got to have willpower is a myth. Willpower is unreliable emotional fuel: experienced at a fever pitch, it may temporarily energize your efforts; once the emotion is gone, however, the train stops. You've had enough false starts in your life to know that there are times when you do not feel motivated, when you do not feel energized. The only way to guarantee forward movement during those downtimes is to design a solid strategic plan that sustains your commitment in the absence of emotional energy. Specifically, your environment must be programmed, your schedule must be programmed, and your accountability must be programmed in such a way that all three support you, long after the emotional high is gone.

Suppose, for example, that your goal is to make physical exercise a regular part of your life. It's easy to get out there and exercise when you're all fired up about your new program. But if it's emotion (willpower) that fuels your effort, what happens on that cold morning in February when you find that you really don't care about exercising and would much rather sleep? Willpower is gone, but the need remains. Only programming your environment in such a way that it is difficult or impossible *not* to do what you have committed to do will carry you through.

Even the simplest programming can be dramatically effective. For example, I am invariably hungry when I come home at the end of the day. For the longest time, I would enter the house through a door that led me through the kitchen. I would tell myself repeatedly that I wasn't going to snack before dinner. Sometimes the emotion would carry me, and sometimes it wouldn't. As I walked through the kitchen, the environment was full of temptation. Maybe it was cookies on a platter one day, a chocolate cake (or some other easily consumable snack food) the next. So, to program myself for success, I just started entering the house through another door that did not take me through the kitchen. The route I took had no opportunities for failure, and I got past that reactive eating that had plagued me so. Believe me, this method is a lot more pleasant, and effective, than relying on the fickle emotion of willpower.

Similarly, if I can influence someone else's environment and program it the way I want to, I can meaningfully influence and/or control their behavior as well. For example, I can cure smoking; I can cause people to quit smoking with 100 percent efficiency, provided that I totally control their environment. Think about it. All I have to do is put them in an environment where there is no tobacco. Problem solved. Unfortunately, probably nothing short of parachuting them into the Antarctic will ensure such a pristine environment. But each and every step in that direction will improve their chances of success.

Suppose you wanted to read and study a five-hundred-page book in a thirty-day period. Notice, first of all, what makes this a workable goal: it's specific, it's measurable, and it has a timeline. Determining how many pages you need to read per day would be a simple arithmetic problem. The *real* challenge would be to make a plan that would program you and your world for literally getting those pages read. This would require:

—Identifying how much time per day you would
  require to read the specified number of pages.
—Identifying the specific time, each day, when the
  reading would take place. (Scheduling is important
  here. Approaching it from the standpoint of
  willpower will not get it done. Setting aside the
  specific time of day, and protecting that time, will
  get it done.)
—Identifying the physical location where you can
  read without interruption or distraction, and where
  you can be sure you will be present at the
  appointed time in your busy day.

The significance of programming is that it recognizes that your life is full of temptations and opportunities to fail. Those temptations and opportunities compete with your more constructive and task-oriented behavior. Without programming, you will find it much harder to stay the course.

Consider here the struggles that alcoholics and smokers undertake in order to defeat their addictions. You would never recommend that an alcoholic who's working to stay sober take a job as a bartender, or that he continue to frequent the bar or other location where he did most of his drinking. If you were programming that alcoholic for success, you would place him in an entirely new environment. You would strongly recommend that he not hang out with his old drinking buddies. During those times when he is most likely to give in to the impulse to drink, you would recommend that he choose incompatible behaviors to perform instead. It's difficult to drink with your buddies when you're jogging around the lake, getting fresh air. In the same fashion, you, too, can program your environment by setting yourself up to behave in ways that thwart negative outcomes.

Don't think that there's any kind of environmental manipulation that is insignificant. If you're a smoker who truly wants to quit, program your environment *in every way possible* to avoid the smoking behavior. You might undertake any number of behavioral changes that avoid the places where you smoke, the times you smoke, and your method of getting tobacco. It is not too trivial to do any number of the following:

—Rid your house of all tobacco materials;
—Stop carrying change or single dollar bills that
  allow you to purchase cigarettes;
—Ask all coworkers and friends to help you by not
  giving you a cigarette, no matter how passionately
  you might beg;
—Schedule activities during the times that your
  temptation to smoke is the strongest, for example,
  immediately upon awakening in the morning,
  immediately after meals, or while drinking alcohol.

Bottom Line: Make a plan, work your plan, and you will attain your goal. Rely on your strategy, planning, and programming, not on your willpower. Arrange your environment in such a way that it "pulls for" that result that you desire. Identify those places, times, situations, and circumstances that set you up for failure. Reprogram those things so that they cannot compete with what you really want.

Step #6: *Define your goal in terms of steps*: Unlike dreams, whose outcomes we pretend will just "happen" one day, goals are carefully broken down into measurable steps that lead, ultimately, to the desired outcome. A dreamworld statement might be, "I'm going to drop down to a size eight from a size eighteen by summertime." A reality-based statement would instead be, "I will take certain steps to lose three pounds per week for the next twenty weeks. At the end of that time, I will be wearing a size eight." Major life changes don't just happen; they happen one step at a time. When someone is considering it in its entirety, the dream of losing sixty pounds and ten dress sizes can be so overwhelming as to be paralyzing. But it begins to look like a decidedly manageable goal when broken down into the steps of losing a few pounds per week.

Bottom Line: Steady progress, through well-chosen, realistic, interval steps, produces results in the end. Know what those steps are before you set out.

Step #7: *Create accountability for your progress toward your goal:* Unlike dreams, which can be entertained at will, goals are structured in such a way that you have some measure of accountability at each and every interval step. In the dreamworld, you might decide that your child should have all B's on his or her report card by the end of the six-week grading period. In the world of goals and realities, that same child would have step-by-step accountability, perhaps reporting to you or a teacher every Friday afternoon to review his or her results on all homework, quizzes, and tests. Faced with this interim accountability, the child is now motivated to perform and adjust, since he or she now expects to be scrutinized on a weekly basis.

Without accountability, people are apt to con themselves, failing to recognize poor performance in time to adjust and keep from falling short. So consider who in your circle of family or friends might serve as your "teammate," the person to whom you commit to make periodic reports on your progress. We all respond better if we know that somebody is checking up on us, and that there are consequences for our failure to perform.

Bottom Line: Create meaningful accountability for your actions or inactions. Some days you might feel like working on your goal. Some days you might not. But if you know precisely what you want, when you want it by, and the time and place are scheduled and protected, *and* there are real consequences for not doing the assigned work, you are much more likely to continue in your pursuit of your goal. Set up an accountability system for yourself that will make it impossible for you *not* to achieve your goal.

Successfully executing your personal strategic plan for change requires that, as you develop your plan, you effectively incorporate these seven steps for attaining each and every goal.

CHAPTER FOURTEEN

FINDING YOUR FORMULA

Potential just means you ain't done it yet.
—Darrell Royal, football coach, University of Texas

Three important events have now come to pass. You have met yourself in an intimate, blinders-off fashion for perhaps the first time in your life. You have learned the real-deal ways of the world in the ten Life Laws that govern your outcomes. And you have acquired critical information about how to set and attain goals, the essence of your life strategy.

Unless I have fallen way out of touch with how people feel when they are taking strategic control of their lives, I predict that you are feeling two parallel emotions right now. On one hand, you are probably feeling some real anxiety and perhaps even an element of dread. That's okay. It is understandable, because if you have done the exercises outlined in this book and truly learned the Life Laws, then the foundation and logic of your life may have been shaken to the core. You are probably questioning or at least examining virtually every aspect of your existence at this point and you may feel a great sense of urgency to quit wasting time. You may be angry at yourself for past decisions and actions or inactions.

Even though such feelings can be constructive, they do clearly call for a tremendous amount of work and willingness on your part to undo and redo major parts of your life. There is no longer room in your life for habit, comfort zones, or rigidity. Taking away those particular aspects of your life patterns can be very threatening and disruptive. But you now know you cannot continue to live with those types of behavior, particularly the rigidity. You are at a point in your life where you have to be as "flexible as a rubber hose," as we say in Texas. You have to be willing to challenge, test, and try virtually everything that up until now you may have treated with habitual and automatic resistance.

Secondly, you are probably feeling a great sense of excitement. And if you're not, you should be. As I said earlier, this is your best shot for taking your life to the next level. This is your chance to put your life together by design and do and be what you want to do and be.

You have had quite a journey through this book as you have progressed through the work presented and gotten to know yourself from the inside out. I hope that you've realized or come to learn anew several important truths about the real state of your life. You should have learned that you may be part of a silent epidemic in America, one that is defined by emotional and behavioral apathy. You most assuredly have learned that your life is governed by ten immutable Life Laws that, if incorporated into your life strategy, can make you a winner. You have likely also concluded, quite rightly, that if you violate these Life Laws, you are likely to suffer severe penalties. Through various tests, questionnaires, and the all-encompassing guided tour of your life, you have highlighted the weak spot that will be your focus.

If you have worked through this book sincerely, you have asked the hard questions and been willing to acknowledge and accept yourself, shortcomings and all. You may have confirmed that you are anything but perfect, and realized that that's only a disaster if you don't work to improve. If you have painstakingly followed your guided tour, you have set priorities and identified the important problems that you need to face and solve in order to not fall short of your goals. And so as not to be left to your own trial-and-error methods, you have learned the steps and conditions of genuine, strategically planned change.

You are now equipped to make a life strategy that allows you to begin changing your life, one step, one goal, one priority at a time. Using the tools that you have learned, you can begin with your top priority and design a knowledge-based, results-based strategy for change, and take the definitive actions to live it.

I predict that you will find that life is a phenomenon dominated by momentum. If your momentum is in a negative direction, it builds in speed and intensity toward disaster. If, on the other hand, you make the efforts necessary to change the momentum to a positive direction, that momentum will build speed and intensity, as well. I predict that you will find that each positive step you take, no matter how small or seemingly insignificant, will stimulate another positive step until the synergy of your efforts reaches a critical mass that will alter your life forevermore. You will reach a level of intensity that will begin to generate positive results and meaningful victories.

As I have said, you have now and have always had within you, every trait, tool, and characteristic necessary to create a quality life. What you didn't have was awareness, know-how, focus, and clarity. You do now. You also have the intelligence, the motivation, and the need. Those are all important building blocks of your life strategy.

Notwithstanding all of the positive elements amassed thus far, your preparation and programming is not yet complete. There is a very important step left. It is a fun and exciting step, but it is an essential one, nonetheless. This step deals with how you will do what you do. It deals with how you approach your life in general, and your problems and challenges in particular. As with every other aspect of your life, you know that you have a choice about how you approach the implementation of your life strategy in terms of what spirit, energy, and attitude you bring to it.

In this final chapter of your preparation for creating a personal life strategy, you will have the opportunity to learn several important aspects of being a winner. You will have the opportunity to learn:

—How to find your "formula" and embrace your personal winning persona, unique to you and only you. This truly makes your life "custom designed."

—How to use successes and failures in building a personal life strategy that works in the real world.

—The common denominators that are present among all winners, from every walk of life: up close and personal, the specific strategies, characteristics, and conduct of some genuine world-class winners.

Finding Your Formula: Your Personal Winning Persona

You will remember our discussing in chapter 12 that you are the only *you* that will ever exist in the entire history of the world. You are unique in the way that you navigate life. Every individual has his or her own personality, attitude, and way of being present day to day. Every individual has his or her own personal best way of being. Every person has their own personal best persona for generating results. Your task is to discover and define your formula and best persona for getting the most out of life. It will be unique to you, unlike anyone else's, and that's okay. It doesn't have to be commonsensical or mainstream conformist. If it works for you, based on results, then that's the test.

So what is your formula? What are the attitudes, intensities, behaviors, and characteristics that will generate peak performance for you? It is like a "zone" you need to find and stay in. You see this in professional athletes on a regular basis. They need to hit their stride and do what works for them. If they get outside their persona, performance will diminish dramatically.

What's right for one athlete can be fatal to the efforts of another. The contrast between Pete Sampras, the number-one ranked tennis player in the world, and John McEnroe, the former number one, could not be more striking. Sampras, as you may have observed, is a very pensive, private, quiet-strength kind of person. When the pressure is on, he becomes very introspective, focused, and calm, at least on the outside. McEnroe, on the other hand, plays tennis with a level of intensity, ferocity, and animation that many people consider to be absolutely out-of-control crazy. Perhaps it would not work for any other person on the planet, but it works for him. He never plays better than when he intensely, ferociously, and angrily attacks his opponent and the game.

To ask Sampras to adopt McEnroe's persona would be absurd. If Pete Sampras started knocking cups off a table, throwing his racket, or swearing at a referee, he would likely feel out of control, lose focus, and suffer greatly in performance. If John McEnroe, on the other hand, were asked to bottle up all of his emotions and constrict himself in the way Sampras does, he would very likely feel shackled and no longer be truly competitive. Each of these world-class professionals has his unique formula for maximizing results, and so do you. It is critical that you turn your attention to discovering your formula for a winning persona.

In addition to deciding what that formula and persona are, you also have to decide that you are entitled to live them. You have to decide that you have the right to be who you are and how you are, so long as it is not at the expense of other people's dignity and respect. You have to be willing to claim your right to uniqueness. If you do not find your formula, or you do not claim your right to live it, all of the training, all of the knowledge, and all of the data that you have worked to accumulate in the course of this book have been wasted. You cannot let people intimidate you or tell you not to be who you are.

So what is your formula? Do you do your best when you are self-assured and maybe even a little bit cocky, or are you at your best when you are quiet but determined? Is high energy your deal, or is yours a more methodical, persistent style? Are you best when you take charge, or are you a strong supporter? Is a positive, receptive attitude your best mode, or do you need to maintain a healthy skepticism? Are you a loner or a team player? Whatever it is, find your formula and live it with pride.

It's often been said that we must learn from our mistakes. That is a true and wise statement. If you approach a situation in a certain manner and make a mistake, you need to take specific note of that unsuccessful attitude or behavior and cross it off your list of options. It never ceases to amaze me that people will continue to persist in an attitude or behavior that simply does not work. They continue the same rigid behavior, beating their head against the wall, over and over again, seeming not to notice that they always come away with nothing. I have frequently pointed this out to such people and have asked what seemed like a pretty basic question: "You have to know that what you're doing isn't working in any way, shape, or form. Why in the world do you insist on continuing to do it?" The answer is almost always the same: "Well, that's just the way I am. I just do what I do because I am who I am." What in the world are they thinking? What kind of life strategy is that? It's the life strategy for losers. It is the life strategy of someone who is so rigidly locked on being right that they would rather lose than learn. They would rather beat their head against the wall and blame the world for the outcome than admit that their approaches and behavior are wrong. They are refusing to learn from their mistakes, and thus will never shape their behavior in the right direction. Don't deny your mistakes; don't even ignore your mistakes. Study them, dissect them, figure out exactly, precisely what went wrong, and you can then avoid repeating them.

Although the admonition to learn from your mistakes is sound, it is only half of the story. You should also resolve to learn from your successes. Study, dissect, and analyze your successes with the same vigor and commitment with which you study, dissect, and analyze your mistakes. The downside of studying mistakes is that you spend a lot of time focusing on the negatives in your life. The upside of studying your successes is that you are focusing on positives. You are acknowledging that there are things in your life that are going right, and when you study them, you will find that they went right because you made them go right.

I don't believe in luck and I don't believe in randomness in life. I believe that what works in your life works because you make it work. I believe that things work in your life because you choose the right attitude and behavior to generate the right results. Only by studying those successful situations can you increase the likelihood of repeating those effective choices.

If, for example, you have a relationship that is working particularly well, it is worth your time to sit down and figure out why. I am not suggesting that you analyze something to death rather than enjoy it, but it is useful if you can figure out what it is about the relationship that is rewarding to you. Do you approach it differently from those relationships that do not work, and if so, how? Do you behave differently? Have you placed this relationship at a priority level that calls for you to invest more energy in it than your other, less successful relationships? Do you get certain feedback and responses in this relationship that are inspiring to you, responses that you don't get from other relationships? What is it about you and this relationship that makes it special? What is it about this relationship that makes it among those things in your life that work well?

By studying this success, you are in a position to identify and repeat attitudes and behavior that work. Maybe you find that you share with your relationship partner a certain candor and honesty that is refreshing. By knowing that, you can seek to replicate it. Maybe in this relationship, you are uncommonly accepting or nonjudgmental, or you feel accepted and not judged. If so, you can seek relationships in which those characteristics are fundamental, and therefore increase your chance of success.

Whether it is a relationship, your job, sports, problem

solving, health, or self-management, if you have areas in your life that are working, figure out why and do it again—and again and again.

   Assignment #18: It would be useful for you to do this kind of analysis now, before you begin to implement your life strategy plans. Use the Life Dimensions chart on page 180 to stimulate your thinking. What can you identify in each of the five life categories that is working for you? If you have created success once, you can do it again.

   In addition to studying your own successes, it can also be highly beneficial for you to emulate the successes and winning strategies of others. There is nothing wrong with identifying traits and characteristics of people that you admire, and then folding those traits or characteristics into your own personality and life strategy. I am not suggesting you try to be someone you are not. There's nothing wrong with who you are. What I am suggesting is that, if there are people you know or have the opportunity to observe who are generating great results, applying strategies and characteristics that you admire, studying those people and using them as role models is a worthwhile endeavor. You may not admire everything about them, but you can choose to emulate those things that stand out positively.

   The study of success in others has always been intriguing to me. It began as a hobby and developed into a lifelong pursuit. Even when I was young, success was fascinating to me. Although I played sports, I never really became consumed by it to the point of studying such things as statistics, rankings, and ratings, but I was much more interested in *why* the top teams and players were leading the league.

   At the professional level, for example, I knew that there was basically very little difference between those at the top of the heap and those at the bottom of the pile. I knew that the mega-millionaire stars, for the most part, could not necessarily run faster, jump higher, or perform feats of strength significantly different from those who were barely hanging on. I knew that there had to be something else that distinguished them, and I wanted to know what it was.

   Who in your life do you admire that is generating successful results? Perhaps it's a coworker or an employer. Perhaps it is someone of national reputation whom you only know through the media or books and articles. Perhaps it is a parent or family member. Whoever it is, it is worth your time to study, dissect, and analyze their formula for success, just as I have suggested you do with yourself. Do they have a certain philosophy that you admire and believe to be the underpinning of their success? Do they have a certain attitude toward problem solving or relationships that you believe distinguishes them from the crowd? Do they have a work ethic or the willingness to make commitments that you admire? Are they the kind of person who will take certain risks to get what they want? Whatever those characteristics, you can help yourself by identifying them and emulating them.

Having spent my life studying success, I can give you a head start on what you will find by studying winners. Over the years that I have studied success stories and the people who star in them, I have found that success is not a random phenomenon. If someone is a winner in business, for example, they have certain characteristics in common with those who are champions in sports, or stars in the arts. People who are consistently winners are not lucky; they make their breaks. They do things that cause the world to stand up and take notice, and thus grant them rewards. They may each have a different goal and specific strategy, but if you laid all of their strategies and maps for success side by side, you would see that there is an invariable common core among those strategies. These are the requirements. Without them, you fail. I share that core group of traits and characteristics with you now, in hopes that you will fold them into your own personal life strategy. They are all a matter of choice, so you can access them as readily as anyone.

These qualities are the all-important "spice" to your strategic soup. Pay close attention, for learning and incorporating this information can make the difference. Here are the top ten elements consistently present in the successful people I have studied:

Vision: People who consistently win get what they want because they know what they want. They see it, feel it, and experience it in their minds and hearts. They envision what they want and where they are going so clearly that they can project themselves forward to that moment of victory and describe it to you as though it were happening. Most people are afraid to let themselves get excited about having what they want, because they fear they will jinx themselves or be disappointed if they don't get it. People who are consistent winners are undaunted by that fear. They take the risk of getting excited, and can describe their moment of victory to you in vivid and palpable detail. They know what it will look and feel like, and how it will change their lives. They have a vision that becomes their North Star: it keeps them motivated and efficiently on track.

Strategy: People who consistently win have a clear and thoughtful strategy for getting that which they envision. They have a map, a flow chart, and a timeline. They know what they need to do, when they need to do it, and the order in which it must take place. Very importantly, they write it down. You will see these people with calendars, flow charts, folders, and other writings that visually anchor their strategy. Their strategy includes an assessment of their resources and appraisal of the obstacles they have to overcome. This written strategy, in combination with a vividly envisioned goal, allows them to stay on course. They don't get off on some rabbit trail, because it isn't on the map. By keeping their eyes on their North Star, they avoid any alternative that does not get them closer to the finish line.

Passion: People who consistently win play the game with passion. They get excited about what they are doing. They get energized about what they are doing. They become passionately invested in the journey as well as the goal, and thrive on it all. For these people, the pursuit of their goal is not work; it is not tiring. The pursuit of their goal is fun and intriguing. These people are reluctant to go to bed at night, and they spring forth in the morning to get at what they seek. Their passion is contagious: those around them begin to share in their excitement and purpose.

Truth: People who consistently win have no room in their lives for denial, fantasy, or fiction. These people "tell it like it is" to themselves and others. They are self-critical rather than self-deluding, and hold themselves to high but realistic standards. They are absolutely nondefensive when they get input and feedback, and they're able to find some value in any information. These are not people who were born on third base and think they hit a triple. They know who they are and what they are, and they build from that truth. They do not kid themselves about the scope or demands of their challenges. They deal with the truth, since they recognize that nothing else will make their vision obtainable. Their attitude is, "If I know where the bottom is, I can deal with it. If I don't, the problems cannot be planned for."

Flexibility: People who consistently win understand that life is not a success-only journey. They understand that even the best-laid plans sometimes must be altered and changed. These people do not remain rigidly fixed on any one behavior or thought pattern. They are open to input and will consider any potentially viable alternative. If A works, they do A; if B works, they do B. They bend, but never break. Because they measure themselves based on results rather than appearances, ego, or intentions, they are willing to be wrong and change or start over.

Risk: People who consistently win are willing to take risks. This does not mean that they are reckless, and it does not mean that they put themselves or their goals in unnecessary danger. It means that they are willing to get out of their comfort zone and try new things. It means that they are willing to plunge into the unknown if necessary and leave behind the safe, unchallenging, and familiar existence in order to have more. It means they are willing to admit that what they have is not enough, even though that very admission creates a pressure to change and the potential to fail.

Nucleus: People who consistently win are not lone rangers. Winners recognize that they become such because they surround themselves with people who want them to win. They recognize that throughout life, you gather around you a nucleus of people with whom you healthfully interact. They choose and bond with people who have skills, talents, and abilities that they themselves do not have. These are people who care enough to tell them the truth, and who take pride in doing so constructively and helpfully. Building a nucleus of trusted friends and allies is critical, and winners do so by giving as well as receiving: They're also part of other people's nuclear groups.

Action: People who consistently win take meaningful, purposeful, directional action. They are not people who redesign the world in their minds and never pull the trigger. Because they are not afraid of risk, these people are willing to step up and do. They take action, and they do so consistently and persistently. They are undaunted if initial actions fail to yield results, because they understand that the world does not give up its rewards easily. If it takes one effort, fine. If it takes ten, that's okay, as well.

Priorities: People who are consistent winners manage their challenges in hierarchical fashion. They set priorities and they live those priorities. They commit to managing their time in such a way that they do not spend time grinding along on priority number two or three or four if priority number one needs their attention. If in the middle of the day they find themselves working on something other than their number-one priority, they stop what they are doing and get back to number one. They choose their priorities carefully because they organize their lives in accordance with them. Once again, they stay off rabbit trails and stay focused on what is most important before moving on to other things.

Self-management: While all of the other nine common denominators of success also involve self-management, this one is more specific. People who consistently win consciously and pointedly take care of themselves as individuals. They are the most important resource they have in achieving their goals. They actively manage their mental, physical, emotional, and spiritual health. They maintain a balance that keeps them safe from burnout. They do not become so consumed by their passion for a particular goal that they forget about the rest of their life. Exercise, recreation, and family time are the focus of their energies, as well. You will not find them languishing in a job or a relationship that is sick and draining. They either make it a priority for repair, or they remove themselves from it. They will not self-destruct. These people take care of themselves, because self is the horse they have to ride to get where they are going.

These ten key elements, consistently found in the lives of people who are winners, are examples of the kinds of attributes that you should emulate in your own life. Make your own success study to validate the pivotal importance of these key elements. Whether it is a sports star or the youth director at your church, if that person is a winner, I guarantee you, you will see evidence of these elements in how they execute their life strategies.

Please don't be intimidated by the lofty sound of any of these qualities. They are not restricted and are not accessible only to famous people. Those people are just like you, and are, in fact, only famous because *you* made them that way. You will find these same key attributes present in schoolteachers and NBA stars alike. You will find them in nurses, clerks, and opera stars. You will find them in your very own home. I did.

I live with a world-class champion. Robin, my wife of twenty-two years, lives her life quietly, anonymously, but meaningfully, with the very same qualities and commitment of heart that you would expect to find in a Michael Jordan or a Cheryl Swopes. Robin is at least as good at what she does as they are at what they do. The only real difference is that a Michael Jordan creates his magic in full view of millions of spectators, while Robin creates her magic for a private audience, consisting of me and our two boys. She has never been on television or played in a championship game, yet I have absolutely seen her perform acts of heroic proportions.

You hear of a Jordan or Swopes "reaching down and finding strength" in the fourth quarter. I have witnessed this woman reach down and find strength when it was not a game that would be over in a few minutes. I saw her depth as she nursed her father through months of a painful bout with cancer that culminated in his death. Yet she was still there every single day for our sons and me. I have seen her keep a bedside vigil lasting ninety hours straight when our firstborn developed life-threatening meningitis, with never a word of complaint.

She is a mother and wife, and she fills those roles with passion and vision. Although she's only five foot two and 115 pounds, mess with one of her children and you have a serious problem. She would fight a bear if he had a buzzsaw. There is no "quit," there is no "tired," there is no doubt. The lady is a winner. The lady is a champ. Nobody brings her a trophy or wants to interview her at the end of the day, yet she plays her game with the same passion, vision, and action as anyone in any game, anywhere.

While Michael and Cheryl are "driving the lane," Robin is driving carpool. Just as Michael Jordan is the heart and soul of his team, Robin, as a loving mother and wife, is the heart and soul of her family. She lives with dignity and quality in good times and bad. She has a plan for our family; she has a vision for our boys. She takes care of herself so she can take care of us. She creates a warm, loving, and nurturing environment that can spawn nothing but success.

These are the true characteristics that define a champion. Recognize them in your daily life. You don't have to look in the NBA to find a star. I predict that there are stars in your life right now. You may not have labeled them as such, you may not have labeled yourself as such, but that is a problem of recognition, not truth. Anyone can be a star, anyone can be a champion in their own life: that is the real truth for you to claim and live. Don't be deceived into thinking that you cannot or are not a champion because there are no lights, cameras, or reporters standing at the ready when you are being who you are. Stop and take a careful look around. You may be closer to greatness than you ever imagined.

Lest you think that there really aren't stories of "daily greatness" in the workaday world and that I only attribute those things to Robin because I happen to have been living with her for the last twenty-two years, let me tell you about Andy.

One of my dearest friends and closest associates, Bill Dawson, got me and my firm involved in a corporate firefight in California that was of staggering proportions. We were representing several Fortune 100 companies in a battle for over $1 billion in cash. The trial would last for almost five months, and hotel living for that long is a strain under the best of conditions.

Bill Dawson was lead counsel, and is one of the finest lawyers in America. When he gets on a case, he is a junkyard dog and tirelessly out-prepares the other side. That means meetings before trial, meetings during trial, and prep sessions for the next day that go into the wee hours of the morning.

Transportation in this city was a nightmare. I met Andy my first night in town. He picked me up in his cab shortly after midnight to take me from the airport to my hotel.

Now, I've been in a lot of cabs in a lot of cities. Some are clean, most are not, and they all smell bad. I knew this cab was different the minute I got in. Although it was after midnight, Andy had that cab sparkling. He had on a shirt and tie and was groomed to match his cab. On the backseat, neatly folded, were current copies of the local newspaper, *USA Today*, and *The Wall Street Journal*. They had probably been read ten times that day, but every page was in place. There was not one doubt in my mind that Andy took pride in what he was doing and the way he was doing it. His grammar wasn't the best, and his shirt was pretty worn, but it was clean and you could tell he took pride in his appearance.

Racing around town the next day, I was in three or four different cabs that made me want to shower with my clothes on the second I got out. I got my previous day's receipt out and called Andy. I explained that I had six or eight people on my team who would be moving around the city on a regular basis, and going to and from the airport for the next several months. I asked Andy if he could handle our transportation needs while we were in town. Thankfully, he agreed.

Over the next four-and-a-half months, I came to know a simple man with simple means at his disposal who had a vision for his life and a passion in his pursuit. Andy covered us like a blanket. He was there early—not some of the time, but all the time. There were times when he picked up some of my team members at six in the morning, and yet was at the airport getting me well after midnight that same day. The cab was always clean; he was always clean. He was professional and he was committed to doing his job.

As I rode with and talked to Andy, he shared with me his philosophy: that if you do things right and you work hard, it will pay off. He explained that his goal was to have his own cab company in five years. He was excited about his goal, there was no doubt. One Friday night when he took me to the airport, there were substantial weather delays, and Andy asked if I would like to see his business plan while I waited. He was in no hurry because he would never leave until he was sure I had made my flight and did not need him further. I was absolutely intrigued to see what this goodhearted but unsophisticated and uneducated man had come up with.

I was absolutely blown away. Words were misspelled, and it was hand-written, but it made sense. He had done the math; he had projected into the future. He had a timeline, and he had clear outcome criteria. Andy was a man with a plan. He was also an integral part of the logistics supporting one of if not the largest lawsuit to be tried in America that year. He moved me and my team, key witnesses, and lawyers in a timely, reliable, and professional fashion. You could tell he was proud to be part of it. He followed our progress each day in the paper and became pretty darn knowledgeable about the facts.

On my last day there, Andy took me to the airport and asked if he could walk me to my gate. On the way, he said, "Doc, I just want to thank you for letting me be part of this deal and making me feel like I made a difference. I learned a lot, and if I never see you again, I want to thank you for giving me the chance and the business." Talk about a class act. I thanked Andy for his help, and told him that I believed in him. I told him that his plan was good, and that I had every confidence that it would work. He was truly a man of vision and a man of passion.

Thank God that there are people in this world like Andy, doing jobs like Andy's, or those of us who get to think we're pretty big deals would be in a whole lot of trouble. As I sat on the plane going home, I thought more about Andy than I did our lawsuit. It was plain to me that Andy was at least as good at what he did as I was at what I did. Andy was a champion and a winner. He took pride in his station in life and bloomed where he was planted. People in Congress, corporate America, and a whole lot of other places could learn a lot from Andy. I know I did.

I could tell you scores of similar stories, but I'll bet that you already get the message. No matter where you are, no matter what you're doing, no matter how far you went in school or didn't, by living the Laws of Life and folding the key elements of a winning formula into your own personality, you can be a winner, too. The choice is yours.